Confessions of a Country Architect

DON METZ

BUNKER HILL PUBLISHING

www.bunkerhillpublishing.com

First published in 2007
by Bunker Hill Publishing Inc.
285 River Road, Piermont
New Hampshire 03779, USA

10 9 8 7 6 5 4 3 2 1

Text copyright © Don Metz

Library of Congress Control Number: 2007926743

ISBN 10: 1-59373-061-6
ISBN 13: 9781593730611

Designed by Louise Millar

Printed in China by Jade Productions Ltd

*To Tom Luckey — incorrigible inventor,
loveable genius, resolute friend, party animal.*

Contents

Author's Note

This book was written during my fourth decade of practice as a residential architect in rural New Hampshire. A few names have been changed in some of the chapters in order to protect the guilty, but the innocent have been properly identified throughout. Occasionally, a storyline may nudge aside an inconvenient fact or merge multiple experiences, but my thesis remains uncompromised: People are more important than the objects they make, and a gainful relationship among the architect, client, and builder is essential to creating a successful house.

Horton

According to his directions, Horton's sawmill "sets in the bushes" across from his house. "Can't miss it," he said.

I missed it. When I knew I had driven too far, I stopped and asked directions from an old farmer digging up potatoes in his garden. It was a brutally hot day, and he was grateful for an excuse to stop working. Pointing back in the direction I'd just come from, he carefully described the turns and landmarks I should ignore. "That second side road won't take you nowhere you'd ever want to go," and, "Used to be a big barn on the side of the road, but it burned down when I was 12 — no, come to think of it, I guess I was 13-years old." He instructed me to go back exactly the way I'd come, and, "Look for a red mailbox welded to a goddamned posthole auger. Can't miss it," he said.

In the mill yard, I parked between leaning towers of lumber and walked through a maze of logs until I found Horton. He was fiddling with something on the big noisy engine that powered the saw. When he noticed me, he shut it off, and instantly the day seemed to shrink down to the smells of diesel fuel and sunbaked sawdust. He wiped his hands on a greasy rag as I approached, and we nodded greetings. A black-and-white dog sitting by his side watched me without stirring. By way of an introduction, I said I had called about buying pine boards.

"Horton Bowles," he said, extending a hand the size of a catcher's mitt. "And the boss," he added, touching the dog's head, "Mr. Jiggs."

At least twice my age, Horton Bowles was tall and angular with a commanding nose and a crusty Yankee accent worthy of the Smithsonian. A master of rural New Hampshire etiquette, his speech was designed to never quite inquire, never quite inform — and always understate.

"Not exactly cool over your way, is it?" It had been over ninety-five for a week.

As a nouveau native, I was a conversational green horn. "Definitely," I replied, and instantly regretted my literal response.

"I should judge she'll cool off substantial tomorrow."

I chose an agreeable, silent nod rather than risk further shame.

And so it went as we (he) discussed the weather, the condition of the roads, unusual wildlife recently sighted, the lengths and widths of the lumber I wanted, the dog's latest encounter with a porcupine, and the Red Sox — in no particular order.

Horton brightened when I asked about the sawmill. He had cobbled it together over a period of years while he worked elsewhere as an electrician, carpenter, welder, and truck mechanic. The log carriage, he explained, was made from a mobile home chassis. The diesel engine was scavenged from a ready-mix truck, the overhead lights rescued from a demolished hospital wing in Plymouth. There was not a single piece that he hadn't rehabilitated, converted, adapted, assembled, and refined himself. The entire sawmill, he said, cost him less than a thousand dollars out-of-pocket. "Plus a few hours labor."

He was in no hurry to sell me lumber, as if to pursue commerce would have been rude. Over an hour of pleasant banter had passed when I reluctantly mentioned the purpose of my visit.

"This fella's got to have some lumber," he sighed to Mr. Jiggs, as if he and the dog were alone. "Guess we got to stop yakking, and amount to something."

After we had loaded the truck, he used a stubby pencil to tally the footage on the clean side of a white pine, 1 x 12 board. I watched him round down the figures in my favor, altogether ignoring three or four pieces he'd decided were not up to standard.

"They look okay to me," I said.

"Can't charge a man for shoddy work," he said. "It don't set right with me."

I gratefully paid him, and climbed into my overloaded truck. As I was leaving, he asked, "And what sort of work do you do for a living?"

I looked past him at the sawmill he had built for a thousand bucks, at the immense concentration of creative energy, ingenuity, thrift, and diligence it represented — and I knew I'd been greatly privileged to meet someone so thoroughly competent as Horton Bowles. "I'm ... I'm just getting started." I was 30-years old and not yet licensed. "I'm ... an architect."

Horton nodded politely and squinted up into the unrepentant sun. There was sawdust stuck to the stubble on his chin, and a hint of pity in his voice when he replied, "I should think that would be awfully boring."

More is More, Less is Not

My first day of architecture school began with gusting wind and rain. One of the first big storms of the season had been lurking off the Connecticut coast for three days, and New Haven was still within range of its torment. But the weather was the least of my concerns. In a few hours, classes would begin, and I was faced with a storm of my own. How would I measure up to the challenges of Yale's celebrated school of architecture? Exactly how much more talented would everyone else be? And as if to compound my anxiety, I didn't own a raincoat or umbrella. My old Volkswagen was parked in a friend's garage across town, and I was too stubborn to call a taxi when I lived only five blocks from school.

I stepped out into the storm wrapped in an old Hudson Bay blanket worn thin by childhood camping trips. With a flap hooded over my head and my arms tucked inside, I sloshed around potholes and puddles like a renegade mummy. Most of the driving rain slid off the tightly woven wool, but from my knees down, I might as well have been surfing. If first impressions meant anything in the school of architecture, I was off to a sorry start.

Waiting for the light to change, I stood across the street from Paul Rudolph's controversial Art and Architecture Building, under construction on the northwest corner of Chapel and York. Due to the storm, work had been canceled that day, but even so, the scene was an exciting brew of steel scaffolding, stacked form

12

panels, framing lumber, and reinforcing bars. The structure's four monolithic concrete towers were so massive and invulnerable, I wondered how they would ever be dismantled when the building had outlived its usefulness — or were they being built so mightily that such an end would be impossible? When a sudden gale momentarily swept back my hood, my eye was drawn upward to the cantilevered arm of the project's hammerhead crane, and I heard its taut cables clattering against cold steel.

On the northeast corner of Chapel and York stood the iconic Yale Art Gallery, designed by Louis I. Kahn — whose name was invariably spoken in reverent tones among "architectiados." Despite the rain, I could see people moving in the warm light behind the windows of the top floor, which I knew was to be the school of architecture's temporary home — and my immediate destination.

While I was waiting for the light to change, the rain seemed to ease up. Peering out from under my makeshift hood, I saw that someone was lending me the shelter of his umbrella. He was tall and handsome and bundled up in a rakish trench coat implausibly fresh and dry. My first reaction was to move away. What to make of such a potentially transgressive gesture?

He smiled, as if to apologize, moved the umbrella a few more inches over me and said, "Damn this weather."

Something about him convinced me the gesture was simply generous, nothing more. It wasn't until I shook my blanketed head in agreement that I realized how pathetic I must have looked, and how cold and wet I really was. "Thanks," I said, through chattering teeth.

"There's a soup kitchen in the basement," he said, tipping the umbrella toward the old gothic church behind us. No condescension in his gesture, not a note to suggest we were less than equals. "And I reckon they might have beds," he added.

I mumbled a few sounds of protest and gratitude. The light changed, he wished me good luck, and crossed Chapel Street with the deliberate stride of someone who knew exactly where he was going — which turned out to be straight into the Louis Kahn building and up the stairs. I waddled after him at a distance, assuming he must be a junior member of the faculty or a visiting critic. When I got to the top floor, I squished into the men's room, hung the dripping blanket over a toilet stall and used a roll of paper towels to dry my shoes and socks. Ten minutes later, I was sitting in a circle of two-dozen students in the first year drafting studio — and there he was, a first-year student, just like me.

About a quarter of the class was made up of my old friends from undergraduate classes at Yale. Foremost among these friends was Tom Luckey, a charismatic, Harrison Ford look-alike who was already displaying a genius for seeing design opportunities where others saw only problems. As an undergraduate, he designed and built a chair in the shape of a capital Z — all in wood. I was sure it would never work: "The joints are going to be a problem," I prophesized. (The chair is still solid, four decades later.) A few years after architecture school, friends of Tom asked him to design a sliding board for their kids, and reconfigure a rickety stairway in their old house. Tom combined the requests and designed their stairway in such a way that it could be transformed into a slide with the pull of a lever. Among other marvels, he built a love seat rocking chair in which the two sitters faced opposite directions and rocked independently.

The instructor asked us to introduce ourselves and give a brief history of how we'd come to the school of architecture. Most of the students gave modest accounts of their lives, but none did so more convincingly than Lamar Jean Finch. Speaking in a soft and faintly southern, genteel voice, my umbrella-toting benefactor projected a sense of self-effacing irony and ease. When his gaze passed my way, I did my best to look powder-dry and dignified, and he gave no sign of recognizing the drowned homeless person at the Chapel Street crosswalk. He offered that he had grown up in Virginia and "bummed around" for four years after college before he'd decided to give architecture school a try. As we became friends in the weeks that followed, I incrementally learned that after he'd graduated magna cum laude from Princeton, spent a year in Florence on a Fulbright scholarship, and then worked for three years in the design department of the prestigious New York architectural firm, Skidmore, Owings, and Merrill. Just bumming around.

When it was my turn to speak, I said I liked to make things. I'd majored in sculpture as an undergraduate, but gravitated toward architecture because designing buildings seemed more challenging than making art for art's sake. Tom Luckey offered that his great-grandfather and grandfather were Brigadier Generals in the army. His father was a Lieutenant General in the Marines. Preceded by three generations of warriors, he said it was only fair that he give his generation's enemies a rest.

In the months to follow, Lamar, Tom, and I spent a lot of time talking about how we saw ourselves progressing, step by step, through our professional lives. Only one of us had it right from the start.

Lamar insisted he wasn't drawn to architecture in order to make art. He was interested because he was curious about how big organizations accomplish complicated tasks. He saw architecture as a collaborative effort driven by a combination of rigorous discipline and the blessing of gifted intuition — not exactly a big business model, not exactly pure art, but something symbiotic in between.

I envisioned practicing an architecture that served the common man, not just those who could afford it. Maybe the aesthetics of affordable housing would be less exciting, but architecture should be obligated to enhance everyone's lives.

Tom was less pretentious. He was curious about the relationship between behavior and design. For instance, why do we feel more comfortable when floors are level and walls are plumb? And why do people always face forward in an elevator?

Such was the nature of our thinking in 1962. None of us thought about making money or becoming famous. Where architecture would lead us, or how long and intertwined our lives would be, was beyond our imagination.

One of our instructors in the design studio was the late John Hejduk. Aside from his teaching duties, he was working on a series of conceptual houses based upon a square floor plan. Within the outer square, a nine-square grid served as the organizational contrivance about which the interior spaces were configured. This formal, deterministic approach to design both annoyed and intrigued me. Why begin with a square? Why subdivide it into nine instead of four, or sixteen? It all seemed so abstracted from the needs and individualities of the householder. But in the end, it was not the didactic variations in those nine indomitable squares that set me free, but the way John Hejduk used language.

I had previously wanted to think of architecture as a hands-on, mind-off enterprise. Hejduk was able to engage me in a way that began to inform my buildings with ideas before I began drawing, beyond structural and aesthetic necessities. One of architecture's great challenges, he suggested, was finding correlatives capable of expressing human feelings. For instance, how might we propose to configure a building that expressed the conditions of love, or hate, or birth and death, of disgrace, or redemption? What kind of window signifies honeymoon cottage? What color brick is most appropriate for a health food store, as opposed to a cancer ward? How do we suggest, through the choices of materials, colors, surfaces, and forms, the nature, purpose, and spirit of a building?

Hejduk's rhetorical method prompted me to think more abstractly and rely less on the practical. "Think about how you might suggest the hierarchy of spaces leading from the public to the private realm," he might say. Or, "How do you express the glory of God in stone?" Or, "What are the shapes left in our collective memories in the aftermath of war — and how do we apply them to the design of a war memorial?"

If John Hejduk taught me how to think within the modernist tradition, Robert Venturi's seminal book, *Complexity and Contradiction in Architecture* taught me how to verbalize the postmodern. Here at last was a practicing architect who used a clear and accessible language by which architecture could be discussed.

I first encountered Robert Venturi when he was a visiting critic at Yale. He and Philip Johnson and various other luminaries were gathered for one of those blood-letting rituals wherein student projects are tacked to the wall, discussed, judged, graded, and de-graded by the faculty jury. One day, I watched a student defend his project as if it were the only choice possible between two competing options, this or that. Venturi rose to his feet and quietly asked, "Instead of the either-or approach, why not look for a way to embrace both-and?" To those of us who had been seduced by mono-causal modernism, this seemingly unassuming question was shocking. Could architecture be so loosey-goosey that it could accommodate both-and?

Orthodox modernist principles of the early sixties held that architecture was a matter of absolute premises. Instead of allowing architecture to recognize cultural contexts and adapt to user sensibilities, cultural/user sensibilities were expected to adapt to modern architecture — and be the better for it. The client was preferably seen as a passive necessity, the architect's vision as sacrosanct, and the only stylistic expression was "international." Moroccan nomads could surely learn to love the same concrete box apartments designed and lived in by stylish, young architects in New Haven, Connecticut. If something was wrong with that picture, we students weren't sophisticated enough to see it — until Robert Venturi came along.

In the decade to follow, Venturi's modest demeanor provided him with an unwitting camouflage. Tie-dyed Hippies and Yippies were making pronouncements with flowers in their hair, but the tweed-jacketed Venturi was far more radical. Perfectly tuned to the times, he dared speak of "... a complex and contradictory architecture based on the richness and ambiguity of modern experience, including that experience which is inherent in art."

By the end of the sixties, the corpse of modernism was moldering, and ornament was back. Allusions to the past were not only permissible, but advisable. Venturi demonstrated, through photos and drawings, how control and spontaneity, correctness and ease, old and new, had co-existed for centuries in our European antecedents. His audacious polemics challenged us to look at the ways in which Michelangelo broke the rules on the rear façade of the Palazzo Farnese in Rome. He showed us the front of the Palazzo del Popolo in Ascoli Piceno, and taught us to see how the contradictions and broken rhythms of the classical orders actually added to the vitality of a design. The banal and the vivid, he insisted, could not only co-exist in architecture, but in fact make it richer. The message we were hearing from this soft-spoken, academic practitioner was, "Up against the wall, Mother Modernism."

And so it would be increasingly revealed to us over the years that life beyond the ivory tower's neat constructs — real life — turned out to be complex and contradictory indeed, much more of it gray than black and white. Why, then, should our architecture pretend it to be otherwise? Re-reading Venturi, I saw even better how he celebrated the quotidian discordances and ironies that defined our lives, how he expressed them as an essential part of his architecture. If watching television is what we do, why not celebrate the TV antenna as a design element? If the automobile is inevitable, play on its impact as an opportunity for richness of meaning instead of a shameful problem to be hidden.

As for the timeworn exhortation attributed to Mies van der Rohe, "Less is more," Venturi dared suggest it wasn't. Although Mies's iconic glass boxes accomplished much as emblems of chaste design, they risked little in their willingness to address the messy realities of everyday life. (Where do we keep the broken bicycle, the baby's car seat, and the extra chairs for the dining room table?) The imperial modernists, finally, were seen to be wearing no clothes. More, in fact, was More, while Less was, indeed, unfortunately, boringly, Less. Thanks to Robert Venturi, John Hejduk, and others, the gates to a humanist, postmodern architecture were opened wide, and the influences of history, context, contradiction, and complexity flooded in.

Stone

"Here's how you do it, boy." Wielding an eight-pound hammer with the grace and precision of a drum majorette, Bo Dabney side-stepped down a line of knee-high, steel wedges set sixteen inches apart, and struck each one in a rhythmic, non-stop, figure-eight loop. When he got to the last one, he turned and repeated his flawless demonstration back to where he'd started. Bling, swish, bling, swish, bling ... Handing me the sledge, he pulled a pouch of Bull Durham from his breast pocket and rolled himself a tidy smoke. "Mind your aim," he said, through the blue haze of a long exhale. "That iron's heavy on the toes."

And so began my first day of work at the French Creek granite quarry in eastern Pennsylvania. First-year classes at architecture school had ended the week before, and despite the raised eyebrows of my faculty advisors, I was determined to spend the summer enrolled in Stonedust 101, eight weeks at hard labor. Several classmates were also working in construction, others were traveling or working as draftsmen. Thanks to his father's military connections, Tom Luckey was stuck in a 5th Naval District architect's office in Norfolk, Virginia, doing boring, meaningless, work. "I spent the first week instructed to find a roll of drawings the colonel misplaced," he told me during a desperate telephone call. "Maybe next week I'll get to sharpen all the pencils he can't find." I had never heard him so miserable.

Lamar was back in Manhattan, apprenticing at Skidmore, Owings and Merrill. The project he was working on involved huge numbers of personnel and would take a decade to complete. His working world was all about huge budgets, huge buildings, and huge amounts of patience. Part of me worried that I should be working in an office, too, but I knew I couldn't sit still long enough to learn what was there to be taught. It was as if I was compelled to process information physically, by way of muscles, bones, and hands.

The big stone cathedrals and palazzi I'd seen on a trip through Tuscany the summer before were, of course, spectacular. But it was the indigenous buildings that impressed me the most — simple barns and houses built of stone dug from adjacent fields and vineyards. Casual rhythms of windows, doors, and archways composed beautifully simple facades with no regard to symmetry, straight lines or formal patterns. Because of its beauty, durability, and availability at minimal cost, it struck me that stone was the most democratizing building material in the world. How tempting it was to endow it with the virtues of moral and aesthetic superiority.

I had built stonewalls for my father and neighbors all through high school — piddling stuff compared with what I saw in Italy. But without knowing why, I was able to look at a stone turned upside down and backwards and know that it would fit into a specific slot in a wall. I liked the string of consequences each piece initiated in the making of a wall, the infinite geometries inherent in the weaving and knitting of a masonry fabric. As for blocks of granite lifted out of a hole in the ground — blocks the size of a VW van and weighing more than a Mack Truck — I had to see for myself how quarrying was done.

On that first day of work, I arrived early at the quarry driving my mother's polite beige Pontiac four-door sedan. It looked prissy parked between two chunky pickup trucks, but by day's end, they would all be equally crusted over with a thick coat of stone dust.

At the quarry's entrance, a couple of dilapidated storage

sheds stood to one side of the chain link gate. Beside them, as if an afterthought stood a small blue trailer with "Offise" painted on its door. I knocked, and when no one answered, I opened the door and looked into a grimy room furnished with a card table desk, a folding metal chair and a two-drawer file cabinet. A "___Days Without an Accident" calendar on the wall had the number 0 scrawled in the blank spot.

I closed the door and walked a few hundred feet to the quarry itself. It was surrounded with rows of granite blocks and slabs, some rough, some sawed and honed and stacked on pallets ready to be shipped. When I looked down into the hole, some fifteen stories deep, a rush of vertigo left me weak: The pit was huge. Roughly fifty yards square at the top, with the sides stepped down in a series of benches terminating at a milky green plane of water at the bottom. At the far side of the pit, a huge wooden mast and boom were held upright by a web of sagging, rusty cables spanning down to anchors bolted into the rock. From a seat in the little engine house, impossibly perched on the lip of the hole, the derrick operator could see everything below.

Bo emerged from behind a cutting shed with a noncommittal nod. Owner, salesman, bookkeeper, and pit foreman, he was a small, bow-legged man, all weathered leather and gristle wrapped around a quiet, shy manner. He was probably in his 60s and was soon to teach me that the energies of youth counted for little when accompanied by inexperience.

The tops of the wedges I was expected to pound were the diameter of a nickel: The striking face of an eight-pound hammer is about the size of a silver dollar. The hammer's handle is three feet long. To each side of the wedges was what Bo called a "feather," a steel shim that permits the wedge to penetrate the hole, steel against steel. As the wedge is driven deeper, it exerts lateral loading to opposing sides of the fracture line until the granite is unable to resist the tension, and splits open.

As per Bo's demonstration, I was going to swing the hammer high over my head, strike a glancing blow off the first wedge, continue the swing uninterrupted to the bottom of its arc, and back up and over my head in one continuous, looping pattern to the second wedge, and so on.

My first swing overshot by an inch, the hammer handle struck the top of the wedge, splinters flew, and I felt a vicious tingle squirt all the way up my arms to my ears.

Bo's long-time helper was a lanky Harley Davidson fanatic whose drowsy accent immediately explained his nickname, "Alabama." He and Bo watched solemnly as I reduced the first hammer handle to splinters, and more than once came within a whimper of clipping my toenails. They must have wondered why they ever hired me — not to mention why a college-educated kid would waste his summer in a quarry — but they were too polite and much too amused to want it otherwise.

When the novelty of my eight-pound hammer ineptitude wore off, they wished me luck and went to work elsewhere while the row of steel wedges were left to taunt my inexperience. My aim became increasingly cautious, but little improved, and I soon demolished a second hammer handle. Halfway to lunchtime, my technique was slightly improved, but not before I had shredded the third and last hammer handle available. It was then that Bo patiently introduced me to the primitive subtleties of the jackhammer.

The holes I was instructed to drill were part of Bo's plan to remove a layer of sedimentary overburden from the north edge of the quarry. He explained that when the holes were at least five-feet deep, they would be filled first with a blasting cap and primer connected to a pair of low-voltage wires: next came six inches of granular nitro. The remainder of the hole would then be tamped tight with sand and pea stone. All I had to do was drill twelve holes, five feet deep, on four-foot centers.

"It's not so bad, once you get the hang of it." Bo laid the jackhammer down flat, unlocked the chuck, and inserted the shank of a three-foot drill rod into the bottom of the shaft. When he'd locked the rod in tight, he uprighted the hammer — the top of which was now shoulder-high — and pointed to two levers near the top of the shaft. "Low speed until you're in far enough so it won't jump out of the hole, high speed to the end of the rod. When you're done with the three-footer, set this five-footer in the hole, lock it into your hammer, and drill it on home."

He snugged the drill bit against the inside arch of his boot, pushed down on the low speed lever, and the jackhammer started to chatter. Within a few minutes, he was in about two inches, deep and steady enough to switch to high speed. "Easy as pie," he said, leaving the hammer to me and walking away.

I continued drilling to the end of the first rod, set up the five-footer as instructed and ran it on down. First hole completed — eleven to go! I wished Lamar and Tom could see me now, working alongside Bo and Alabama with a weapons-grade jackhammer in my hands. Whatever they might be doing in their stuffy offices today couldn't possibly measure up to this. This was education at its finest. I could feel the steel cutting the stone!

As I started hole number two, I discovered that a carborundum bit rotating on a bumpy, sloped granite surface refuses to behave predictably — for me. While the instep of Bo's boot had steadied the bit long enough to get the hole started, my boot seemed more like a target than a guide. In the same time that it took Bo to drill a two inch-deep starter hole, I had pockmarked a square foot of stone, and came close to cutting the air hose in half. By the time I finished the twelfth hole, it was quitting time, and I was in a world of hurt.

Whatever I did in the next few weeks, I seemed to do badly. When I lost my grip on a sledge hammer and sent it spiraling past Bo's head, Alabama gave me the nickname "Rosin," as in, "Put some rosin on your hands and hang onto that danged hammer 'fore you kill somebody." Bo never flinched. He was stoically tolerant of my ineptitude and continued to show me how things were supposed to work. Alabama thought my daily performances were proof positive that a college education was "... 'bout as useful as tits on a mule." But he always brought an extra slice of homemade pie for me at lunch, and graciously mumbled, "There you go," when I did something right.

Without once sounding like a teacher, Bo taught how to look for grain and changes in color and density in the stone, how to rig, move and place huge slabs with simple machinery, and how to survive the lethal dangers of working in the pit. By mid-August, I was beginning to feel genuinely useful. I could hammer down a line of wedges without a miss, and had more or less mastered the wicked ways of the buck dancing jackhammer. When Alabama was on vacation, Bo let me operate the derrick, casually cautioning me to keep away from the open cable drum spinning inches from my right elbow. As an afterthought, he mentioned that a previous employee had lost his right arm to that same spinning reel.

I ran the forklift in the loading zone. I made wooden crates for shipping and replaced saw blades in the cutting shed. I tamped sand and got headaches from the nitro, but I could claim, 63 Days Without An Accident, five weeks without breaking a hammer handle! By the end of the summer, I felt I had redeemed myself enough to ask Bo a favor: "Next time we shoot, could I push the plunger?"

The impulse came from the Westerns I'd watched as a kid,

especially the scenes in which someone would tie explosives to something that needed blowing up. They'd string wires to a hiding place behind a boulder and attach the wires to a battery box with a T-shaped plunger sticking out of the top. The hero (or villain) would hover steely-eyed over the apparatus, waiting, waiting. When the time was right, he would push down the plunger, and all hell would break loose. Hero or villain, I wanted to be that guy.

Bo scheduled a shoot for my last day at the quarry. He showed me how to braid the wires and attach them to the terminals, which were about two inches to either side of the plunger on top of the shoot box. Following his instructions, I wrapped the wires around the terminals — red on the right, blue on the left — and tightened them with the brass wing nuts. When all was set, we prepared to hunker down behind the company's ancient Diamond Reo flatbed truck, maybe seventy-five feet from the shoot. Bo blew the truck's horn in the standard three blast warning signal, and waited sixty seconds before he said, "Okay Rosin, let her rip."

I locked my elbows over the plunger — and froze.

"Rosin?"

A collage of thoughts compressed themselves into that defining moment: I wasn't imprisoned in a suit and tie, bent over a drafting board in a big city firm on such a beautiful summer day. How blessed was I to be exactly where I was. I wished everyone I knew could watch as I created thunder. I thought of a recent lecture by the peerless historian, Vincent Scully, in which he proposed the existence of axial sight lines between distant hilltop temples in Greece. Temples made of quarried stone. (And what was the connection?) I was a quarryman! I was Vulcan, Zeus, and Thor combined, about to shudder and erupt the earth. Every blister, every aching joint and muscle suffered during the hot, dusty summer counted as nothing compared to the glory attending this deifying performance.

"Rosin?"

I plunged the handle down, and as my unsuspecting thumbs made simultaneous contact with the brass wing nuts, 100 amps of indiscriminate current coursed through my mortal meat and bones and jolted me silly. I landed in a cockeyed heap, but just in time to hear a mighty, joyous BOOM and see the dust and flying chunks of splintered rock sail upward through a perfect August sky.

A week later, I was back at school waiting in line to register for second-year courses when I found myself eavesdropping on a third-year student. He was explaining how he had spent his summer as part of a design team working on an inner-city museum, "Interesting challenges, ambiguous site, funding nightmares, but we're still in the game." I was suddenly uncomfortable, and I decided he looked underfed, and his hands, I noticed, were as fragile and thin as a child's. How awful. I listened as he described the ingenious cost-cutting proposals his employer had promoted — that he had helped create. He also mentioned that he'd learned to write specifications and review contracts.

Ouch! I had spent a summer without drawing a line or studying a blueprint, without thinking. Could I really equate a working knowledge of a two-speed jackhammer with the experience of writing specifications?

Better yet, did I need to compare them?

In the days to come, I limited myself to sharing with Tom and Lamar the amusing highlights of the summer. Tom was envious, so awful had his summer been with the naval district architects. Lamar was graciously supportive, but I knew what he thought about manual labor, and so I held back from him the parts that meant the most to me, my respect for Bo and Alabama's utter proficiency, the pride I felt hitting wedges dead-on, the satisfaction of watching a ten-ton slab of granite separate from a shelf like a slice of bread cut from a loaf.

The nasty aspects of quarry work I kept to myself — how stone dust chokes the air, how the walls of the quarry act as a reflector oven. Did anyone really want to know that I spent most days marinating in a hot, noisy lather of dust and sweat, that the jittery pulsation of steel cutting stone disarrays the body's cells with no discrimination? That the staccato of the jackhammers and the background howl of the diesel-powered compressors anesthetize your hearing? Would anyone be impressed that these assaults on the senses tend to draw the edges of perception inward so that the awareness of danger — which is grave and everywhere — is greatly compromised? Or that when the noise stops, its sudden absence is simply shocking; the silence is almost painful. All of this for low wages, pureed kidneys, and permanent hearing loss? If they asked me why I wouldn't have rather worked with talented people on an exciting project in a cutting-edge office, I would have been hard-pressed to explain why not. I was coming to architecture through my feet, from the bottom up, through the perfected skills and competence of men like Bo and Alabama, who would recommend I never let my education become an obstacle to learning.

First Building

A framed cartoon that's hung on my office wall for years depicts a bow-tied chimpanzee holding up an Escher-like blueprint of an impossible-to-build staircase. The caption below the chimp/architect reads, "All we do is put it on paper. It's your job to build it."

Imagine the contractor who receives a drawing that can't be properly executed. For example: When a string of dimensions indicates a wall is eighteen-feet long, but, drawn to scale, the wall is only sixteen-feet long, which of these contradictory commands should the builder follow? In an ideal world, the builder and architect negotiate the intended solution. But in the deadline-driven, too-much-to-do, too-little-time-to-do-it world of contracting, such meetings don't happen too often. If the contractor takes a chance and builds in the eighteen-foot wall as dimensioned, ("It was on the *%#$&* drawings!") he may be ignoring issues of aesthetics, safety or budget, and aggravate the building inspector, the architect, or the client — who is unknowingly paying extra for the delay and confusion created by the architect's mistake.

American architecture schools have traditionally emphasized a curriculum based on aesthetic and intellectual rigor. Hands-on, practical skills are seldom taught. Unlike our European counterparts, American architects can be licensed to practice their profession without ever having opened a toolbox, lifted a brick, or touched a 2 x 4.

Fortunately, my three years in architecture school coincided with an unprecedented student initiative. Although the school offered no formal training in the building trades, a surge of interest in construction led many of us to seek hands-on experience wherever we could find it. My summer jobs in the quarry, and later, in construction, were typical of a growing trend. Several classmates took a year off to build houses they had designed. Some refused to dirty their hands. Lamar, by nature, kept a respectful distance from tools of any sort, and dedicated his summers to perfecting a lethal serve on the tennis court. Tom Luckey was teaching himself to weld, carve wood, and use a wide range of power tools to transform his increasingly eccentric ideas into gorgeous toys and furniture.

I had been married for three years, to my wife Cora, when we moved to Cambridge, where our daughter, Oona, was born. We liked Cambridge — at first. Drafting jobs were plentiful, rents were cheap, and the streets around Harvard Square were buzzing with architectural chitchat. After apprenticing at a prominent firm for a year, I switched to another well-known collaborative, as if the change would somehow lessen my growing distaste for office life. Meanwhile, a modest inheritance from my grandmother allowed us to buy a dilapidated farmhouse on thirty-five acres in the little New Hampshire town where I still live.

Weekends and holidays were immediately consumed with a three-hour drive to the farmhouse, a flurry of work, and a three-hour drive home. At the office, I was drawing toilet partition details for a huge high school project in western Massachusetts. In New Hampshire, I was learning to build. At the office, I was secretly sketching my next weekend's project — as well as a modest design commission of my own. If there had been an award for Employee of the Month, I would have been last on the list. A few colleagues remarked on my calloused hands, and on my time-consuming interests outside the office. As the farmhouse restoration neared completion, I began to imagine how I might make a living in New Hampshire, designing and building small projects. When a second, larger commission appeared, it seemed like a promise of things to come. I began drafting at home before and after work, and arriving at the office late.

My apprenticeship was technically completed, and although I would have learned so much more had I only applied myself, my thoughts and energies were elsewhere. After Oona was born, Cora and I decided to make the move real, and I began calling in sick on Fridays — from New Hampshire. On Mondays, I told stories about the north-country loggers and farmers I'd met and admired, while my co-workers applied themselves to their work in reproving silence. Hired as a promising prospect from a prestigious school, I worked my way straight to the bottom in less than a year.

With the arrival of spring — which to me meant the beginning of the building season — I wanted nothing more than to be up in New Hampshire banging nails. By the middle of June, I had become, not entirely by accident, an insufferable, insubordinate, underachieving burden to my employers. They had no idea how much I appreciated being fired, and I'm sure I've vastly underestimated how grateful they must have been to see the last of me.

Once we moved to New Hampshire, I worked night and day to finish remodeling the farmhouse we'd bought. Running water, an indoor bathroom, central heat, and an upgraded electrical system were just the beginning of what had to be done. My wife and infant daughter were admirably tolerant of the initially rustic living conditions and my consuming obsession. We slept and ate in rooms fluffy with sawdust and stacked with building materials. I had to discipline myself to finish eating breakfast before beginning work.

We sold the house that August for a price that reflected the cost of my months of sweat equity, plus a hefty profit. Having subdivided the property before the sale, we were left owning a sizeable parcel of land across the road, and funds enough start on the first building I would design and build from scratch. Within a week of the farmhouse closing, I hired Ray Uline and his D-8 Caterpillar to clear the new site.

When I first watched the D-8 at work, I was convinced that Ray was a genius. It seemed inconceivable that such a huge machine, with its wide cleated tracks and squeaky, steel-on-steel pins and bushings could be made to perform such precise choreographies. Mechanically, it appeared primitive, an unlikely combination of hydraulics, geared-down drive train and a small-displacement, low-RPM motor. But oh, how it worked. Like a king on his throne, Ray played with a handful of push-and-pull levers that controlled the speed and direction of the machine as well as the angle and depth of the cutting blade. I watched him slice across a patch of lumpy terrain and leave it as smooth as icing on a cake. Boulders yielded, stumps succumbed. Sixty-foot-tall trees toppled over with a push and a shove were nudged into a pile as neat as a stack of carrots.

Watching him strip the site was like watching a one-sided war. I was both thrilled and uneasy — thrilled with the progress and the anticipation of what was to follow, but at the same time apprehensive about seeing Nature so ruthlessly ravaged. An innocent tree caught in the wrong place was instantly pulped. A patch of wild blueberries ripening in the sun was, in the next moment, replaced by a carpet of fresh, fragrant dirt. The machine was invincible, the destruction breathtaking, and the excitement palpable.

There was something almost erotic about the sudden nakedness, the vulnerability of all that raw dirt, and I confess that newly opened ground continues to have its Pavlovian way with me decades later. Part of the attraction must be that the digging of dirt naturally foreshadows the pleasure of the building to follow, and part of it also must be the fecundity of the earth itself, as if its capacity to grow and nourish grass and trees extends to the nurturing of buildings.

In a single day, Ray cleared half-an-acre around the house site, dug the foundation, and roughed in a driveway. What had been, early that morning, a young forest of hardwoods and conifers, was by late afternoon a coherent building site. When he asked if I wanted the area in front of the house "cuffed off level," I said yes, and offered to set up my newly acquired surveyor's transit to check the grade.

Ray declined. "Got the transit right here," he said, tapping his temple.

I had no idea what he meant.

"I can feel it when the dozer sets level," he said. "Then I blend in the slopes and back drag everything smooth 'til it's all eye-sweet."

Eye Sweet.

As he left that evening, Ray told me he would be back in the morning with his lowboy trailer and move the D-8 to his next project. "Meanwhile," he said, "The keys are in it. You want to dress off the rough spots, don't be shy about it."

"I don't know how to operate a thing like that," I confessed.

"Sure you do," he insisted. "You got the touch. I can tell."

"If anything broke ..."

"We got only two rules," he said. "Always look behind you when you back up so's you don't run over your dinner pail — and we never blow hoses on Saturday 'cause we can't get replacements 'til Monday."

I stayed on the site long after Ray left, cutting up fallen trees along the driveway with my new McCullough chainsaw. I had stacked close to a half-cord of firewood when darkness made it impossible to continue — but I couldn't go home just yet.

Climbing up onto the 'dozer, I tried to remember which controls he had used to do what. I made engine noises like a kid and groped in the dark for the key. Ray wasn't kidding: the key was in the ignition. Permission had been granted, so why not? And wasn't this a hand throttle on the right hand side of the dash, where it was located on my dad's Ford tractor? With the clutch pedal engaged, I held my breath, turned the key, and felt a thrill run through me as the diesel engine chugged to life.

For the next half-hour, I played a PG-13 version of Ray. Deciding it was too dangerous to move the dozer in the dark, I limited my puny experiments to the six-way blade — lifting, lowering, and angling in endless combinations. As I soon discovered, the levers were ergonomic in design: pushing forward on one lever pushed the blade down; pulling it back lifted the blade up. Pushing forward on a second lever tilted the blade down to the right, pulling it back dropped it to the left. A third lever, using the same logic, moved one side of the blade forward or backward. When I thought I'd squandered enough of Ray's fuel and good will, I found the key again and shut the diesel down. The silence was abrupt. Stars speckled the sky, and a new moon poked up through a tree-spiked horizon. A whippoorwill repeated its three-note song. I was way overdue for supper. The cool night air left me suddenly shivering in my T-shirt, and I noticed for the first time that I was half-eaten by mosquitoes. In a few days, I would be pouring concrete. This wasn't just going to be an idea of a building, or a drawing, or a thick sheaf of specifications, or an abstract text explaining the ideation of a building — but a thing I would build with my own hands. How difficult could it be, anyway?

Ray had already left with his D-8 when I got to the site at seven the next morning. I set up the transit and shot a few elevations along the terrain at the front of the house. The grade was within an inch of dead level over the hundred-foot length of the section he'd flattened with his God-given transit. I'd admired many instructors throughout my academic training, but after watching Ray for one short day, he joined Bo and Alabama in my growing pantheon of hands-on heroes. Because of Ray, I've since owned and operated three bulldozers. My last John Deere actually paid for itself while I built a road and shaped the landscape around my latest house. The others, as I earnestly explained to my accountant and my wife, were far less expensive to maintain than a sailboat or a Ferrari. My one regret is that I still need a transit to tell me when the grade is dead level.

I had the footing forms laid out by mid-afternoon, and the ready-mix truck was on its way from the batch plant, twenty miles away. Footings act as the foot or base supporting a foundation wall. The forms are simply two parallel, level planks, usually 2 x 10s, placed sixteen inches apart.

How quaint it seems now to think that I pushed on these 2 x 10 form boards with my foot, imagining I was testing them for sturdiness. Wet concrete weighs about 150 pounds per cubic foot, or, 4,000 pounds per cubic yard. Each lineal foot of concrete in my footings, for instance, would weigh close to 200 pounds. And, because concrete is fluid before it sets up, its effect on its container is dynamic. Imagine the difference between carrying a gallon of water in a bucket, versus carrying a gallon of water in a garbage bag. Imagine my pathetic 2 x 10 form boards buttressed by no more than an occasional stake — and me testing it with a shove of my boot!

After checking my watch for the hundredth time, I finally heard a truck turn into the driveway and roar mightily up the grade. (Most ready-mix trucks can carry up to nine cubic yards of concrete — hence the term, "The whole nine yards." Fully loaded, a truck's gross weight can approach 65,000 pounds.)

I'd passed plenty of transit mix trucks on the road, and watched them at many construction sites, but now this was my truck, summoned up with no more than a telephone call. As I watched it approach through the trees — a dazzling snow-white body on ten huge rubber tires, sparkling chrome and glass — I thought, how beautiful! The loaded, tapered drum on its back rotated slowly, inexorably. The air brakes hissed and the truck rocked forward as the front wheels stopped at the edge of the excavation. My addiction to building was abruptly and forever irreversible.

The driver took in the site with a glance, calculated where he would position the truck so that his chute could reach the forms and, after some tricky maneuvering, backed into place. We assembled the chute and swung it down into the hole. I was so excited I had to remind myself to breathe.

The driver set the drum rotating at a higher speed before adding water to the mix. "How wet do you want it?" he shouted.

Concrete is weakened with too much water. Because highly watered concrete flows quickly and easily, an impatient driver or lazy contractor might ask for a soupy mix. Why? Since the delivery chute often can't reach distant parts of the forms directly, some of the concrete must be moved into place by hand, with a shovel or hoe. The stiffer the mix, the more backbreaking the hoeing and shoveling. The wetter the mix, the better it flows and the easier it is to shovel — but the concrete will be weaker. "Not too wet," I said, recalling my engineering professors' warnings.

For the next several minutes, the truck's big drum was spun faster as it mixed the added water into the cement and aggregate. While I watched, I raced through a mental checklist of everything I knew (not much) about footing design, and comforted myself with the recollection that in all but the worst of soils, light-residential footings are virtually non-structural, serving more as a platform for the wall-form panels than part of the structural scheme. When I saw how short the chute was relative to the most distant forms, I began to calculate how much shoveling it would take to move the concrete to the farthest corners: The answer? A lot. A whole lot. Maybe the concrete could be wetter and weaker after all. "How about medium wet?"

The driver nodded, and added more water, but I could see there was something else on his mind. "Those forms," he said, when the drum stopped spinning, "Ain't gonna hold."

I assumed he'd seen a million yards of concrete poured and knew more than I ever would about how it was done. I was a rank novice, and we both knew it. He sensed my hopelessness, grabbed a shovel and climbed down into the foundation, where he began shoveling dirt against the sides of the upright 2 x 10s, tamping it into a firm, sloped ramp with his boots as he went. I followed his example, shoveling furiously, abashed at my naïveté. Twenty minutes later we began the pour— medium wet. Okay, wet medium wet. I shoveled and hoed the sticky, leaden mix to every corner of the forms. A furious half-hour passed in slow motion — but it was done. We had just enough concrete, and the forms held firm. I shook the driver's hand, perhaps longer than necessary, but I was grateful. He hosed down his truck until it gleamed, and drove away under a bright and consecrating sun.

Back down in the hole, I used a two-foot length of 1 x 4 as a trowel, and screeded off the concrete so that it was level with the tops of the forms. (I would learn sometime later that finishing concrete with a wood trowel brings sand to the surface; a steel trowel brings up water, and a magnesium trowel — or "bull float" — brings up a thick soup of sand and Portland cement called "cream".)

When the surfaces were level, I scooped out a rough "keyway," a shallow trough down the centerline of the basement wall-to-be. Next, I poked short pieces of #4 re-bar (dowels) vertically into the keyway at two-foot centers along the keyway. Once the basement walls were poured on top of the footings, the keyway and dowels would serve to lock the wall to the footing.

When I'd finished placing the dowels, I stopped for a moment and watched the occasional dribble of water seep out from between the form boards; the entrapped concrete was still an infinitely pliable, viable medium. Before curing, it could assume the shape of any container strong enough to capture it — flat or rounded, thick, thin or compound-curved. Within a few hours, mine would be fixed forever, flat, square-cornered footings.

While the concrete set up, I busied myself cutting more firewood from the toppled trees Ray left around the edges of the site. Every hour or so, I stopped to look for changes in the concrete. Concrete cures as a result of hydration: the exothermic reaction between Portland cement and water causes the cement to form a chemical bond between the sand and aggregate. On a warm day, a freshly poured slab can withstand foot traffic within three or four hours. Wall forms can be removed within twenty-four. The curing strength curve rises steeply in the first few days. Full-rated strength is achieved in tewnty-eight days, and it continues to harden indefinitely. For me, just watching the increasing solidity of what was so recently a wet flow of lumpy lava seemed miraculous. It smelled like wet lime, and to the touch — I couldn't help touching it — it radiated heat produced by the hydrating process.

The first step of many to follow had been taken. A house would rise from these footings, and if all went well, it would nourish the eyes as well as the hearts and souls of its inhabitants, my family, and others to come. I scratched our initials into the hardening surface and left the site as dusk settled over the hills.

Within two weeks, the basement's concrete walls were formed up and poured without further incident. I now stood on the plywood deck of the first floor. None of the first-floor exterior walls were in place yet, no periphery established, no interiors defined. When I looked up to where the second floor would soon be, I tried to imagine what it would be like to be standing ten feet higher, what the view of the valley would offer, how the perspective of the landscape would change — but my imagination couldn't approach the sensory particulars of physically being up there. Drawings are useful — interior perspectives, CAD facsimiles — but even video tours are an inadequate shorthand for defining the physical experience. Until I could make the step-by-step transition of bodily climbing the stairs and transforming one perspective to another, until I could stand on that second floor and feel it vibrate as I walked across it — until I could sense a ripple of vertigo when I looked down to the floor below — I would never truly know the space.

My friend Peter Anderson and I framed up the rest of the house in four frenzied weeks. Peter was a recent Dartmouth graduate who had majored in drama and shared an interest in building. His willingness to humor my architectural fancies was a flattering testimony to our friendship, which endures to this day. He came to work every morning full of enthusiasm, eager to begin the next adventure. It was my dream we were building, but somehow Peter made it his as well.

I lived those days on adrenaline and slept little at night. There was so much to think about, so much to learn, and it all had to happen as soon as possible; winter was on its way. Because the electric company was late bringing us service, we worked without power tools. It never occurred to us to rent a generator: we were in a hurry! A retired carpenter in the village sharpened our hand-saws every Sunday, pleased to see someone still using traditional tools, sweetly unaware of the circumstances driving our stubborn choice.

Ordering materials from the lumber yard had the guilty flavor of forbidden pleasures. Where else would I permit myself to spend such sums of money on so much enjoyment? Each time a delivery truck arrived with another load of lumber, it felt like Christmas morning. A stack of plywood was a gift of unlimited potential, ripe for exploitation; a bundle of shingles was another few square yards of reprieve against the rain. Converting these materials into tangible form felt like nothing so much as sanctioned play.

We worked in the rain and under a scorching sun, ever-driven by the prospect of seeing what would happen when the next floor, the next wall, the next roof pitch took shape. Snapping a chalk line down the length of a sheet of 5/8ths plywood and attacking it with an eight-point handsaw became routine, repeated many times a day. Due to a self-imposed, Calvinistic notion of construction etiquette, it seemed to us that a certain degree of misery was to be expected, if not mandatory. If the task was back-breakingly difficult, the ultimate product was bound to be better than something gained with ease. Exactly how our moral advantage would be revealed was never made evident, but we were so possessed with progress that progress itself seemed more important than reflection on what it meant. We used rickety ladders instead of staging and hung upside down over windowsills to nail the siding below. We clung to the steep roof like spiders and balanced on tiptoes to perform spectacular feats that would, today, bring OSHA to apoplexy. At times, our anthem seemed to be, I cut it off three times, and it's still too short! We became the inadvertent poster boys for on-the-job training without a trainer, doing everything the hard way before eventually learning to do it right.

Partway through building the house, I realized we needed to dig a well. Ray suggested I hire his uncle, Squeak McGoon, to dowse for the location. Squeak's nickname originated with the involuntary sound he made when he inhaled. His remuneration for a water witching session hadn't changed in thirty years — a six-pack of Budweiser.

When Squeak got out of his truck, he walked to the back, hitched himself up onto the opened tailgate and unlaced his shoes, one by one. His socks were shockingly clean and white, as if the science of dowsing required sterile laboratory conditions. Moving with the cautious economy of the elderly, he arranged his shoes perfectly parallel next to him before gingerly stepping into a pair of worn red carpet slippers. "Better feel for the ground." As thrifty as he was in his movements, he was equally generous with advice about how to find water. "Hard maple likes their soil well-drained. Don't even bother looking for water in a sugar bush." For his dowsing rod, he had brought along a forked branch from an apple tree. The bark had been whittled away because, "Bark acts like insulation. No use for it a'tall."

After painstakingly walking a grid back and forth across a gully above the house, he found the tip of his apple wood wand repeatedly pulling downward in the same location. "See that?" The stick was defiantly twisting in his grip.

"She's down there, all right," he said. "Can't tell you how deep, or how much," Squeak's trademark peep punctuated his pitch, "But, mister boy, you got all kinds of water."

I must admit that the place he pointed to was no surprise. Fast running melt-off each spring had scoured out miniature basins between the rocks and roots, and left little clutches of twigs along the freshet's erratic borders. White alders, buttonbush, and hay-scented ferns were abundant, sure evidence of wet soils. If I'd had to guess, I would have intuitively picked the same spot, but I wouldn't have had the chance to watch a Yankee water witch at work, or discover that Squeak's apple dowsing rod pulled down in the same places for me as it had for him.

There are numerous theories on how dousing works, but there is nothing so convincing as the inexplicable pull against your hands. I once met a douser at a writers' workshop who claimed he used a dousing rod to choose his literary agent from a list on a page. When I saw him a few years later, I inquired — expecting the worst — how the writing was coming. His stick-doused agent had found him a premier publisher, a fat advance, and the book was soon to be in the bookstores. Go figure.

When Ray dug for water at Squeak's designated spot, he hit a layer of gravelly sand about six feet down, a natural hydro-logic conduit. "Water just sapped out of the sidewall," I heard him say, when he brought uncle Squeak back to see the proof of his witching.

"All the water anybody'd ever need," Squeak said proudly.

"How deep d'you go and how much d'you get?" he asked.

"Vein six foot down, seven gallons a minute," Ray said. "Cold as ice."

"Seven gallons?" Squeak repeated, "Just like I figured."

On a practical level, I wanted my house to be dry in a rainstorm, warm against the cold, and comfortable among pleasing sur-roundings. But on a loftier, architectural plane, I needed to experiment with every gesture of form, space and light imagina-ble: tower, arch, balcony, bridge, cantilever, soaring ceiling, slop-ing wall, curved chimneybreast — I coveted them all. These were the conditions by which architecture was defined, and so it seemed to me that I needed at least one of each.

Once the roof was tar-papered, the windows in place, and the rooms walled up, I had no one to blame for the results but myself. Viewed with kindness, the house might have been described as, "Energetic." A less sympathetic spin might have been, "Jugular-vein modern" or "Feral naïveté." Whatever it was, there were eleven level changes, three stories, two sleeping lofts, two balconies, a cantilevered bathroom, angled windows, and a front door accessed by a bridge with no side rails. What surprises me now is the ease with which I concocted plausible excuses to justify so much exuberance. The design was driven by an eat-it-all approach I would later repudiate, just as I would later embrace and repudiate other styles. But for the moment, like it or not, it was all mine.

And the roof did not leak! When the first rainstorm fell on the finished house, I prowled every room, looking for water. The harder it rained, the more wonderfully symphonic the thunderstorm became to my ears. Water cascaded off the eaves, thunder boomed and lightning flashed, but my little fortress was secure in the storm.

Before winter began, I stuffed the walls and ceilings full of insulation, installed the heating system, and finished the interior trim. The first howling blizzard sounded more like a confirmation than a threat. Lying warm in bed and hearing the furnace rumble to life in the dead of night, or turning on a hot water tap and knowing where the water came from made me feel I was working in concert with forces large and powerful instead of against them. I liked that feeling and have spent most of my life trying to duplicate it. As for my first work of architecture, I was mightily pleased, of course, but the pleasure immediately segued into planning the next house, and how it would be even better.

Pigs

Earning a master's degree from the Yale School of Architecture involved mastering an immense amount of information about building design, structural engineering and the history of art, but virtually nothing — oddly — about raising pigs.

When I abandoned the Cambridge debacle and moved north, my former classmates thought I was committing professional suicide. Tom thought it was a fabulous idea, of course, but Lamar and the others were aghast. For them, trading a "Starchitect's" office for the wilds of New Hampshire seemed like reverse acculturation, a renunciation of truth and light. But I couldn't help myself. Despite its countless attributes, Cambridge suffocated me. In a climate-controlled office with no windows, my necktie became a noose. Each successive year of internship only increased my yearning for the free-range childhood I'd enjoyed in the rolling hills of Pennsylvania. There had to be a means of practicing sophisticated, creative architecture in a rural setting. It wasn't that I wanted to go barefoot and build log huts. I was hoping to combine what I'd learned with what I wanted to learn, to lead a double life, Vitruvius and Tom Sawyer united with a T-square. And it seemed to be working. My first few houses were surprisingly successful, and within a few years, I had built up a loyal client base. Designing good buildings and living a good life weren't mutually exclusive pursuits after all.

My friend Garrett lived off the grid, way out in the Vermont woods across the river from our home in New Hampshire. He wore his hair in a pony tail and drove an old truck. Garrett heated his house with wood, used an outhouse, and drew water from a spring. He worked forty hours a week as a finish carpenter, played bluegrass guitar like a pro, and raised most of his food.

It was 1971, the dawning of the Age of Aquarius. Counterculture icons Timothy Leary, Van Morrison, and Ken Kesey were ascendant; bourgeois ambition was not.

Leary's siren call, "Turn on, tune in, drop out was in the air," and the back-to-the-land movement was filling the north woods with pilgrims. I was too straight-laced to be tempted with the self-conscious high jinks of Ken Kesey's Merry Pranksters, but I was also a pilgrim, looking for mentors in the tradesmen I met, looking for a context for my work. Imitating everything Garrett did wouldn't suit me, but he embodied the possibilities of living outside the limits of the city, and that was appealing.

He also raised pigs.

I loved the idea, not so much for the pork (which would prove to be so plentiful that we gave much of it away to friends with a cheery, "Hi ! How about a home-grown picnic ham!"), but for the pungent metaphor: Raising pigs would be deliciously contrary to anything I had done during my painful tenure in the fair city of Cambridge.

I talked to a few pig-raising neighbors and read a United States Department of Agriculture pamphlet on how to be a patriotic pig farmer. The first thing I learned was that two or more pigs will gain weight faster than one alone. Companionship is probably part of the equation, but being a pig is all about eating, and competition for food boosts the weight gain for all. Pigs are clean. Pigs need shade. They seek the coolness of mud holes because they can only perspire through the skin on their snouts. Pigs defecate neatly in a specific area of their pens. Pigs are smart. And raising pigs might (I hoped) help convince my neighbors that I was more than just an over-educated, college boy, flatlander. All of the above convinced me to proceed with my pig farming folly.

Garrett bought his pigs that year from a commune in Wentworth, New Hampshire. I'd never been to a commune before, and I was curious. The person who first welcomed me was a quiet walrus of a man who called himself Zero. A giggly 2-year-old boy sat atop his huge, disheveled head, pulling on Zero's ears. The sound of a tentative violin wafted through an open widow of the nearby house, accompanied by the musty-sweet incense of marijuana. Out in the garden, a ragged flock of communards pecked at the rocky soil with shovels and hoes. I saw a rib-rippled mule with a painful limp, browsing on bushes at the edge of the clearing. Half-a-dozen cannibalized vehicles were strewn about the yard, two of them crippled VW vans splashed with paint box colors. The tattered house, the cars, the farm tractor — the mule — all seemed to be in a static state of dysfunction. Zero led me around and showed me the chickens, goats, and guinea hens and a teepee covered with tattered polyethylene plastic.

Everybody at the commune seemed friendly enough — and tediously slow and earnest — as if they were trying to blend psychedelica with a Hollywood version of farm life, circa 1885. With the exception of Zero, the men tended toward scrawny, pale, and bearded in their muddy overalls, while the women were healthily plump and mostly naked, as though a party of agrarian strippers had been airdropped into the backyard of a backwoods bachelors' home.

Zero talked about organic gardening and the concepts promoted by Scott and Helen Nearing in their back-to-the-land books. He made it sound seductively simple, but I'd spent enough childhood summers in a vegetable garden, coping with woodchucks, slugs, and potato bugs to make me wonder if Zero had grown things before. I later learned that his given name was Irving. He had grown up in New York City and was a recent Vietnam veteran. I'd demonstrated against the war, and was spared the draft due to the birth of our daughter in 1967, but I always felt guilty when I met someone who had nobly served our country and returned so visibly damaged, trying so hard to survive. Living close to the land at the commune was Zero's chosen therapy — a good choice, I'm sure. One could only hope that he'd soon find the peace he deserved.

Overall, what I saw that day seemed lugubrious, except for the children, who were gloriously alive. I wondered about the adults, most of whom were college graduates from advantaged backgrounds, like me. Where were the working-class communards? Actually working? Did the prerequisite of a collective mindset automatically deaden individuality, or was everybody just too stoned to stand up straight? All by himself, Garrett managed to do everything well that they were trying, and all but failing, to do as a commune. Lamar thought of commune living as, "Digging-a-hole-with-a-spoon," but that seemed too harsh. Something good was happening here — wasn't it? Tom Luckey would have loved the unfettered freedom and the naked ladies, but he was far too inventive and industrious to tolerate the deliberate regression to nineteenth-century gratuitous hardships.

At the time, I wanted to admire communes more than I did. We all knew that America was polarized by the war, lied to by its leaders, struggling with issues of women's rights, race and poverty — but was dropping out the solution? I thought not. I had no perspective; I was too close to it all to see that we were in the midst of a cultural revolution, and cultural revolutions begin with extremes.

Zero led me to the back of the commune's barn, where a huge sow and her weaned piglets were shading themselves under the ravaged carcass of a Mercedes Benz. The piglets I chose weighed about thirty pounds each, and were frisky and cute as puppy dogs. One was black with a white belt around his middle, the other was two-toned tan. I paid thirty dollars for the pair, said my farewells, and put the squealing Oreo and Pig Newton in the trunk of my car.

The majestic quarters I'd built for them was cobbled together with selected scraps of lumber liberated from various jobs. The floor plan measured four by eight feet, one sheet of plywood. A mason's discarded formwork used to shape a brick archway made a cunning Romanesque entrance. The walls — embellished with one port hole each — soared upward to at least three feet above the floor, and the pitched roof was crowned with a discarded cupola topped with a flying duck weathervane — 100% recycled materials. I sited my creation in a shady grove beyond sight and smell from the house, and attached to it a thirty foot-square yard surrounded by a four foot-high fence. It amused me to imagine that this goofy little folly precisely represented the nadir to which Lamar assumed I would tumble. I dubbed it The Hambone Hilton.

I'd like to believe that Oreo and Pig Newton were impressed with the architecture, but as pigs will do, they immediately began roto-tilling the yard with their amazingly powerful snouts, ripping up roots and dislodging rocks the size of soccer balls in their search for edibles. I fed them pig pellets and table scraps constantly. The water bucket was regularly tipped over until I nailed the handle tight to the inside corner of the fence.

As they settled in to their new home, Mr. Newton devised a brilliant competitive eating tactic: He would lie down lengthwise in the trough, covering all the food except the portion under his snout. Oreo was frustrated at first, but quickly learned to root for his supper under Pig Newton, and consistent with the two-pig theory, they both gained weight fast and equally. By the middle of June, they were twice the size they were when they arrived.

It's always been a mystery, though, how Oreo escaped. When I came to the pen one morning, Pig Newton was lying in the trough, as usual, fast asleep, and Oreo was just plain gone. I checked the fence and found no holes in it, no holes dug under it; there was no gate to be nudged open. Had Oreo jumped or climbed over a four-foot wall? I'll never know. I scouted the woods around the house for hours and found no tracks, no traces of rooting, no pig. It was the fourth of July, and Oreo had declared his independence.

He lived out in the wild for weeks. I found where he'd foraged — hillsides that looked as if they'd been ploughed up by a drunken farmer — but Oreo himself became a phantom. During the first week, a neighbor called to report a sighting, but by the time I arrived, Oreo had disappeared. The second and third week brought more callers. Some of them were justifiably irritated as the increasingly infamous fugitive was found to have excavated a vegetable garden or a patch of cornfield. Each time, I apologized effusively, rushed to the scene and made amends. I saw him on three occasions, but when I tried to sneak up on him, he'd lift his head, sniff the air, and bolt through the woods as if he had wings. As the weeks went by, it was my neighbors I worried about far more than the pig. My desire to assimilate was backfiring. I was the new kid on the block — an architect flatlander, at that — who couldn't even build a working pig pen.

I gave up chasing and entertained other options. A lasso? A snare, a net? A tranquilizer gun? How about a blowgun with soporific darts? Aerial bombardment with hypnotic smoke bombs. Drugs? But then, where did one find such things, let alone the pig for whom they were meant?

A close neighbor, Tony Foster, called one evening to report that he'd seen Oreo among his Herefords. "Little guy must be getting lonely," he ventured. Oreo was following Tony's cattle on their daily rounds of grazing. "You can see them along the roadside fence around noon," he said, "Like clockwork." Tony knew where his cattle were every hour of the day. "Kind of cute how they let little piggy tag along."

Now that I knew where and when to find Oreo, how would I capture him? I poured myself a glass of wine and looked up at the stars — and down at the glass in my hand. Eureka! I would set a trap — using food — soaked in alcohol. Jack Daniels and slops in a tub. Perfect. A pig's nose is almost as fine-tuned as a dog's. If a pig could smell underground truffles from twenty yards away, Oreo could smell this concoction from across the county. No need to take the trap to him; he would come to it.

The next morning, an hour before noon, I laced a tub of slops with a fifth of Tennessee's best and drove over to Tony's where I left the tub just outside the barbed wire fence, beyond the Herefords' reach.

The telephone rang at one-thirty. "Don," Tony said, "You can come get your pig," Pause ... "And you don't have to hurry."

The Herefords were gone when I arrived, but I found Oreo lying on his side next to the half-emptied tub, passed out cold. As I hefted him into the trunk of my car, I could tell he'd had plenty to eat these last four weeks. He was every bit as big as Pig Newton, almost too heavy to lift. He was also crusted with dried mud and his breath stank, but I thought he looked beautiful.

Back at the Hambone Hilton, I opened the trunk lid with extreme caution, imagining that he would burst out and escape once again — but I needn't have worried. Oreo was snoring. His front hocks were crossed in the manner of a delicate ballerina *sur pointes*. Now and then, his legs twitched, as if he were dreaming about being on the run again. His eyes fluttered and closed. I imagined he'd had fun being a celebrity, a free-ranging bandit dodging me at every turn. A smart, fast pig he'd been indeed. As I lay him down inside his pen, the grin on his stubby pink snout was simply beatific.

Out the Window

We lived in that first house for eight years and always looked forward to Tom Luckey's visits, but we never knew what to call the dogs and people coming with him. As a re-inventor of forms and functions, it logically followed that Tom was also a re-inventor of people and animals' names. Reproducing every alias he's assigned to his loved ones over the years would be impossible, but the list goes something like this: His son, Spencer has answered to: Wise-E, Rich Rolling, Boyim, Rotten Brown and Schwazz. Spencer's sister, Owen, was aka Nugget, Nugg-Nuggs, Bar Mitzphee, Mrs. Berman and Mrs. Hoomer. The first family dog was Snippety, or Associate, followed by Cue-tip, Squinch, Diner's Club Card, Zone, Spunkeeney, Pla-Doo, Snack, Oomrix, Lily and Cornsoolian. There's a family Donkey named Victor and two horses, Zephyr and Pee Do Wabbit. Tom fondly refers to his mother as Grackle. His lovely second wife, Ettie, is Mol, The Commander-in-Chief, Peeky, Stanley or Hooly Mol. (She calls Tom, Nutty.) Their daughter Kit answers to: Wacky, Shark, Shocky-P-Gik and P-Unk. Their son Walker is Bean, Creamy Booskin, Old Mr. Pollutie, Slow Pokey Guy or Slooge. Yours truly is Mertzenberger, or, if Tom is in a hurry, Mertzen. Dignity always intact, Lamar remained Lamar.

Lamar's career path was such that he was able to visit us just once, which I confess was exactly the number of times I'd visited him. (So much for my illusion of being immune to the hustle and stress of being an architect in the city.) I hadn't seen Lamar since school, and he looked older and broader than I remembered, but his hair was still thick and blond and perfectly tousled as always. His French girlfriend, Simone, would have come with him, he said, but she was rehearsing for a new off-Broadway comedy written by a young British playwright I'd never heard of. Lamar and Simone had met at a party given by a corporate client in Paris, and as Lamar explained, "sa va de soi," which I took to mean he was pretty well done for.

Compared to ours, their lives were filled with urbane excitement including, I inferred, star-studded soirees in their Greenwich Village loft. I pictured them dining out at chic new restaurants, knowing exactly when to order a crisp Pinot Noir instead of a fruity Merlot. Their week's vacation in Argentina the year before was entirely devoted to the tango. Lamar mentioned he was learning to speak Italian — which was "easy" because, thanks to Simone, he had learned to speak French. I decided not to mention that up in the woods behind the house, I had learned to raise pigs a few summers ago.

Although I was swamped with increasingly interesting commissions, my exposure to cold winters, carpenter talk and the sound of coyotes at night was a far cry from Lamar's concerts, art galleries, and museums. We occasionally went to the only movie theater within thirty miles, but other than listening to NPR and lots of reading, we were strictly from Hicksville compared to Lamar and Simone.

There was an authoritative rasp in Lamar's voice I hadn't heard before; maybe it was the Gauloises he smoked. But his genteel manner was now shaded with a tone of greater certainty, and it was easier than ever to imagine him managing a team of architects, engineers, and contractors. Still, it took only a few minutes to feel as if we were back in school again, as if nothing had changed.

While we were hungry for news of his life in the city, he insisted we first take a tour of the house. From level to level, room-to-room, I tried, but failed, to sound modest. "Peter and I built this cantilevered loft without staging," I boasted. "On a windy day." As Lamar glanced out the window at the ground below, I imagined him calculating the personal injury award for one of his fallen union carpenters. "Thirty feet off the ground," I added shamelessly. "And it was spitting rain when we slid the window in."

"You're still an idiot, I see." I took it as a compliment. "I can't even climb a step ladder," he added.

I wanted to convince him that my move north had not been idiotic. Lamar was the poster boy for the loftier cultural virtues I'd turned my back on, but since I admired how suitably he'd applied his education, I was inevitably led to seek affirmation for how I'd applied mine. Before he might think poorly of my skills as a finish carpenter, I showed him our dining room table.

"You made this?" he asked.

"From a walnut tree cut down at my folks' place in Pennsylvania."

He smoothed the surface with his hand and stooped to examine the trestle below. "Mortise and tenon? Very nice ..."

I think he meant it.

"And now that I've seen the house for myself," he said, "I must say that it looks even better than it did in print."

I hoped he'd seen the article, but didn't want to ask. My house had been featured in *The New York Times Sunday Magazine* soon after it was built. I was dumbstruck to see my work published in such a flattering venue — as was my mother. She liked the house much better once it had been published, and passed around copies of the article to strangers.

"You must have been swamped with fan mail," Lamar said.

As I was to learn when other houses were published in multiple journals in the years to come, the response ratio was underwhelming. After the first house appeared in the *Times*, for instance, I got exactly two responses. One was a phone call from a woman in Maryland who wanted to know where she could buy a table lamp shown in the photos, and the other was from a celebrity I didn't care for at the time. "Bob Dylan wrote me," I said, "Asking if I might be interested in doing a house for him in Woodstock."

Lamar was impressed with his country bumpkin friend. "And you designed him a masterpiece, I presume?"

"I never answered his letter," I said.

"Excuse me?"

My wife shot him a supportive glance, confirming that she, too, knew I'd been a fool to pass up such an opportunity.

I said, "Have you ever listened to the lyrics of Mr. Tambourine Man?"

Lamar threw up his hands. "What's the song have to do with it? You bonehead. We're talking about Bob Dylan!"

In a splendid display of hubris that I can only marvel at today, I declared, "Just listen to him sing the stupid song, okay? The guy is such a loser."

Lamar's sixty-hour weeks at SOM suited him perfectly. He was enthusiastic about the sixty-story, glass-and-steel office tower he'd been working on for the past three years. At the time of our conversation, the design phase was done. Engineering, working drawings and specifications were partially completed; the project would be let out to bid in another six months. Six months later, the project would begin. From the time SOM was awarded the commission to the day the occupants moved in would span half-a-dozen years.

I understood the sixty-hour weeks, but mine seemed somehow less onerous because I was self-employed. My time was my own, or so I thought. I'd completed twenty-some houses since leaving school with the help of one draftsman. Lamar hoped to become a junior partner at SOM within the next five years. Another ten years might see him in charge of overseeing multiple projects and flying around the world selling SOM's services to ambitious clients. He seemed comfortable with the idea of working at SOM until he retired, as if no other options were feasible. For the first time since I'd met him, I felt a twinge of pity when I imagined the all-too-predictable arc of his life. Working for a huge organization, fitting in, behaving well, promoting the brand — it all seemed to me like an abdication of freedom.

As we finished lunch that day, Lamar gazed out the window and said, "That's too bad."

I wondered what I could have missed looking out across the valley at least a dozen times a day. What was too bad? "Where?"

He pointed to the corner of a pasture, a mile away. "That house trailer. Would you call that pink, or fuscia?"

"That's Tammy and Leon's," I said. "Our closest neighbors. You'd like them." I explained that when I cut down some trees for the view and first saw their trailer, I felt a connection, even though we were still strangers. I barely noticed what color it was. When we moved in, they dropped by to welcome us with an apple pie and a six-pack. When we saw their lights twinkling at night and the smoke rising from their chimney on a cold winter's day, we felt part of a community. I occasionally played guitar in their pickup country band, "Tammy and the What Knots," and got to enjoy her renditions of Patsy Cline's "Blue" and "Crazy". When Leon's Holstein was out grazing the summer pasture, we could almost make out her black and white spots. Two vehicles in the driveway meant Tammy and Leon were home from work. They owned two snowmobiles and a camper trailer, and they didn't read *The New York Times*.

Lamar saw nothing but a pink house trailer because he'd never heard Leon yodel off-key, or sing a George Jones duet with

Tammy. From Lamar's point of view, the house trailer signified an aesthetically unfortunate, economic necessity. What I saw wasn't about the failure of aesthetics, but about the success of making a life. He argued that what we "see" is, by default, culturally programmed, as well as contextual, literal or figurative. Depending upon the expectation, Tammy's pink trailer might mean many things to many viewers, just as looking east across the Hudson toward the skyline of Manhattan could be as awe-inspiring to a New Yorker as a back-packer's wide-angle prospect across a Colorado mountain range. It's the lens through which we "see" that endows an image with meaning, not necessarily the image itself.

So much for the figurative: What about the deliberate, architectural devices calculated to frame and manipulate the viewer's experience? English Romantics of the nineteenth century went so far as to build ersatz ruins and "follies" (miniature Grecian temples or Dutch windmills) as a means of teasing the eye into the landscape. In the early part of the twentieth century, Frank Lloyd Wright promoted the idea of integrating a building's inside with the outside, living with as well as in nature. The concept was inimical to a frontier culture accustomed to wolves and blizzards howling at the door. How could nature be trusted? Wright insisted it could be. Modern construction methods and a tamed wilderness made the indoor-outdoor concept suddenly attractive, and architects of every stripe adopted the idea. Walls extending from inside to outside, deep overhangs, patios, arcades, arbors, pergolas and trees in the foreground all provide a three-dimensional means of stretching the view from the man-made to the natural.

Blah, blah, blah! Bringing the outside in was just talk between Lamar and me; Tom Luckey had done it all when he renovated an old house in Branford, Connecticut.

The house he bought had been built as a summer cottage, circa 1900, with the era's trademark, double-beaded Douglas fir on all the interior walls and ceilings. Forty yards from the beach, the house was quasi-Queen Ann in style, two stories high with a big front porch and a view of the Long Island Sound. Twenty-five feet behind the house, a cliff rose almost vertically, well above the roof. Tom brought in the outside by extending the side walls and roof of the house rearward until it met the cliff. The result was a spacious two-story living/dining room dominated by a massive, ivy-covered granite monolith. The new back wall of the house was literally the cliff.

The old downstairs back wall (separating the new and existing spaces) was removed so that the kitchen was now part of the two-story living/dining space. Above the kitchen, Tom left the original outside wall of the cottage — salt bleached shingles and two rear windows looking out at the now-enclosed cliff. One of these windows served a bedroom, and Tom's children could always keep the sash shut when the adults were making too much noise at the table below. The other window admitted light into the upstairs bathroom, next to the toilet. The sill of that window was less than two feet from the floor. The sash was never replaced when the addition was completed, so that anyone using the toilet could easily continue a conversation with dinner guests twelve feet away at the table below.

Which bothered Lamar. "I hold it 'til I leave," he said. Lamar was as fond of Tom as I was, but he admitted to some discomfort with Tom's casual manners and was worried about Tom's career. "Where exactly is he going?" he would ask. Tom had abandoned architecture soon after graduation, and instead was making the most brilliant, uniquely-crafted — and un-commercial objects imaginable. Toys and furniture spilled out of him. They were idiosyncratic enough to deserve art object status, but too unique to become marketable. And anyway, he made the toys as gifts for his children, little wagons, see-saws, scooters, and a perfectly proportioned, full-sized pony with a real mane and tail. Not for sale.

For three or four years, Tom worked relentlessly on a series of mini-merry-go-rounds — ingeniously portable, foldable contraptions designed to be towed on a trailer from playground to playground. Some of these were designed in such a way as to require the children themselves to crank the revolving platform into action. Tom liked the idea of encouraging each child to participate in both the fun and the responsibility of making the fun happen.

The merry-go-rounds turned out to be less than merry. Clients were scarce, money was tight, and his marriage was failing. Tom moved into a waterlogged catboat on the Connecticut shore, cooked his meals on a Coleman stove, and slept in a damp galley hammock. But he was still upbeat, ever ready to compensate for a loss with a new enthusiasm. "You should hear the waves drumming on the hull at night," he said, when I worried about his homelessness. "It's just fabulous, down there in the dark, living below the water line."

It got worse: Tom describes applying for unemployment benefits as the low point, standing in line alongside badly broken people whom he felt deserved to be there so much more than he did. He kept himself sane by rowing far out into Long Island Sound every morning at dawn. He occasionally changed his clothes and shaved, and never stopped making toys and furniture and intricate sculptures carved in wood. He made plans for playgrounds that no one would buy. Our tenth-year architecture school reunion was a year away. Unlike many of our classmates, Tom had never once stopped inventing, pushing ideas and forms into new configurations, constantly asking, "What If ... ?"

When Lamar finally left for the five-hour push back to the city, I was sorry to see him go. As he drove away, the trees along the driveway framed his car in a series of strobe-like vignettes, sunlit and shaded, light and dark. When he passed from view, I wondered how we would frame ourselves in the years to come, how we would reconcile the disparate architecture of our lives. I imagined him driving under the shadow of the George Washington Bridge and down the West Side Highway to where it had begun to crumble north of the Lincoln Tunnel, to the last permitted exit where a river of cars poured out onto lower Manhattan's local streets. I walked through the trees to my office and imagined the heat and the noise of the city in August.

Everything For
Which It Stands

A decade after moving to New Hampshire, my professional life had taken root. I had enough work to justify hiring full time help with the drawings, and another two projects had been published in national magazines.

Among the more engaging projects at the time was a vacation house for a couple from Boston. They'd been dreaming about a small, rustic retreat in the woods for years, and when their children finished college, they bought five acres on a remote pond in Vermont and were ready to proceed. I felt comfortable with them from the moment we met, although it took a while to understand that their version of "small" meant twice the size of Tammy and Leon's trailer. Their notion of "rustic," I soon realized, required the spending of considerable sums to achieve an effect that would look as if little had been spent.

After our first few meetings, I was confident that I understood how they approached problem solving and how they interacted with one another. Elaine, a civil rights lawyer, deferred to Bob in most aesthetic matters, which in turn, he negotiated with me. Bob was a research biologist. Elaine confided in me that even though he had received a MacArthur Foundation genius grant before his thirtieth birthday, he was prone to forgetting their zip code. Bob deferred to Elaine in all things financial, and they both, almost reverentially, deferred to me in all matters structural.

Bob loved their old Labrador, Bud. Elaine was graciously tolerant of the pooch, even though Bud habitually smelled as if he had rolled in something toxic. Elaine was a principled vegetarian, her husband a hairy omnivore. They wore fashionably unfashionable clothes and laughed loudly at my worst jokes. How couldn't I like them? They were passionate about music, fresh baguettes, and liberal politics. They drove an old, rumpled Volvo wagon so bulging with discarded research papers and leftover picnics that it could have doubled as a recycling bin. In their mid-fifties, they still held hands. Their respect for one another was palpable, and their marriage was alive and durable, which left me both fascinated and envious.

The first thing I asked Bob and Elaine to do was to write up a "program." What was their vision of the house, and how would it function? What did it want to look like, feel like to them? How many, how big, and what kinds of rooms did they want, and how would the spaces relate to one another? Did they want a Jacuzzi, a green house, a fireplace, or perhaps a laundry room next to the bedrooms on the second floor? Or, would all the bedrooms be on the first floor? Were there important rugs or furniture or paintings that needed to be accommodated? The program, I explained, was a client's wish list, and there was nothing too trivial to be excluded. If the wish list overshot the budget, we'd go back to the items on the list and embark on a sequence of surrender.

Bob and Elaine's program covered two pages. Since they wanted a compact design, we talked a lot about the difference between proportion and size, how size is not absolute, but is dependent upon the relationship of one thing to another. We decided this "tiny" house should have a generous, open feel to it, and discussed how we could play with proportions. Smaller panes in a window make a room feel bigger. Larger windows extend the inside spaces outward into the landscape. A low ceiling in a small room will expand the sense of space and size in an adjacent room with a high ceiling. Wide floorboards tend to miniaturize a small room while narrow floorboards will appear to enhance the dimensions. Dark colors shrink a room; light colors expand it. Size matters, but proportion matters more.

Even before I began drawing the first line, it was understood that several design parameters were predetermined by the setting: views of the lake lay to the south of the house site, the sun's path moved unobstructed from east to west, and the driveway came in from the north. All of these worked in our favor.

Like so many clients before them and since, Bob and Elaine talked about creating the perfect, tasteful house. But what did that mean? If we were to poll a hundred people, each of whom lived in what they considered the "perfect" house, how few would trade for another's version of perfect? Taste is a complicated acquisition. Understanding the bubbling stew of one's aesthetic history requires a kind of rigorous, personal archeology. "I don't know why I like it, I just do," is not much help when a hundred interrelated decisions have yet to be made. But to leave taste unexamined limits the design process to the expression of a few subconscious particulars.

Perhaps the first step of understanding taste involves identifying what we like: I like the way Greek fishermen's houses use asymmetric openings in their masonry walls. I like my grandfather's library, my neighbor's kitchen, my best friend's living room.

The difficult question is: "Why?" Why wood instead of stone? Why green instead of ochre, why large and rough instead of small and smooth? What is being satisfied within us when we see a certain material, texture, color or shape? Taste is the reflection in the mirror of our pasts, but it has many faces and is never entirely transparent. Many contemporary Greeks and Italians, for instance, live surrounded by monumental heaps of antiquity, and yet they renovate their homes and businesses with gaudy objects and flimsy plastic materials totally inappropriate to their revered cultures. This apparent disconnect seems both unforgivable and logical. To many modern Athenians and Romans, the insular inconveniences of the past can't compete with the ubiquitous ease of the present.

Of course, taste isn't the only thing Bob and Elaine were bringing to the party. Their positive outlook was exemplary. They couldn't wait to see each new set of drawings, each wall newly raised. The simple pleasure of designing from scratch excited them. By attitude alone, they encouraged their architect to dare. Because they were rich with enthusiasm, the depths of their pockets were immaterial. Their intelligence, passion and curiosity were contagious, and made me want to do the very best I could for them.

Some clients approach the process with the glass half empty. Convinced the project will be a painful experience, they invariably find that self-fulfilling prophecies aren't easy to dismantle. Some clients expect a new house to provide a surrogate solution to family problems. (If only raising a complicated teenager was as simple as building a complicated house.) Others think of design as a check-off menu — granite counter tops here, a hot tub in the garden, a fireplace under a curved staircase over there — without ever seeing the composition as a whole. Others leave every decision to the architect and move into a house that bears no traces of them. And like some architects, some clients are simply eccentric.

I was once interviewed by an engineer who wanted to build a house for himself entirely held together with adhesives. No nails, bolts, screws, hangers, staples, or metal fasteners of any kind: just sticky stuff. I've been asked to design a house for a woman allergic to wood, plaster, concrete, stone, brick, metal, ragweed, and glass. I declined. Another would-be client wanted a subterranean bomb shelter home for himself and his family. After discussing the niceties of family life in a cave, I inquired how he imagined he'd seal himself in if a nuclear event occurred. His caretaker, he explained, would bulldoze a mound of dirt over the entrance, leaving only the pipelines for filtered air exposed. What would become of the loyal caretaker was never discussed.

By the beginning of May, Bob, Elaine, and I had been telephoning frequently, and sending sketches back and forth for a couple of months. We followed our combined logic through many iterations of the floor plans and elevations; Bob and Elaine were unfailingly enthusiastic and flexible. By early summer, we were in agreement that nothing was missing, nothing was redundant, nothing too big or too small. As small as they were, all the pieces — two bedrooms, one bathroom, a laundry room, entry hall and great room, interacted harmoniously. The massing was simple, the detailing witty, and we liked very much how it looked — a big little house. I had sweet dreams about it, and was about to begin working drawings when I received a letter.

Dear Don,

We're terribly excited about how well the plans are shaping up. Can't wait to see the cabin nestled in the trees and Verdi soaring on the stereo. We've shown the plans to a part-time architect-artist friend of ours who makes marvelous bird houses — a few local nurseries carry his work — and he's doing some sketches suggesting how we might move some spaces around, maybe add a room or two and make the place a little more jazzy.

All the best,

Elaine and Bob

I felt like a cuckolded lover. Marvelous birdhouses? I'd never heard Elaine and Bob use the word "jazzy" before, and now this part-time architect-artist was going to move some spaces around, add a room or two and make the house jazzy? I suppose I should have been grateful that he was an "architect-artist" and not an accountant-artist, but if this was where we were headed, I imagined it wouldn't be long before aunt Iola would be sending along Formica samples (avocado) from the house she and Uncle Vern built in Omaha in '56.

There is always a point in the design process when the project begins to drive itself. The critical mass of coordinated decisions reaches a point when it makes subsequent choices almost immutable. The four legs on a horse are essential to all the other parts, and vice versa. If adding a fifth were to be suddenly proposed, the entire anatomical premise would require re-thinking. In houses, as with horses, good design is driven by the accretion of symbiotic ideas, not the random assembly of disparate parts. Elaine and Bob's friend may have proposed valid ideas (we would see about that!), but he hadn't been with us, week after week, as we evolved an anatomy from the conceptual to the particular. It offended me to think that someone would presume to dash in at the eleventh hour without having been privy to the incremental logic of our labors.

My only consolation was that the letter hadn't arrived after I'd begun the working drawings. At least I wouldn't have wasted hours of work on an obsolete design. We had signed the typical architect-owner contract, which refers to three basic stages of work: design, working drawings, and construction supervision (since changed to "construction observation" in an attempt to lessen the architect's liability for errors committed by the builder.) Working drawings are a means to an end, a protocol serving the building process in much the same way that a screenplay serves a cinematographer or a recipe serves a chef. Working drawings, like invitations to a wedding, are best postponed if any of the parties are having second thoughts — as Bob and Elaine apparently were.

No matter how perfect a design may be, some clients interpret the ease of a natural birth as some kind of capitulation. Had Bob and Elaine begun to doubt their experience? Had they assumed I was less than adequate because I had thrown no artistic tantrums? Could True Creativity be realized without overcoming great obstacles? Maybe Don was being lazy and hasn't explored all the options!

I splashed strong waters over ice, took courage, and composed my reply:

Dear Elaine and Bob,
Jazz is good, Charlie Parker is a genius and Miles Davis is a giant, but I must confess your sudden interest in redefining your plans takes me by surprise. I'll hold off on the working drawings until I see your friend's sketches.
All the best,
Don

Of course there is always the fear that you've overlooked the obvious, or worse yet, exalted the mundane at the expense of artful opportunity. And then there's the ultimate paranoia, the fear that despite all your patience and attention to the client's needs, you've not understood them; after all the hours you've spent together planning the trip, you missed the boat. I scolded myself for feeling off balance. I wanted this house to be the best it could be. Someone else's good idea might be perfect, but why was it so threatening when it came unannounced from someone unknown? Who cared from where it came?

I did.

The sketches arrived a few days later. To be fair, they weren't bad, but Mr. Birdhouse hadn't participated in the lengthy back story that drove so many of our decisions: the kitchen/dining area was on the southeast corner precisely because the clients were early risers and wanted morning sunshine as they drank their coffee looking out at the lake. His kitchen was in the middle, away from the windows. In my scheme, the bathroom, stairs and entry were at the rear of the house, where sunshine and view were minimal. The great room and the bedrooms above had full sun and the view of the lake. His great room faced the woods. (Did that make it jazzy?) He'd missed those sessions in which we decided, after careful negotiations, which of the bedrooms was to face east and which was to face west, not to mention the reasons we separated them with closets (noise attenuation) as well as complicated issues involving Bud the dog, early risers/late risers, their daughter's allergies, and Bob's snoring — among others.

Mr. Birdhouse had not been present when I explained the elegant economy and logic of the exposed framing pattern. Every post and beam and corner brace landed exactly where it needed to be without compromising windows, doors, or structural integrity. His plan would have been chaotic to frame, expensive to build, and paid no attention to the layout of the energy efficient mechanical system that drove so many of our decisions.

His sketches contained several nice ideas I would endorse and thank him for, but the house he drew was an altogether different house, designed for clients I didn't recognize, on a site and within a budget not our own. The extra rooms would have added significantly to the cost of the house, and I knew Bob and Elaine's funds were limited. His ideas were jazzy? Given the evidence, he may have once taken a lesson, but he was no musician.

Dear Bob and Elaine,

I got the drawings today and look forward to discussing them with you as soon as possible. I like the way your friend flared out the bottom two steps on the stair. It makes a more graceful transition into the great room. I also like the idea of the transom window above the front door as the hall might be a bit dark without it. As for the other suggestions — let's talk.

Ciao,

Don

When Bob and Elaine next called, they began by explaining that they were exhausted. They'd been up late the last few nights puzzling over the plans and had a lot to talk to me about. (Was this a preamble to a long rationalization about why the house wasn't right for them? Had they decided to sell the land and move to Arizona?)

"We've been looking at Raphael's plans," Bob began, (His name was Raphael? Wasn't that a bit much for someone who makes birdhouses?) "And we're comparing them back and forth with yours."

"Good idea ..."

"We see some big problems."

Fine. I had other work pending, a house in the Berkshires, a house in northern New Hampshire. There was plenty to do if this project fell through.

"We're having a lot of trouble seeing how his ideas fit," Elaine said. "Yours make much more sense."

On second thought, I decided Raphael was a name anyone should feel free to use.

"We're not too smart at this," Bob (the MacArthur genius grant recipient) said, "But it seems that we'd lose all the things we worked on with you if we were to jazz up the plans the way he wants us to."

"He drew a jazzy house," I said. "And you are smart at this. I'm just not sure these new ideas address your concerns."

"We're so relieved to hear you say that," they answered in unison. "It looked so interesting when Raphael first showed it to us," Elaine added. "It's too bad he never finished architecture school."

"He was a first-year student at M.I.T and dropped out to make sculpture," Bob said. "A friend of my son's."

I felt suddenly magnanimous. "I liked his idea about the bottom stairs," I said.

"Is that a pipe railing thing?"

I wasn't sure what she meant; there were no pipe railings in my plans or Raphael's. "The flared steps at the bottom," I explained. "It eases the flow into the great room."

"Really?"

I was reminded that Bob and Elaine had difficulty reading drawings. Lines on the paper simply did not translate into spaces for them. Their failure to comprehend was clearly not related to intelligence, or even training. A dear friend and client of mine was a guest at my house every few months for fifteen years. A man of great intellect and accomplishments, spatial relationships were an infinite mystery to him. From the first visit to the last, he had to ask where the bathroom was.

"And I liked the idea of a transom window over the front door," I said.

"Is that what that was? We wondered ..."

Trust in an architect can be difficult enough when the client is drawing-literate. Trust in an architect as a seeing-eye dog requires unadulterated faith. What is apparent on the drawings to some must be translated verbally to others. Talking about space can be a little bit like trying to talk about wine or perfume — but sometimes there is no option, so we talk about expanded space: pinched, compressed, generous, borrowed, elongated space — foreshortened, soaring, dead, dynamic, asymmetrical, unsettling, proportionate space; ennobling, humble, sacred, and profane space. The words help, but they fall short of the feeling. If needed, I look for full-scale approximations of what I've drawn — an existing room or combination of elements in an existing building — but it is a time consuming and potentially inaccurate enterprise unless I'm lucky enough to find a perfect copy. Least effectively, I hold my arms this wide apart to demonstrate the width of a hallway. In the end, my client will live in a house defined by very specific quantities and qualities space, light and form, not in a house made of my inadequate adjectives, adverbs, and nouns.

There was more to the phone call: "We had another idea," Bob said.

I began chewing my pencil.

"Actually, it was our daughter's boyfriend's idea," Elaine added. "He's just started his MBA at Harvard," which I assumed was code for, he's really smart. "And he rooms with an architecture student."

The first corollary to the Last-Person-I-Talked-To Syndrome is that there never is a last, Last Person. "Really?" The false enthusiasm with which I replied was meant to convey a dutiful, non-judgmental and open-to-all-ideas-from-all-comers frame of mind — MBAs, architecture students, and diesel mechanics included.

"He thinks we should put a bathroom downstairs as well as the one upstairs."

"We could do that," I said, although I knew we couldn't possibly squeeze in a bathroom without expanding the current floor plan. In any case, we had many times discussed a second bathroom, and decided it wasn't worth the expense.

"Didn't you say an extra bathroom would cost about a thousand dollars extra?" Elaine asked.

We all have episodes of selective amnesia, but my dear clients were afflicted with the variety that forgets only the prices of things they've wanted but couldn't afford. If we'd been talking about a part of the house that only I wanted to include, Elaine would remember the cost to the cent. When I reminded her that the extra bath would cost multiple thousands more, she seemed genuinely surprised, but the issue was immediately settled — no second bath.

"Anything else we should be talking about in the way of changes?" I asked.

There was a long pause, and then, "We were wondering about a tower."

"A tower."

"A cousin of ours built a house in the Adirondacks," Bob said, "And the view was out over a lake, like ours. They have this clever little tower-cupola thing on top that they go up to for cocktails."
"Has your cousin seen our plans?"

"We described them, sort of." They laughed when they heard themselves say, sort of. "Not a good idea, huh?"

"I like the idea. It would be a nice element, but ..."

"It would cost a lot, I know," Elaine said. "Just checking."

It would cost a lot, I explained, and we'd need either a stairway or a ladder to reach it, and ladders are not easy to negotiate with a tray of cocktails in hand. Stairs are expensive and take up space in a small house — especially from a room less than ten-feet square. Aside from cost, lack of space, structural, aesthetic, and practical concerns, the idea was excellent.

After our next few conversations, it appeared that Bob and Elaine were truly ready to commit to the plans we'd made. If they had more ideas from well-intentioned friends and relatives, they never mentioned them. Our design solutions had withstood months of scrutiny. We had put all the pieces in place, and even if we had reinvented the wheel a few times, it was finally prepared to roll, round and true. I finished the working drawings by the end of August and began calling contractors.

Contractors are selected for a project by two basic methods: competitive bidding or negotiated contract. Competitive bidding involves two or more contractors who assign exact figures to every aspect of the project, add a "cushion" for unexpected contingencies, plus a fee (or a percentage) for profit and overhead, and then submit a final, not-to-exceed bid for the work. The client reserves the right to accept or reject any or all bids, but usually awards the job to the lowest bidder. The advantage to competitive bidding is that the client and builder agree contractually to exactly what the building will cost.

A negotiated contract begins with a chosen contractor and proceeds on the premise that each portion of the job will be negotiated with the best price in mind for both owner and builder. Because it is a cost-plus arrangement, (cost of materials and labor, plus profit and overhead) the builder needs to add no "cushion" for unforeseen contingencies. Although the owners have only an estimate of what the project will cost, they can proceed knowing they will be charged only for work accomplished. Elaine wanted to let the drawings out for competitive bids so that she'd know to the penny what the house would cost. Bob preferred to gamble on the negotiated contract, reasoning (optimistically) that if everything proceeded as it should, they would save money. Elaine prevailed.

I suggested we limit our bidding list to three candidates. With such a small house, the profit margins would be scant, and there would be less incentive for anyone to bid against six or eight competitors. I found two reputable contractors who were interested, and was about to engage a third when Bob called.

"I don't know if we ever mentioned our friend Stanley Paige," he said, "But Elaine and I would like very much to include him on our bid list."

There were plenty of builders in the area. I had worked with half a dozen and heard the usual builders' gossip about others, but if Stanley's name didn't sound familiar, I wasn't worried. After all, I was the eternal flatlander who had much to learn about who was who. "Where's Stanley from?" I asked.

"Perkinsville," Bob said. "He's an awfully nice guy."

"So you've known him for a while?"

"Three or four years. We met him at the Old Mill Restaurant in Woodstock when we used to come up looking for land, way back."

"And he does residential projects?"

"We're sure that he could."

I conveniently assumed Stanley was a commercial builder, and began to mentally frame several questions about his qualifications: Could we see some examples of his finish work? Was he associated with subcontractors who worked on residential-scale projects? Was his crew used to wood-frame construction and post-and-beam details?

"Where's he working now?" I asked, assuming we could answer all my concerns if we interviewed him at his current jobsite.

"He just got laid off," Bob said. "That's one of the reasons we thought this might be a timely opportunity."

When I asked which construction company he'd been working for, Bob paused a moment. "He was the chef at the Old Mill Restaurant. Been there for years, but it was just sold, and the new owners are bringing a French guy down from Montreal."

In the conversation that followed, I learned that Stanley Paige was a very large, bountifully bearded, former English professor who had traded academia for the saucepan. Over the past couple of years, while working at the Old Mill, he had also been building a 16 x 16 foot library tacked onto the side of his house, and it was "almost finished." The bookshelves, Bob explained, were made from pieces of recycled church pews stacked atop recycled concrete blocks. "Quite beautiful, really." I tried to picture the aesthetic — and failed. According to Bob, Stanley Paige was honest to a fault, creative, ingenious, resourceful, hardworking, funny, literate, down-to-earth, strong as an ox — and his crêpes were "to die for." He apparently also did some carpentry.

I advised Bob and Elaine not to include the chef in the bid process, but they were determined. If hiring a friend as one's contractor was risky, hiring a friendly cook had to be worse. Bob and Elaine were older and presumably wiser than I, so I argued my case as politely as possible. In the end, they thought I was being unnecessarily cautious, and I thought their friendship for Stanley was as admirable as their judgment was flawed. Stanley stayed on the bid list. For the next couple of weeks, all I could do was wait until the bids came in and hope Stanley would price himself out of the game.

The best outcome in competitive bidding happens when the numbers are closely bunched together. The client sees that the price is truly market-driven and has the luxury of choosing the builder with the nicest smile. When the bids are spread slightly apart, the lower or lowest bid is usually chosen. When one bid is far, far below the others, we have the dilemma called Stanley Paige.

Stanley's bid was almost one-third below the other two, which were less than 5% apart. I tried to convince Bob and Elaine that Stanley had obviously left something out of his calculations — the entire second floor, perhaps — but he fervently assured them he had covered everything with room to spare. "Plus," Bob argued, "Stan doesn't have all that expensive overhead to worry about like the other guys do." It didn't seem to matter that the "other guys" had built dozens of houses, had more than fifty years of experience between them and were known for good craftsmanship and timely completions. Stanley had never built a house, but that seemed to mean nothing. "That's like saying you shouldn't have built your first house," Elaine said. "It turned out nicely, so why not give Stanley the chance to do the same thing?" It didn't matter when I explained that on my first project I was both builder and client, that my cost overruns would (did) hurt no one but me — and that, frankly, the house wasn't very well built due to my inexperience. But nothing seemed to matter except the seductive appeal of a 33% discount. Penny wise, pound foolish — there's no free lunch — I tried to dissuade them. I knew I had finally lost the battle when I overheard Bob whisper to Elaine, "With the money we save, we can trade in the Volvo." I not only lost the battle, but I lost the other two bidders as well. I'm not sure they believed me when I told them how hard I'd resisted awarding the bid to Stanley Paige. When I invited them to bid on another project a few years later, they were conveniently "too busy."

The good news was, I liked Stanley. As a person, he was everything Bob and Elaine said he was — funny, enthusiastic, erudite and down-to-earth; Falstaff in overalls. He agreed to start the project by the first of October, which would allow him time to have the building closed in and roofed over before the first snowfall. I gave him six sets of blueprints so that he could distribute them among his subcontractors. He seemed to understand the drawings perfectly, and I began to wonder if I'd judged him too harshly.

After considerable prompting from me, he also agreed to sign an owner-builder contract, a document both he and my clients referred to as paranoid paperwork. For them, a contract was a symbol of mistrust. I proposed it was more about clarity, and they responded as if legal strictures among friends insulted the friendship. But both parties signed it. Among other particulars, Elaine asked that all the bills be sent monthly, directly to her. When I suggested that an architect's review of invoices was a standard practice, she and Stanley traded a weary smile, a gesture I later interpreted to mean I would never see a single invoice. October began with a few days of light rain followed by two full weeks of glorious weather. Three phone calls to Stanley went unanswered, so I drove to the site. The maples were turning to brilliant oranges and golds, the lake was diamond-bright and the sky was improbably cloudless and blue. The layout stakes we had driven into the ground at the end of the summer were twined with morning glory vines, but there was no sign of Stanley, not a scrap of lumber, not a spade's worth of dirt turned, not a tire track in sight.

I decided to wait another week. If Stanley hadn't begun the job by the third week in October, I'd call Elaine and Bob and suggest we look for someone else — and try my best not to say, "I told you so."

"Stanley had to fill in at the restaurant for a few weeks," Elaine explained when I finally called. "The new owners are having trouble getting a green card for their new chef. Stanley says he should be digging the foundation by the first of November."

"I've tried to call him, but ... "

"He's phobic about the telephone," she said. "It's perfectly natural. Some people are like that."

"It's going to get cold."

"He'll come through, I promise," she said. "Don't worry, okay?"

The next time I saw Stanley was on a Saturday morning at my local lumber yard. It was now the beginning of November. There had been zero progress on the house and a few near-zero temperatures at night. I was beginning to resent his irresponsibility, but he seemed so pleased to see me, as if we were old friends with no undone business between us. When he'd finally finished asking how I was, how my kids were — followed by a long and literate soliloquy on how the weather had been "preternaturally wintry," I turned the conversation to the obvious.

"And the house?"

He put a big paw on my shoulder and moved closer, as if to shield our conversation from spies. "Monday," he said. "First thing Monday morning, we dig the hole. Once that's done and my concrete man does his thing, it's a piece of cake."

Two Mondays passed and the site was dusted with the season's first snow when I called Elaine and Bob in Boston. If there was an edge to my voice, it was warranted. "It's the middle of November, the ground is freezing up and it's starting to snow. We really ought to reconsider if you ..."

Bob cut me off. "Hold on. We're driving up to see Stanley tomorrow. He's had some setbacks, but he's ready to roll."

I began to protest, but it was useless. "Hope you've got good snow tires."

"Of course," Bob said. "Bear with us, okay?"

The foundation was finished just in time for the biggest Thanksgiving snowstorm in fifty years. Our original schedule would have allowed Stanley to complete the outside of the house before the first snow so that he could work inside all winter. Now, the inefficiency and discomfort of working in the cold was a true disadvantage. Several hours would be wasted shoveling out from under each new snowfall. Keeping warm and dry took time and energy; at temperatures hovering near zero, every aspect of the construction process invariably slows down. The best I could do was to anticipate problems, keep abreast of the work in progress, and help Stanley wherever I could. The bond between him and my clients seemed so indestructible that I sometimes felt like a heartless bureaucrat — not to mention a little envious of their friendship. I had become the skunk at the picnic, and I simply didn't know how to do my job and feel more like part of the team at the same time.

Stanley hired his old friend, Todd, to help him with the framing. They seemed to not mind the cold, and their carpentry was much better than I had anticipated. I stopped in two or three times a week to check on their progress. They always seemed pleased to see me, and were open and gracious about suggestions or changes. The house was going to be what I had hoped for, and more. Stanley called it, "Versailles de Bob." I was beginning to call it a miracle.

By Christmas, they had the house roofed over and the windows installed. Bob and Elaine were ecstatic, which made me happy. It was only when I heard how pleasingly surprised they were by certain elements in the house that I realized how little they had understood the drawings — but never mind. We were on a roll. The electricians and plumbers showed up on time, and Stanley and Todd were working five full days every week. With Stanley's initial procrastination behind us, I was pleased with everything I saw.

By Valentine's Day, the boiler was hooked up and the heat turned on. The house was insulated, the wiring and plumbing were roughed in, and the walls were ready for sheetrock. Stanley was a pleasure to work with, and I unequivocally understood why Bob and Elaine liked him so. Bob took pictures of the work in progress and Elaine baked batches of cookies from one of Stanley's recipes — fabulous oatmeal-raisin-walnut cookies I can still taste.

By Easter, the snow banks were beginning to melt, the house was about two-thirds finished, and Bob had already invited guests for the Fourth of July weekend. I was at my drawing board early one morning, sketching up some of Elaine's ideas for a simple landscaping plan, when I got one of the few calls I had ever received from Stanley. In a voice I barely recognized, he told me had used up every cent of the funds in the budget.

We all met at the jobsite at noon. Bob was speechless. Stanley seemed shrunken to half his enormous size and even the house seemed suddenly diminished. I felt rotten because I hadn't insisted on seeing the invoices. Elaine was mortified. Determined as she was to make a success of Stanley, she had somehow ignored the relationship between the work completed and the payments rendered.

We agreed to meet at my office late that afternoon and discuss what to do next. Stanley arrived first in his battered Chevy pickup. We were awkward and overly polite with each other. I closed my eyes when I saw Bob and Elaine drive up in their new Volvo wagon.

I believed Stanley when he said he was sorry. I believed him when he offered to pay them back when he got another job cooking. I also believed he had no idea how he'd managed to spend all the money so soon. The contract he signed obligated him to deliver Bob and Elaine a completed building for a specific sum, but it was clear that nothing of the sort would ever happen. Stanley had no resources beyond his heavily mortgaged house. Bob and Elaine liked him too much to see him homeless. If they took him to court, what would they gain?

After several more meetings without Stanley, we decided to hire another contractor — a firm with a proven track record and AAA credit who would finish the work on a guaranteed, not-to-exceed-cost basis. The trick was to find someone willing to finish someone else's project: Who knew what hidden errors and omissions might emerge? Luckily, Stanley's work was presentable enough to persuade Alton Construction to finish the job. I kept quiet when we saw that their contract price, plus what Stanley had spent, was almost exactly what the other two bidders had calculated nine months before.

Alton's style was competent, professional, and unimaginably devoid of personality. The joking and goodwill were absent, and the personnel changed weekly as the various subcontracts for flooring, tile work, kitchen cabinets and painting were completed. I saw plenty of proficiency, but it was accomplished in such a grim manner that I wondered how anyone could work like that day after day. Any pleasure taken in a finished product — the winding stairway, for instance — seemed measured by its speed of completion rather than the beauty of the object itself. Watching the work proceed as a matter of unadulterated business, I found myself missing Stanley.

Except for one brief stopover, Bob and Elaine stayed in Boston and left the site visits entirely to me, as if their intrusion might lead to further misfortune. They needn't have worried. Alton finished the job in six weeks. The final punch list consisted of half-a-dozen items, which Alton dispatched in less than a week — done deal. They loaded their tools and went off to the next project with hardly a goodbye. The final invoice was paid by Memorial Day, and the moving van was parked next to the house a few days later. After they'd moved in, with all their books and rugs and furniture, we all agreed that the house fit Elaine and Bob perfectly — a little house with big heart.

A year after the house was finished, Elaine and Bob invited me to join them for dinner at the Old Mill Restaurant. The Canadian chef had apparently never materialized, and Stanley was running the kitchen again, much to the satisfaction of his old customers. We had a nice dinner and talked about books we'd read and movies we wanted to see. The fourth chair at the table looked empty, but the spirit of the house filled it amply. I imagined it was disappointed to not hear its name spoken once. Before we ordered dessert, Stanley appeared at our table in his white chef's smock and food-smudged apron. Elaine insisted he come see "his" house the next day — please, anytime — soon. Bob praised the work Stanley had done, especially on the stone fireplace and chimney, where in fact he had done an exceptional job.

The frustration, time, and money spent on Stanley's miscalculations seemed suddenly trivial compared with the pleasure we took in one another's company. We had designed and built a good house, suffered, and learned, and through it all, remained good friends. As a correlative to living life fully, the process had served us all well — even Stanley — who would always know he'd built a house with no shortcuts, with each and every nail driven completely home.

I missed seeing sawdust on his massive shoulders, and complimented him on the grilled salmon. We were begging him to sit with us for a while longer when a waitress brought out a beautifully ornamented cake crowned with a single candle.

"Someone's birthday?" Bob asked.

"Let's just say it's a first-year tribute to the house," Stanley said, bowing grandly to Bob, Elaine and me, "And to everything for which it stands."

Building to Survive

In his fascinating book *Animal Architecture*, Karl von Frisch writes about the instinctive behavior that compels certain species to build sophisticated structures. For example, the male orange-crested gardener, a small bird found in the rain forests of New Guinea, builds an elaborate bower to attract his mate. With fastidious care, he decorates his forest-floor showcase by gathering colorful bits of flowers, shells, and iridescent blue beetle parts. At the entrance to his love nest he erects a plaited grass fence and "garden" where he will dance provocatively in hopes of convincing a female of his charms. He knows how to build his bower and dance his dance from the moment he is born; his hard-wired instincts are critical to the survival of his species. Accordingly, when his efforts are successful, a female will follow him into the bower. After their mating is concluded, the purpose of the bower will have been served, and the female will thenceforth ignore it and build a utilitarian nest in a nearby tree, in which she will raise her young.

Unlike the bowerbird, my building skills served to satisfy the implacable ethics of John Calvin, Euclidian aesthetics, and to attract new clients, not mates. It wasn't until after my misplaced efforts helped ruin my marriage that I saw how the unexamined instinctive behaviors I might have shared with the bowerbird were much more to his benefit than mine.

Tom and I talked on the telephone every few months or so with news of our lives. His divorce was final, and he had met his future wife Ettie, a gorgeous, vivacious cellist with a seductive southern drawl and a sense of adventure equal to Tom's. When we attended Lamar and Simone's wedding in New York, Ettie stole the show.

Tom had sensed the fault lines in my marriage, but was wise enough to suggest no glib solutions. "This is a fertile time for growth," he said. "I'm excited for you."

I was stunned at the remark, overwhelmed with the mixed-up feelings of sadness, inadequacy, guilt, and anger consuming the divorce. And he was excited for me? "Are you kidding?"

"You learn a lot when you're living below the water line, trying to keep afloat. Trust me. That's when you see what matters most."

"I'm too busy to be swimming this hard," I complained. For the last few years, I'd flung myself headlong into busy-ness as though my identity would dissolve if I were to stop. The slow-cooked recipe for acting like a human being — instead of a human doing — was not yet clear to me. My marital model was summed up in a photograph I'd saved from college: The painter Georges Braque, handsome and elderly, is serenely posed in a chair with his loving wife leaning over him. She has her arm wrapped protectively across his shoulders in a gesture of unconditional adoration and love. That's how it should be, I thought at the time; his work comes first. The harder he works, the greater the rewards for them both.

Faced with divorce, I decided what the family really needed were two white-faced Herefords. In the earlier, happier days of our marriage, we had raised pigs and chickens, but they were relatively small compared to two Herefords. Now that our problems were huge, wouldn't adding a ton of cattle be an appropriate counter balance? And, grass-fed beef would be good for us!

Other than what I'd observed in my neighbors' barns, I knew nothing about raising cattle. But what did that matter? Buried far beneath my superficial focus on cattle was (unbeknownst to me, of course), a behavioral instinct to build something, to substitute what was most difficult with what was instinctively easi-est, and — better yet — to justify it with claims that I was serving the common good. When I should have been busy talking and listening, I was the busy martyr designing and building a perfect barn. Should the roof pitch be as steep as 12/12, or would a 10/12 pitch suffice?

Among the many other birds who build to attract, the male weaverbird of the African savannas weaves his complicated nest in the shape of a spherical basket. If he fails to attract a mate within a week or so, he demolishes the nest and weaves another in the same tree. His weaving skills are unlike those of any other species, and yet they are essentially identical to every other weaverbird, all of whom know what to do from birth. Less self-critical than the weaverbird, the male wren hedges his bets and builds a number of nests. The European blackbird often leaves his multiple nests unfinished because he misplaces his work-in-progress and begins yet another, and another anew: in the worst of circumstances, a final nest is never completed.

While I had no time to shore up the collapse of my marriage, I found time to build the barn and begin work on a book (*Superhouse*) that explored the pros and cons of various energy-efficient building types. My research for the book and its even-tual publication led to teaching workshops on the subject. One day after class, a student approached me and spoke of his inter-est in architecture. "I'm thinking about going to graduate school next year, and I was wondering, what courses should I be taking if I were to choose to become an architect?"

If he were to choose? For me, the pull to architecture had been irresistible — invisible, magnetic. There was no choice. My bowerbird instincts, such as they were, were apparently hard-wired. But the student's question made me wonder: Was a hard-wired human's behavior capable of change? Could someone choose between multiple professions and be as successful as someone whose career was not so much chosen, but pre-ordained? Lamar was enough of a chameleon to have been a success in a variety of professions. I believed Tom would find his path soon enough; there was no stopping his voluminous flow of ideas and energy. Whatever he did would incorporate all the skills he'd accrued, and it would be fabulous. He was amply hard-wired, and, so I imagined, was I. So, what would happen if I couldn't continue defining myself through architecture? How could I risk stopping, even for a day or two?

The great architect Louis Kahn was fond of asking his students, what does a building want to be? Redirecting the question inward, the more important question for me was, who do I want to be? And while the story of the weaverbird's hardwired conduct was fascinating, it was the multiple, unfinished nests of the European blackbird that became my cautionary tale.

On the day the cattle arrived, I was stringing the last of the wire fence when a barb snagged the inside of my forearm. A deep gash filled with a surge of crimson, but I was numb to the wound, as if injury to my flesh had no right to appropriate the pain of a greater loss.

The barn I built was solid and handsome enough, but unlike my other buildings, it failed to engage me. The old, reliable connections between building and pleasure were suddenly faulty. My spouse and children had moved back to Cambridge, and the house was eerily empty. Never sick, I came down with the flu. It seemed to rain a lot. The gash in my arm got infected. For the juggernaut Herefords, my fence was a joke; they found the weak spots immediately, and gorged themselves on clover in the neighbor's pasture. I sold them within the month, before I even named them, and the barn would never see an animal inside it again.

Tom was right after all. It was an exciting time, in a siege-mentality kind of way. Living below the water line for a while was, indeed, instructive. I wasn't a bird. Even if the instinct to build was hard-wired, I had the option of finding an off-switch when the situation demanded. I had fled the city to avoid becoming the myopically busy architect I had become, and now it was time to recalibrate the machine and live the integrated life I knew I was meant to live.

The barn still stands, but the fence has all but disappeared.

A Day in the Office

In architecture, as in medicine, law, accounting, engineering, and hairdressing, a prescribed amount of education and apprenticeship is required before one can peddle one's services as a legally registered professional. Since my three years of obligatory indentured servitude had been fulfilled when I moved to New Hampshire, I was eligible for the five-day inquisition devised to test one's knowledge of everything from contractual procedures to site planning to structural engineering. I procrastinated for six years before taking the test — most municipalities don't require house designers to be licensed — and then one day drove down to Manchester, my head crammed full of eleventh-hour facts and figures I might never use again.

For the daylong segment on design, we were instructed to bring food and drink, as if to leave the clammy examination room for anything but nature's calls might somehow lead to cheating. Accordingly, I arrived with a paper bag containing two sandwiches, my daily ration of oatmeal cookies, and tea. At mid-morning, I noticed my fellow supplicants unscrewing thermos bottles, and I was suddenly thirsty. Since I hadn't been able to find a thermos that morning, I'd poured my tea into an empty Jack Daniels bottle and wrapped it in a dishtowel. Four hours later, I was pleased to see that the tea was still warm. After I'd slugged down a couple of audible swigs, the earnest-looking guy in front of me turned around just as I plunked down the bottle and wiped my sleeve across my lips. Eyeing the demon jug with contempt, he hissed, "You don't think that's really going to help, do you?"

Maybe it did: After waiting months for the licensing board to spend a few hours grading the tests, I was solemnly informed that I had passed the exam with more than a few points to spare. In return for a $60 annual fee, and my solemn vow that I had committed no felonies lately, the State of New Hampshire issued me a genuine, certified rubber stamp bearing my name and license # 860. I was now an official architect, but the distinction was oddly anticlimactic. I felt exactly as I always had — eager to design and build as best I could, and wholly indifferent to the necessity of official sanction. Moreover, my professional status now exposed me to the possibility of a bankrupting range of lawsuits that would not have been actionable before I was officially licensed. I wasn't sure if I'd moved one step forward or two steps backward.

Geoffrey Thornton came to work for me and stayed for the next twenty-two years. He and I occasionally remarked that we spent more time together in the office than we did with our wives — which does not account for the fact that he's been married twice and I've been married three times. (More on that in my next volume, *Confessions of a Country Serial Monogamist*.) He's more of a math geek, I'm more artsy-fartsy, and we're both naturally predisposed to competitively race anything with wheels on it. Call it yin-yang, professional symbiosis, whatever — it worked. When one of us needed to specify a steel beam, Geoff would reach for the handbook while I gazed out the window. If we came up with different answers, I deferred to the dreary handbook, but mostly we chose the same beam, and none of our buildings have fallen down. Yet.

After Geoff was licensed, we became full partners. Geoff gravitated to commercial and institutional projects, while I stayed mostly in the residential field. Such was the reach of our vast empire that we eventually hired two (2) apprentices, Pi Smith and John Vansant, who stayed with us for six years before setting up an empire of their own.

Our office consisted of two large rooms on the second floor of a building in the village of Lyme. Pi and John shared the north-side studio while Geoff and I had the sunlit south-side space, next to a big window that looked over the road and into the fields and wooded hills beyond. When I first showed Lamar the office, he had one of those, "Is that all there is?" expressions on his face. When he finally understood that this was it, he remarked that the men's room (on his floor) of SOM's head-quarters in NYC was about the same size as our entire office. I asked him how many trees he could see from his drafting board.

Our "conference room" was generally understood to be the least cluttered surface closest to our respective drafting boards. Privacy was non-existent. We had neither a coffee machine, nor a water cooler, nor a secretary, which may be why we produced more work than most firms twice our size. If Geoff's phone rang while he was "in conference," I answered it, and vice versa. Despite the interruptions it caused, it was our deliberate policy to be available and accountable to our clients and builders when-ever they needed us. Everyone in the office knew what everyone else was up doing, and we all benefited by way of our self-imposed brand of collective osmosis.

The romanticized image of an architect's workday has him or her toiling in sacrosanct silence, gathering lofty ideas from munificent muses, and spending chaste creative hours in search of the perfect solution. Hah! If an office like ours were to log in the time we spent each day communicating with clients, builders, job applicants, and salesmen, preparing contracts, approving requisitions, reviewing shop drawings, writing speci-fications, producing drawings and driving to on-site construc-tion meetings — the portion allotted for "creativity" would amount to five or ten percent. And ours is a design-driven office.

A typical day goes like this: With four phone lines and faxes eerily quiet, all four of us are potentially "being creative" at our drawing boards at 8:01. At 8:05, John's phone rings, and I can overhear him talking to a client who is calling because her builder has not shown up for work. The project is small and the builder works alone, and John patiently suggests that perhaps the builder is at the lumber yard picking up materials for the day's project. Behind John's voice, I can hear Pi talking to a contractor about leaky flashing around a skylight: The owners want to blame someone, and it sounds as if the finalists in the "blameathon" are going to be the architects.

Meanwhile, I am sketching an elevation of a two-story house, and playing with the idea of making the second story windows about four-fifths the height of the windows below. Or would three-quarter work better? I've almost got the proportions I want when my phone rings: Irma wants to know if the elaborate built-in dresser that's just been completed in her dressing room could be six inches lower — and store the same amount of clothes. It takes about fifteen minutes for me to convince Irma that as much as I'd love for it to work out differently for her, making the dresser shorter makes it smaller, and making it smaller means it won't hold as much as it would if it were bigger.

Where was I?

I get to spend about eight-and-a-half minutes on my window proportion question before I take a call from Barry, an attorney I'd recently consulted regarding a possible lawsuit against me. My client, Abe, had been perfectly reasonable throughout the process of designing and building his house, but when he moved in, he threatened to sue me because the hot water tap in his kitchen sink didn't deliver hot water immediately after he'd turned it on.

"Don't worry about it," Barry says. "If he wants to proceed, we'll request a jury trial in Chelsea, and when twelve dairy farmer-jurors hear that a flatlander wants to sue you because he has to wait thirty seconds for hot water in a house he uses only three months of the year ..."

I've barely put down the phone when I realize Laura is about to arrive for an 8:45 appointment. I shovel off my drawing board, glance out the window, and see her pulling into the parking lot. By the time she's up the stairs, I've removed her drawings from the flat files and spread out the relevant sheets, neat as can be.

Laura's house has been finished for a few years, and she loves it. Now, I'm designing a built-in cabinet for her dining room. She's recently inherited an heirloom collection of Spode china, and the cabinet has to be perfect. With its walnut paneling, glass shelves, and concealed halogen lighting, we've spent almost as much time on the cabinet as we did on her entire kitchen. Today we're talking about hinges and knobs — perfect hinges and perfect knobs. Laura's taste is a product of living well — in Vienna, Palm Springs, and Manhattan — and I always learn something from her that makes my life in New Hampshire seem both provincial and redeeming.

We spend an hour looking at exotic hardware catalogs, and then something outside catches my eye, and as I glance past the pearl necklace draped over Laura's Shantung silk blouse, I see Mort Bailey's ten-wheeler pull into the parking lot below our window. Is he here to see the construction firm downstairs, or one of us at Metz & Thornton?

Mort moves dirt for a living. Acres of it. He builds driveways, digs cellar holes, and installs septic systems for most of the contractors in the area. A true Yankee genius, he maintains and operates his equipment himself, and he works longer and harder than anyone in the business. Mort is also the local weather prognosticator: When he starts appearing around town without his shirt in early April, we know that spring is just around the corner. When the first snowflakes stick to his bare shoulders, winter is on the way. Mort is tall, ferociously strong, and one of the gentlest, nicest people I know.

His trip up the stairs is preceded by a distinctive scent. Laura's nostrils flare as she picks up her first whiff. Because I've smelled it before, I can imagine he was repairing on one of his rigs this morning and soaked his pants with diesel fuel.

Standing hugely in the doorway to our office, he nods politely to Geoff and Laura before he turns to me. The toe of his left boot is bound with old duct tape. He has a nasty-looking gash across his wrist, and he's smiling the sweetest smile imaginable. "Sorry to interrupt," he says, "but I wanted to stop by and let you know the water line up to Worthington's is dug."

I've been waiting for Mort to dig the ditch for days and welcome his report.

"Thing of it is," he says, "I cut the underground electric that leads to the house."

While I imagine sparks and smoke, Laura stares agape at Mort. "Hope you didn't get scorched," I say.

Mort grins and shakes his head, no. "She shot some dinky little flames and smoke, is all. Must have tripped the breaker at the pole, but seeing as how you were in such a yank to get it done," he sighs and turns to go, "I just thought I'd let you know."

I thank him for stopping in. When he is down the stairs and out of earshot, Laura says, "I like that guy."

Laura leaves shortly after Mort's departure, and I look at my calendar and realize I've got a site meeting scheduled for 10:30 with my client Linda Lewis, whose house plans I'm about to begin. The purpose of today's meeting is to determine the house location, an absolute necessity before the design phase begins. I tell Geoff I'll be back for lunch, follow the lingering scent of diesel fuel down the stairs, and jump in my car.

A twenty-minute sprint brings me to Linda's property, where I find her waiting with an expensive-looking magnetic compass and a geodetic survey map spread out on the hood of her car.

"I read somewhere that we should have these," she says, pushing the map and compass toward me. The gesture is fraught with apprehension, as if ridding herself of these mysterious devices will protect her from the black magic they might summon.

I was born with a good sense of direction. Linda was not so lucky. For her, a map is an instrument of deception, deliberately designed to put her on the missing-persons list. For Linda, north is up.

I glance at my watch. Pointing toward the sun, I adjust for the difference between 10:30 and noon, and drop my arm to the horizon. "South is right about there."

"Just a darned minute," she teases, unwrapping the compass. "No fair. This thing cost me twenty bucks, and you've never even looked at it."

I spread out the map and open the compass. Magnetic "south" on the compass points slightly to the east of where I'd pointed — by about fifteen degrees — which it should have. I explain that the difference: the "declination" acknowledges the difference between "true" and magnetic bearings — fifteen degrees in New Hampshire.

Linda suddenly says. "I get it! East is left."

"If you're looking south, yes, east is to your left. But if you're looking north …"

She extends her left hand and turns a complete circle. As she passes the four points of the compass, she repeats, "Left is east, east, east and east."

After we've sited the house, Linda leaves with my directions back to the interstate, which will take her south to Boston in less than three hours. When I ask if she wants to repeat the instructions, she looks down at her notes and says, "Take the first left, go three miles and take the left fork onto River Road. Go right at the stop sign at the end of River Road. Nine miles later, take a right onto the interstate's southbound ramp."

"Perfect," I say, convinced she'll get home safely.

"Two easts and two wests," she says as she drives off. "I'll be up in Boston before the traffic down there gets bad."

I get back to the office at a quarter past noon and join Geoff, John and Pi on the porch downstairs, where we like to eat lunch during the summer months. John tells me that the final section of Sandy Kelsey's barn foundation is about to be poured, and the concrete contractor wants to talk to me ASAP about the re-bar in a retaining wall. Also, there is a call from Rick and Linda Roesch, two of the most enthusiastic, bighearted clients an architect could ever wish for. The thank-you party they're holding for the crew who built their house — all the workers and all their families — is scheduled for the Fourth of July weekend. Could I help with a few addresses? There is also a call from Barney about the setback variance for his addition. His planning board hearing is tomorrow night and he wants me to be there. Also: Geoff reminds me to call back the steel fabricator who's suggested a substitution for the open-web bar joists my engineer has specified. We hear the phone upstairs and let it ring as Mort's ten-wheeler roars by in a cloud of black smoke, and we all wave like children.

It takes two minutes to eat my sandwich, and just as I finish, the conversation turns to Junior Johnson, the lead-footed southern moonshiner who notoriously outran revenue agents on rural back roads in the 1950s. Junior's signature maneuver was a 180-degree turn at high speeds: Geoff has been practicing the same move in the tricked-out Honda CRX he races in sports car events on weekends. Once or twice a month, we encourage him to show us a Junior Johnson on Route 10 in front of the office. Once or twice a month, he obliges.

Geoff drives off northward, down the hill, where he will turn around for his approach, and we scan the road to the south for oncoming traffic. All is clear. I hear the phone ringing again upstairs, but there's an answering service, and more important things to attend to at the moment. We hear Geoff zooming toward us up the hill and onto the flat. As he comes abreast of the office, he jams on the brakes, which unweights the rear end of the car. In the next nano-second, he flicks the steering wheel to the left, and as the car begins to rotate, he locks up the rear wheels with the emergency brake. The back end of the Honda whips around with a screech, and Geoff completes a prefect Junior Johnson without crossing either edge of the southbound lane. Talk about architecture!

Immediately after lunch, Geoff, John and Pi and I are all on our phones, returning calls. Among many, I call the jobsite-phone at Kelsey's barn, but no one answers, so I reluctantly think about hooking up the new computer that's been sitting under my desk in its unopened box for the last three months. Geoff has the same model and uses it daily. Like a kid confronted with a vegetable he hasn't tried, I don't like it. I like machines with visibly cause-and-effect parts of substantial weight and shape, chunks of metal that I can see, touch and manipulate with a hammer or a wrench. The computer's invisible logic leaves me stupid, but its practicality is too compelling to ignore, and, yes, we will eventually form a partnership with Christopher Smith, whose uncanny skills with computer assisted drawing (CAD) revolutionize our means of producing, filing, and delivering documents — none of which will ever separate me from my old, reliable, never crashed, never updated 3H lead pencil.

Thank God the phone rings before I've read halfway through the computer's setup manual. It's Harlan.

"I still don't know if it's too high or too low," he begins, "But it just doesn't work for me."

Over the last several weeks, we've been discussing his living room, eighteen-feet wide by twenty-six feet long. Harlan's been a repeat client, likes beautiful houses, and pays well for good design, but sometimes he gets stuck. This is his fifth or sixth call on this "too-high, too-low" subject. The carpenters have framed up the new room, but there's no interior finish yet. Harlan thinks the thirteen-foot ceiling is either too high, or too low — by two inches — but he can't decide which. I've repeatedly told him I don't think the two inches matter one way or the other, and I explain, once again, that if he wants to change it, making it two inches lower would be relatively quick and inexpensive (by shimming down the rafters), while raising them two inches would cost a lot. Harlan isn't interested in the time or money involved. These two inches — up or down — have become a matter of absolute truth for him, and my failure to share his concern seriously bothers him.

"You're supposed to be the expert," Harlan says, after rehashing the same old pros and cons. "I'll leave the decision to you."

I'm exhausted with Harlan's obsession, and I don't want to burden the project with unnecessary costs and re-scheduling, but I'd also like to put an end to his disproportionate fixation on an irrelevant issue. I can think of several parts of his project with which I'd love to wrestle another few rounds, but this one is definitely not a contender. "I think the ceiling would be perfect," I say, "If it were an inch-and-a-half lower."

"An inch-and-a-half?" He sounds so relieved. "You really think so?"

I look at my watch. We've been on the phone for fifteen minutes and accomplished nothing. "In fact, an inch-and-a-half would be perfect,' I say. "Wish I'd thought of it earlier."

Whenever I tell Lamar about clients like Harlan, he shakes his head and swears he'd rather perform eye surgery on himself than get involved with the idiosyncrasies of residential work. I feel the same about Big Architecture when he tells me he hasn't slept in his own bed for three weeks because he's traveling around the globe soliciting huge commissions for SOM.

The moment Harlan hangs up, I write up a change order and fax it to Harlan and the builder for their signatures. With any luck, we'll get Harlan's approval and drop the ceiling one-and-a-half perfect inches before Harlan changes his mind. I'm about to begin drawing again when a Pella window salesman walks in. He wants to tell us about some new features, and he has a fat new insert for the catalogue. Geoff looks at me, I look at Pi, Pi glares at John and poor John, he understands: he's it. Fifteen minutes pass while the Pella sales guy drones on about northern low-E film with John.

Creativity anyone?

It's 3:30 by the time I've returned my lunch-hour phone calls, and I begin work again on the window proportions I started this morning. Fifteen minutes later, I get a call back from Rich Saffo, the concrete contractor at Sandy Kelsey's barn. Could I come over? It's practically next-door; I jump in the car.

Sandy's huge historic barn has a sloped ramp at the east gable end. At the top of the ramp is a wide barn door that once provided hay wagon access to the loft on the upper level. I designed a twelve-inch-thick retaining wall to replace the crumbling stonewalls under the door and to each side of the ramp. The question today concerns how the upper ends of the retaining walls will be attached to the wall beneath the door. When Rich poured the wall under the door, he cast in keyways (indented slots) to provide stability to the ninety-degree intersection — instead of the contiguous re-bar I specified. Structural continuity is what I wanted. We both knew that doing it his way was easier, but not as strong.

"What happened to the rebar?" I ask.

Rich is a very smart guy. He knows exactly what I'm looking for and wants to make the best of the situation. "How about if I drill some # 5 bars six inches into the keyway — twelve inches on center up the height of the wall? I'll leave two feet sticking out — and then I'll tie them into the horizontal bars in the side retaining wall."

Given the circumstances, it's a good idea. I'm tempted to ask if it wouldn't have been easier to lay the bars in the original pour and leave them extending out through the end gates, but I don't need to: Rich reads my mind. "I didn't have a drill with me at the time," he says. "But I'll fix it. No biggie." And he did.

I'm back in the office by 4:15. Geoff is on the phone. He points to a post-it on my drawing board that says, "Call Harlan, you lucky duck."

I crumple up the post-it and shoot a three-pointer across the room into Geoff's wastebasket as I dial. Harlan answers on the first ring. He wants to know if I really think dropping the ceiling an inch-and-a-half is better than dropping it two inches.

"I do," I say. "I really think you'll be happy with it."

"Then I'll sign the change order." He pauses. I close my eyes and cross my fingers. "If you really think an inch-and-a-half is best."

I take a very deep breath, snap a yellow wooden pencil in half, and assure him most wholeheartedly that I do, absolutely, positively, one hundred percent. I say "cheerio" and try to put the phone back in its cradle gently, and I am proud to know that I have just contributed enormously to another great moment in the history of architecture.

Now I get to spend fifteen, maybe twenty, minutes on the window drawing I started eight hours before. I like what is happening, and print out a copy to send to my client. On my way back from the print room, I find Danny standing at my drawing board.

Danny works for the construction firm downstairs, as well as doing the lawn work and snow removal around our building. He's a hard, loyal worker, loves to hunt and fish. This is the first time he's been in our office in years.

"I thought they was somebody downstairs, but they all went home," he says. "So I figured I'd come up here and show you fellas."

He is holding an enormous mounted fish, a northern pike well over three-feet long. The under-slung jaw with its multiple rows of teeth looks as if it's capable of shredding sheet metal.

"Where'd you ever catch that thing?" Geoff and I say in unison. I'm thinking, Northwest Territories, clouds of mosquitoes, a three-week-summer kind of place.

"Post Pond," he says.

Post Pond is less than a mile from our office. Our children swim there. "That thing was in Post Pond?"

"Reeled him into the shallows and jumped on his back," Danny says. "Fought me something wicked hard."

Geoff says, "That thing is a monster."

"Grabbed him by the gills and threw him in the back of my pickup truck."

"Wow."

Danny enjoys an audience. The account that follows is the perfectly rehearsed set-piece rendered by hunters and fishermen everywhere when it comes time to glorify their trophy. Danny begins with what time he got out of bed that morning, what he had for lunch (two olive loaf sandwiches), and what he used for bait (chicken gizzards). The unabridged epic, we learn, takes about fifteen minutes. When he's finished, I decide I'll never go swimming in Post Pond again. Or eat an olive loaf sandwich. Or eat fish.

By 5:00, I'm the only one left in the office. The phones have finally stopped ringing, and I finally sit down for a period of uninterrupted pleasure. Of course it has occurred to Geoff and me that we could move to a bigger office, hire more people, and compartmentalize duties, but we've both agreed that we'd rather be disorganized generalists than organized Generals. We like the immediacy of knowing everything that's going on and solving problems on the spot. Our clients seem to like it, too. When Sandy Kelsey dials my number, I'm the one who answers, and I'm the one who is able to report, first hand, exactly what's going on at his barn. Big offices like Lamar's obviously can't afford our approach; their projects are huge and complicated, and the multi-layered staff required to run them require careful coordination, a strict chain of command and a well-paved paper trail. Big offices can't suddenly decide to close their doors on a beautiful day and hike up the mountain. Ours can — and does. Our projects are big enough to excite us, but small enough to allow us the luxury of coordinated chaos, and we work hard to keep it that way. In any case, whether we work in a big office or small, the true limitation to the quality of the work we produce is located between our ears.

Time to finally get to work. I turn off the radio, sharpen my pencil, and tack Linda Lewis's program to the wall above my drafting board. At a glance, I can check my progress against her requirements. I begin to sketch a diagram of the site, taking into consideration the slope of the land, important trees, rock outcroppings, drainages, and waterways. I keep in mind close-up and long-range views, opportunities for public and private domains around the house, the sun's path, and the direction of the prevailing winds. I also sketch in the probable routes of driveway and utility lines, and the most likely location of the well and septic system. Only after these essentials have been added to the written program can the house design begin.

My second task is to unravel Linda's list of requirements and transpose them into workable floor plans. When I first became interested in architecture, I began by visualizing houses from the outside in. The "look" of the house seemed like the logical place to start, but I soon discovered that this approach led to the tail wagging the dog. A building of any complexity needs to be designed from the inside out, by which I mean that the utility, circulation, and site-driven logic of the floor plan — the organs and the skeleton — are what drive the plans.

As always, the process consists of questions built upon questions: What if? If this goes here, will this fit there? What is the appropriate hierarchy between this sequence of rooms? What are the sight lines and sources of light inside the house? What are the views from inside to outside — and from outside to inside? If I arrange the bedrooms at opposite ends of the house instead of above or below, how would that alter the client's expectations of interior zoning? Are there ways to profitably impose or disrupt a rhythm of elements (windows, doors, posts, beams, corners, casework, stairs), expand a space, or condense it down? Can I gain a sense of openness by letting a wall stop short of a ceiling — and still retain a sense of privacy? Some ideas begin to suggest others, some lead nowhere. As I prove and disprove each thesis, the search will lead to something that may work. Or not.

Part of every design process includes the argument between the forces of logic and the temptations of delight. It would be delightful to tilt the walls outward and curve the entire front of the house to take advantage of the panoramic view, but the budget says no. Linda would like to divide the dining and living rooms with a huge two-sided fireplace, but its chimney would make the logic of the upstairs hallway impossible. Eliminating the railings on the bedroom deck would make the view stupendous — but the codes say we need a railing through which a four-inch diameter ball cannot pass. Could we afford tempered glass panels instead of rails? Logically, the four children's bedrooms are most efficient to build and heat if I configured them foursquare instead of the offset, linked pattern that would make them so much more — delightful?

I work up a scheme that seems to have promise. All the primary rooms have a view to the south. Entry hall, stairs, closets and bathrooms take up most of the north wall. A tall ceiling over the big, screened porch off the dining area will allow light to reach far into the house. Water and snow coming off the dormered roofs won't land on decks or entryways or in front of garage doors. The rooms programmed for the second floor approximate the total area of the rooms on the first floor. The overall massing promises to be interesting with three intersecting volumes of varying heights and widths. Floor spans across all the spaces can all be achieved with standard lengths and depths of lumber. What is emerging is beginning to look exciting. Tomorrow I'll sketch up a few cross-sections and elevations and see what the floor plans imply about the exterior. For now, it's enough to know that I haven't exceeded the maximum square footage (i.e. cost) we'd planned for, and there still appears to be real possibilities for art within the architecture.

It's a quarter to seven, time to get home and help with supper. I leave the office feeling grateful that I get paid for doing something I love to do, and promise myself that tomorrow, if it's a sunny day, I'll play hooky and hike to the top of Smart's Mountain.

Errors and Omissions

A popular architectural legend goes like this: At the opening ceremonies for a university library, the trustees are sharing a celebratory glass of champagne. Proud of their achievement, they heap praise upon the beaming architect and enumerate the multiple accomplishments that led to this crowning moment. During a pause in the conversation, someone inquires, "How did you calculate the weight of all those books?"

"The books?" The architect's stricken expression tells the rest of the story.

My local phone book weighs a pound and serves fifteen adjacent towns in Vermont and New Hampshire. Almost half of the book consists of yellow pages, which begin with glossy, full-page advertisements shilling the services of injury-claim attorneys. Posed photos of these justice jocks strive for a square-jawed, sensitive-to-the-client but tough-as-heck-on-the-bad-guys effect. If these costly ads are any indication, taking someone to court is our area's most profitable industry.

A few pages before the listings for attorneys, wedged between "Archery Equipment" and "Armored Car Service," the careful reader will find "Architects." There is no bold face type here, not a single display ad or hint of self-promotion. Architects don't advertise. Instead, we hope to find work via published examples of our projects, competitions, word-of-mouth, and the benevolent patronage of wealthy relatives. Could it be that modesty warns us away from self-promotion? More likely, it's a matter of ego. We wonder how interested in serious architecture these potential clients could be if they pick a name at random from the yellow pages, as if they were shopping for the nearest Roto-Rooter service.

Every architect's career is at some point visited by the nightmare of a collapsed building. Just imagining the loss of lives and a building collapsed in ruins can load the drawing of a single line with a ton of anxiety. Most engineers and architects, like physicians, carry professional liability insurance. They pay hefty premiums to protect themselves against the possible outcome of unintentional, but ultimately inevitable lapses in judgment, errors and omissions. These insurance policies, ironically, cover the insured party only during the period in which premiums are being paid. Having dutifully sent off a quarterly check for forty years does nothing to protect against liability after the policy is closed. If, for instance, in year forty-one, the architect cancels the policy — and a claim is presented relating to a project completed fifteen years before — the insurance no longer covers the claim. Some architects with small practices, myself included, decide the cost of professional liability insurance is too high for the protection offered, and proceed into the litigious world of looming disasters stark naked.

I've occasionally wished I were better dressed. Lamar was appalled when he first learned of my decision. "There are people out there who would love to bankrupt you." His employer spends obscene sums every year on insurance to cover the multiple millions of work they produce. Tom Luckey, on the other hand, thinks the insurance industry is purposely designed to ruin a good party.

Over the last three decades of practice, I've committed my share of minor errors and omissions, but all of them have been turned either into auspicious opportunities or equitable alternatives. One such problem almost didn't, and but for the good will of my clients, might have led to first-hand experience with one of those square-jawed phone book attorneys.

In the early 1970s, I designed and built a series of earth-sheltered houses. The first of these houses, the Winston house, was sited in a high alpine meadow with infinite views. A stand-up structure would have been a violation of a beautiful pastoral setting. I figured that by tucking the house into the hill and generously planting the roof and foreground, I'd be able to obscure much of the building and minimize its visual impact. Today's energy-saving, sustainable mindset was a few years short of being articulated; in 1971; heating oil cost 19 cents a gallon.

When OPEC cut production in 1973, the cost of oil tripled. Overnight, energy-efficient strategies became architecture's compelling cause célèbre, and earth-sheltered houses suddenly became the bulk of my work. In 1974, *Architectural Record Magazine* recognized the Winston house with an award for excellence in planning and design. Along with architects such as Malcolm Welles and John Barnard, I developed the earth-sheltered concept into a viable building option. Among other popular approaches (super insulation, double envelope, and solar heated) the earth-sheltered concept was conceptually the simplest: earth (dirt cheap) can be used to isolate a building from the effects of extreme hot and cold weather. Five feet below grade in New England, earth temperatures hover around fifty-degrees Fahrenheit year 'round. A typical building entirely exposed to the weather loses and gains heat at exponential rates as the weather outside gets colder or hotter. Covering that same building with a mantle of earth removes it from the extremes of weather, which for us in New England, is the equivalent of moving the building to Virginia.

For those who have never seen a well-designed earth-sheltered house, the idea evokes images of a dark, moldy cave. A well-designed plan dispels all such fears the moment one walks in the door. For example: imagine a rectangular floor plan placed on a southerly sloping site. The south-facing wall (the long dimension) receives sun all day and is generously glazed, while the north wall is buried into the side of the hill (i.e. Virginia). The northern portions of the east and west ends are also tucked into the hill. A foot or two of earth covers the low-pitched roof, which can be interrupted with skylights where required. Properly designed, there is no sense of being "underground." With more than half of the house enveloped within a snug mantle of earth, the effects of icy storms and hot, humid summers are significantly mitigated, as are reduced costs of heating and cooling.

And so it was that Ray and Pam came to see me on a sunny day in June of 1976 with the intention of building such a house. Ray had recently retired from a medical practice and was anxious to spend his time gardening with Pam and making sculpture and jewelry. Pam couldn't wait to get out of their quaint but drafty farmhouse and into a cozy new home with new flower beds.

The building site we selected was at the northern edge of a pasture above their old farmhouse, a sloping hillside with generous views of the mountains to the south. With three modest bedrooms and a study, our final scheme resembled the approximate proportions of a shoebox attached to a smaller, similar shape — the garage — offset to the northwest corner of the house. Walking up the hill towards the house, you see mostly glass under an overhung roof with tufts of greenery creeping over the rim. Walking down the hill from above, a stubby chimney and two skylights provide the only hint of the dwelling below until you reach the edge and look down at a patio.

Ray and Pam were commendably supportive, relaxed clients. They had seen and admired several other earth-sheltered houses I'd designed, and our collaboration proceeded quickly and smoothly. By October, all the working drawings were completed and a builder selected from among the three who submitted competitive bids. Wayne Pike had already built several earth-sheltered houses with me, and was well-qualified for the job. Concrete was poured in early November, the foundation was backfilled, and the heavy-timbered roof system (6 x 12 hemlock timbers spaced eighteen inches apart) was begun by Thanksgiving. By the time the roof decking (2 x 6 tongue-and-groove fir) was nailed in place, and the insulation and waterproofing applied, winter was upon us and Ray and Pam had left for warmer climes.

It wasn't that they weren't interested in their house-to-be. They'd watched the walls go up and they took lots of progress photos — the kind that get stuffed into fat albums for the dubious entertainment of captive relatives — and they liked everything they saw before they left. As we waved our goodbyes, it never occurred to me that we would soon earn their trust many times over.

Most residential clients understandably want to be on the site as often as possible, trust notwithstanding. Being privy to the everyday progress, the inevitable glitches and triumphs, is part of the excitement of seeing a dream come true. With the client present, eleventh-hour decisions are more easily negotiated, and changes can be made while they are still most cost-effective. ("We had no idea the fireplace mantle was that high off the floor ...") With Ray and Pam absent, an ambiguous sense of freedom set in: we were free of the extra effort it takes to deal with even the best of clients — but we were also free to stumble into errors and omissions all on our own.

Progress continued apace as December turned to January, and even in February it still hadn't snowed more than a few inches. The old-timers called it an "open winter," cold and dry, and without the protective cover of snow that typically insulates the earth from frost penetration. Open winters are known to be tough on rootstock, insects, burrowing animals, and the replenishment of aquifers. As it pertains to buildings in New England, a lack of snow and seasonal cold can drive the frost down more than four feet. Conversely, a few feet of constant snow cover can result in a frost line only inches deep.

Wayne's finish carpenter, Eddie, who had worked on many projects with me, first noticed the problem in early February as he began installing the large glass doors on the south wall of the living room. The sides of the doors are attached to jambs attached to the bearing walls. As Eddie began to fit the jambs, he noticed the jack stud — and hence the bearing wall itself — was more than an inch out of plumb. Disbelieving the evidence, he checked the other four bearing walls and also found them to be tipped — westward — by the same margin.

Eddie's phone call to me was brief. "You know who this is?"

"Sounds like Eddie."

"You best get over here."

My usual twenty-minute drive took fifteen.

Eddie's discovery, and the ego-numbing forensic exercise that followed, soon pointed to our problem: the earth used as backfill against the east wall had frozen and expanded. As could be expected, it had moved what was easiest to move — in this case, the entire heavy roof assembly. Designed to address worst-case scenarios (fully saturated soils followed by a record-breaking snow load topped with a teenager in a wayward Jeep), roof loads for earth-sheltered houses are calculated at over two hundred pounds per square foot. This amounts to four times the design load for conventionally built, northern New England homes. In our case, 150 fifty tons of roof and earth cover had slid westward more than an inch, shearing off the anchor bolts at the top of the concrete bearing wall which, miraculously, was still standing plumb. This frozen freight of timber and earth had migrated westward fraction-by-fraction over a period of weeks, and we never knew it until Eddie held his level plumb to the wall.

The good news was we hadn't completed any finish work that would have to be removed. Additional good news was that Ray and Pam were somewhere warm and innocent of the evil machinations of frost. Our open winter had allowed frost to penetrate down through the depth of the earth covering the roof (sixteen inches), past the depth of the insulation (five inches), plus the depth of the deck and timbers (thirteen inches). Had the frost gone deeper than those thirty-four inches — and it might have with another week's artic weather — the concrete wall would have been pushed westward as well. As for why the frost along the north wall didn't push the roof assembly southward, our theory went as follows:

Backfilling around a house means dumping dirt in against the foundation walls. It takes less than an afternoon's work if the material is on site, as it was at Ray and Pam's. As usual, there were several big piles of material heaped up around the building's perimeter. Some of them were heavily laden with clay; some of them were sandy and porous. It was the latter material that was meant to be used as backfill. Sandy soils hold little moisture, allowing minimal frost expansion. The stockpiles of clay were intended to be used as fill on the slopes leading up to the roofline. As Wayne and I reconstructed the most likely scenario, we concluded that some of the sandy material was put in against the north wall, and material from the clay pile was inadvertently dumped against the east wall. The lack of snow cover and subsequent deep frost line completed the story.

Neither Wayne nor I were present when the backfill was put in place. Should we have been? In retrospect, of course, but supervising all the trades at all times requires an expenditure of manpower that few clients can afford. Our excavator, Howard, was one of the best. He had been in business longer than Wayne and I put together, and he knew well the dangers of placing clay against a foundation wall — but he had somehow picked the wrong pile of dirt for part of the job. Would Wayne or I have seen something he didn't? Given the season, all the piles would have been covered with a frozen gray crust. The cold, dry weather would have made it difficult to identify which pile was which. There may have been one of the season's rare dustings of snow that day, making visibility less then ideal. It may have been Howard was late for his supper.

The late Niles Lacoss, a self-taught jack-of-all-trades, was fond of referring to structural engineers as "blacksmiths with glasses." Niles was known for his ability to back up his innate common sense with whatever arcane engineering formula pertained to the problem at hand. One of his last projects was fabricating parts for the Mt. Washington Cog Railway steam engine. All the design work and machining was accomplished in his sooty little blacksmith shop nestled down in the hollow below his house. Had Niles still been living, he would have been the first person I'd have consulted about our little problem with Jack Frost. Next in line was Hank Woodard, a structural engineer with (glasses and) a knack for crunching numbers.

Before I telephoned Hank, I spent a sleepless night pursuing answers. There are situations in architecture where an inch or two of discrepancy means little, but an eight-foot-high wall out-of-plumb by more than an inch is intolerable. Equally intolerable would have been leaving the roof where it was. By midnight, I had exhausted the notion of shimming out the walls, or moving the tops of the walls back to plumb. (Unfortunately, we had already completed a clever detail, whereby the blocking between the beams above the walls had already been routed into the sides of the beams before the roof was decked over.) Shimming or moving the tops of the walls would have meant that the blocking would have been inboard of the wall plane on one side and outboard on the other, instead of flush on both sides, as it was meant to be. Moving the bottoms of the walls would have meant moving all sorts of plumbing — the roof drain drops, baseboard heat, sewer and water lines penetrating the floor slab within the walls — a huge undertaking.

By two in the morning I was through with the use of hydraulic jacks. If we had wanted to push the roof farther westward, we could have pushed against the frozen earth to the east easily. But pushing the roof back to the east required something to push against, and there was nothing but air on the exposed, west end of the house. Furthermore, the hill sloped away from the building towards the west. I finally concluded that no practical combination of triangulated trusses, posts and fulcrum points could ever provide 150 tons of resistance to the jacks.

By four in the morning, I was warming to the might of giant winches.

The winch on a bulldozer is located at the back of the machine, behind the drive train, between the tracks. It feeds out a reel of braided cable, which is turned hydraulically on a drum. The force of the hydraulics is unimaginable. For instance, if the cable were to be attached to an immoveable object, the winch is strong enough to reel in the bulldozer as if it were a Tonka Toy, even when it's mired up to its floorboards in mud. So why not hire the most colossal bulldozer we could find, anchor it at the east end of the house (I pictured the rear end of the machine chocked firmly against beefy steel columns planted deep into the frozen ground) and winch the roof back into place?

A ragged dawn found me conceptualizing a second pair of steel columns, which would be planted below the west-end roofline. It was to these two columns that the cable would be attached. When the winch pulled against the columns, they would in turn push against a horizontal beam positioned so as to transfer the pull to the ends of the 6 x 12 roof joists. Eureka!

Fundamental to any of these procedures was an open a ditch along the east side of the roof. No matter how we moved the assembly back into place, I knew we had to make room for its relocation as well as replace the clay with sandy fill to prevent future movement. In order to salvage some small portion of my bruised self-esteem, I also knew I would insist on doing the work myself, partly because I didn't entirely mind the drudgery of the ditch, but also because I felt Ray and Pam deserved some kind of redemptive gesture. A long afternoon with an 80-pound jack-hammer would bring back some memorable days at the quarry, and, I hoped, deliver my penance.

Hank returned my call and listened politely to my winching scheme. "How big a cable on the winch?" he asked. For calculating purposes, we guesstimated the cable's size and tensile strength. "And the machine would be anchored how?" The steel columns/posts would provide adequate stability if they were of sufficiently thick section and buried deeply. Hank was kind enough not to ask why the roof ended up where it was.

Then came the bad news: When a cable is stretched, he explained, it behaves like a taut rubber band. The heavier the load, the more it elongates — until it ultimately fails. The first bit of stretching comes easily, but as the load increases, the degree of elongation decreases in inverse proportion to the load. According to Hank, our hypothetical one-inch cable was strong enough to slide the 150 tons of roof. So far, so good. But then Hank delivered a brief discourse on axial fatigue and static strength tests — and dropped the bomb: In essence, the cable's elasticity made its behavior unpredictable. If we'd wanted to move the roof an indefinite distance with no precise stopping point, we could do it. But we needed to move the roof an inch and a fraction, no more, no less. It was impossible to accurately predict the point at which the cable would stop stretching and begin to pull — and when it did overcome the inertia and begin to pull; it was impossible to regulate the winch so that it would pull only the distance desired. We discussed providing structural stops, blocks, beams or posts that would somehow stop the movement of the roof at the precise spot we intended, but the idea quickly became too impractical to pursue. As usual, Hank ended our conversation with "Let me do some numbers and call you back."

Still without a solution in mind, Wayne and I nonetheless rented a compressor and jackhammer later that morning. At least we would prevent the roof from moving further while we searched for a solution. At least we were doing something. The temperatures that day were just above freezing, but the work was so grueling, we were quickly down to our shirtsleeves, trading off five-minute spells with the beast.

As I'd learned from Bo at the quarry, the jackhammer is not a subtle instrument. But I'd forgotten how it sets up a peculiar resonance with the tissue at the tip of the nose. The itchy, jiggly sensation is impossible to appease while clinging with both hands to the chattering hammer. Was advancing age making it worse, or had I simply chosen to forget? Every time I took over the hammer, my nose itched like hell. Shrugging it into my shoulder was the best I could do to reduce the sensation.

We finished the ditch just in time to fill it with sand before darkness fell. I collapsed into bed that night at the mercy of tender regions of my body I'd never heard from before. Ten hours later, I awoke still exhausted, but with a vision so providential and compelling that I was on the phone to Wayne before I'd brushed my aching teeth.

The dump truck driver must have been puzzled. The house was obviously still being built — even if it might have looked to him like a walkout basement with dirt on the roof and big windows. He certainly saw the big yellow crane with the forty-foot boom parked alongside the driveway. And there he was with a two-ton wrecking ball in the bed of his truck — the type used to demolish old buildings. Had he driven to the wrong address?

My brainstorm was so unsophisticated I hadn't dared call Hank for fear that he would talk me out of it with a line of reasoning too levelheaded to ignore. Thirty-six hours had passed since Eddie's discovery, and I had to fix the thing — now. I knew my impatience was dangerous, but my instinct felt right. Yes, I was acting unprofessionally: no calculations, no lawyers or insurance agents, no structural consultants, but I was prepared to risk ridicule, not to mention a big chunk of money, if only to satisfy a stubborn curiosity. Blow by blow, I was sure we could pound the roof back into place with a two-ton wrecking ball.

Prior to the crane's arrival, we rigged up a double thickness of 6 x 12s along the west end of the roof. They were bolted to the butt ends of the 6 x 12 roof joists, and would serve to absorb the blows from the wrecking ball. The impact load would be then transferred to the ends of the joists, which were lined up serially, the length of the house. The roof's structural decking, tongue-and-groove 2 x 6s spiked to the joists, would act to tie the joists together in a relatively dimensionally stable rectangle. Such was my theory. And to chart my theory's progress, if any, I dusted off my old surveyor's transit.

A transit is generally used to establish elevations, compute angles between compass points, and measure distances. Looking through the lens is akin to looking through a high-powered rifle telescope, with fine-lined cross hairs superimposed on the targeted image. My target was a 3 x 5 file card. With a razor-sharp pencil, I'd drawn a row of vertical hash lines one-sixteenth of an inch apart. A thicker line, my base line, zero, was at the right (east) end of the pattern. I stapled the card to the south side of the house. With the transit steadied on a tripod thirty feet away, I hoped to track the movement, fraction-by-fraction, blow-by-blow, as the roof moved eastward back to where it belonged.

When I explained what we were about to do, the crane operator was dumbfounded. "You want to do what?"

Excited by the prospect of seeing an architect do something
delectably stupid, the dump truck driver couldn't wait for the
folly to begin. "You heard him, Ellis," he said. "Pound it."

Once he had been reassured that he was not responsible for
damages, the crane operator lifted the wrecking ball from the
bed of the truck and moved his rig to the west end of the house.
When the crane's stabilizers were secure on the frozen ground
and the cab leveled, he lifted the boom to a forty-five-degree
angle so that the ball hung next to our battering beams. After
another brief explanation of what we intended, he swung the
boom away from the house, and then brought it back.

Thump. The house shook. The crane operator looked guilti-
ly pleased at the shocking effect.

I ran over to the transit and peered through the lens at the hash
lines. Nothing. The transit crosshairs were still on zero. After a few
more futile swings, we speculated that the ball was not moving
with enough speed to deliver the punch we needed. Wayne suggested we raise the boom to almost vertical, which would give us
more radius, more leverage, more thump. The new geometry
worked to our advantage, but the old crane's clutch was sticky, and
swinging the boom at such a vertical angle was awkward and jerky.
On the third swing, the two-ton ball rebounded in an unexpected
trajectory and grazed the crane cab with deadly indifference.

The operator was now convinced we were nuts. "Jeesum!"

I saw where a patch of paint had been scraped off the corner
of the cab, and began to wonder if I'd made a fool of myself.

The dump truck driver covered his told-you-so grin with his
glove. Wayne called time out and fetched a rope from his truck.

We tied the rope to the cable just above the wrecking ball and
asked the crane operator to lower the boom to about seventy-five

degrees and leave it stationary. A few test pulls suggested we might have better control and accuracy if we swung the ball ourselves. Wayne, Eddie, and I began pulling the rope. The truck driver, overjoyed by the lunacy of our enterprise, jumped in to lend assistance. I imagined him telling the story that night at the Elks Club bar.

With enough rope played out, the four of us were able to draw the ball almost fifteen feet away from the building. Swung through its forty-foot radius, it made a deep, booming, hollow sound as it whomped against the timbers. After three or four tries, I checked the transit, and it seemed we had advanced — maybe a sixteenth — or was it a thirty-second of an inch? Three hits more and the evidence was unmistakable: the hammer was working.

For the next hour, we pounded the cross timbers with a grim kind of glee. Trial and error soon taught us that four or five hits in one location gave us a sixteenth of an inch, but additional pounding in that same spot yielded no further progress. The roof system was apparently flexible enough so that it became temporarily concaved at the point of assault, like a stiff trampoline might behave when struck with a bowling ball. A series of poundings at consecutive, four-foot intervals along the length of the roof's edge, however, gained us roughly a sixteenth of an inch at each location. Countless trips to the transit charted our inexorable progress. The announcement of each successive sixteenth was greeted with cheers. The big ball was working. When we'd reached the full distance, we whomped it one last time for good measure and traded high fives all around. Now the truck driver would have an even better story to tell. Ten minutes later, it began to snow hard for the first time all winter, a perfect, soft, white coda to our brutal performance.

Hank was appalled when I called to report on our success. How could we have proceeded without his calculations? "What'd you say the ball weighed? (As much as a compact car loaded with three Vikings' linemen.) How far did you swing it?" I could hear him furiously clicking at the buttons on his calculator — and then a long pause. "My numbers say it doesn't work."

Niles Lacoss once told me that according to aeronautical formulae, bumblebees can't fly. I had seen such examples in sports, the four-minute mile, the sixty-yard field goal, and I knew he was right: It can't be done, but then, it is. Flushed with the success of our improbable flight, I said, "But Hank, if we had done the numbers first, the roof would still be back where it was, right?"

Hank's tolerance was more than I deserved. "What did your insurance people have to say?"

I respected Hank, and relied on his engineering expertise without hesitation. We had worked together often, and I wanted him to respect me, too. I just couldn't tell him I had no insurance, so I fudged my answer: "Not much ..."

I'm not sure how much Ray and Pam wanted to hear about what had happened, but I was so pleased with the course we'd chosen that I felt compelled to tell the whole story from beginning to end. To be sure, I'd been lucky, but if we'd pursued the conservative route, gone through the standard procedures of errors and omissions insurance claims, and all the attendant expert witnesses, engineers, and lawyers who come along for the ride, the remedial process would have been enormously time-consuming, tedious, expensive and, worst of all, entirely out of my hands. As it was, I chalked up my expenses in dollars, anxiety, and time as an affordable withdrawal from my personal insurance fund. I had applied the flinty values of thrift, self-reliance, independence, and accountability that I admired so much among my adopted Yankee mentors, and the outcome was as good as it could be. In other words — to the extent that it was possible for an over-educated flatlander to presume local status — when the chips were down, I'd gone native.

Green Architecture

When Jesse came to my office one summer, he had been an elementary school teacher for most of his 46 years. Bearded, tall, blond, and skinny, he looked the part of the archetypal hippie, notwithstanding his master's degree in education from Harvard. His desire was to design a self-sufficient house on twenty acres in Vermont. "I want to build Green," he said, "and I'm willing to make whatever sacrifices are necessary."

It was immediately evident that Jesse had read a lot about photovoltaic panels, solar gain, thermal mass, water turbines, and recycled-content building materials. He mentioned, with some passion, that he wouldn't be caught dead in polyester or an SUV. A single father of two sons, 17 and 19, Jesse hoped to live off the grid and build a compact, environmentally responsible house. He was excited about raising chickens and growing organic food. He wanted to create what he described as "an accountable life based on responsible custodianship rather than reckless dominion." This guy was serious. No one is entitled, he insisted, to use more than his or her share of the Earth's resources.

As energy prices surged in the early 1970s, Jesse's predecessors promoted an awareness of a global ecosystem whose health and welfare were symbiotically linked to the choices we make in our everyday lives. Those pioneers were typically frugal, educated, natural fiber-wearing folks, and they were trying to save much more than money. The back-to-the-land, self-sufficient movement was glamorized in publications such as *Solar Age* and *Mother Earth News* ("The original guide to living wisely").

Innovative, energy-saving solutions flourished along with contra dances, handcrafted sandals and macrobiotic diets. Helen and Scott Nearing's seductive, back-to-the-land bible, *The Good Life*, sold hundreds of thousands of copies.

Much of the home-grown, alternative house design of the period was driven by a commitment to save energy and "do the right thing for the planet." The ungainly design of many "sustainable" houses was justified in the name of energy conservation, and the idea of efficient housing began to permeate the marketplace.

By the end of the 1980s, the trajectories of idealism, pragmatism, and aesthetics had merged; energy-efficient houses could be made to look as good as any other. Mandated by national energy codes, insulation values for windows, doors, walls, and roofs improved two and threefold. Hot water heaters, clothes dryers, refrigerators, air conditioners, and heating systems became significantly more efficient. Light bulbs burned longer and brighter while consuming less electricity, and certain passenger cars were soon to travel fifty miles on a gallon of gas.

Jesse knew all about all of that, but he also wanted a house that reflected his willingness to sacrifice comfort for ideology. I believed him: From September to June, he jogged three miles to school through every kind of foul weather Vermont had to offer.

Like the scholar he was, Jesse had collected information from a variety of sources for years. Among the dozens of books on alternative housing were three of mine: *Superhouse*, published in the late 1970s, discussed the pros and cons of earth-sheltered, double-envelope, and super-insulated houses. Editorially, the message was that no single solution was likely to serve everyone equally well. I'd also put together two editions of *The Compact House Book* , compendia of small, efficient house designs. Jesse knew them all, chapter and verse. As our conversation continued, he chided me for reversing an opinion I'd held years before in an article about the use of bentonite as a waterproofing product for roofs (it failed), and suddenly I was reminded of the fundamentalist flavor I often encountered at earth-sheltered housing conferences.

The attendees at these conferences were mostly earnest, want-to-do-the-right-thing folks. Interspersed at the fringes were always a few somber survivalists whose self-centered zeal scared me. "I'll have enough food and water for my family for a year underground, and I can guarantee that anyone who tries to break into my bunker will be looking at the business end of a 12-gauge." The compassion, intelligence and long-range perspective among the established leadership, however, was compelling, and the health of the planet would be better off with them in charge as opposed to the profit-motivated, anti-science ideologues who scripted the short-sighted policies of the imperial administration of George W. Bush.

When it comes to signing on the dotted line, Green Architecture is a hard sell. If I were to compartmentalize my practice into categories of houses — low-cost to unaffordable, ambitious to utilitarian, prosaic to poetic — the clients I've encountered in the Green arena are most liable not to build once the project is formally defined. Several theories might explain this phenomenon, foremost among which are the added initial cost, size limitations and the incidental sacrifice of creature comforts. Other contributing factors may be that I am impatient when Green sounds like voodoo, and reluctant to sell shoes that don't fit.

I discovered early on that an over-inflated approach to a Green, cure-all panacea implodes the moment it becomes evident the windmill has no wind. Sensational magazine articles, selectively researched and puddle-deep, encouraged their readers to run ground water through heat pumps for heating and cooling — without mentioning the cost of drilling a deep well, installing an expensive pump and operating it twenty-four hours a day. "Dig into a hillside and stay warm all winter!" they propose, without specifying the expensive, high-strength wall and roof structure, tricky waterproofing details and costly insulation required. And yes, you can cover your south-facing roof with photovoltaic shingles and run the electric meter backwards — if you have $50,000, a sunny location, low wattage requirements and a very large roof. Do I sound grumpy yet?

Some clients are surprised when I ask what kind of car they drive, or if they use a frost-free refrigerator. I enjoy hearing about an eco-tour through Mexico, but flying 6,000 round-trip miles on an A/300 that burns 11,000 pounds of fuel per hour is unfortunately part of the picture, and the equations of Green mathematics are grimly unforgiving. The question is not whether or not we go to Mexico (my bags are packed), but how the sum of our decisions affects the world we live in. Triple-glazed windows are no more or less important than maintaining proper air pressure in our automobile tires, or turning off the hot water heater when we leave the house for a week. In most cases, the most effective and efficient strategies for saving energy are just not all that sexy.

As our conversation proceeded, Jesse began to fidget as he saw how his wish list, consisting of photovoltaic panels, a windmill, ground water heat pumps and composting toilets, would quickly be reduced to the more prosaic — and dollar-for-dollar, more effective — fluorescent lights, super insulation and a high-efficiency, wood-fired boiler. When he became discouraged that he was not wealthy enough to be doing his part in the war against energy, I reminded him that the Greenest approach to building is not to build at all — or, most ironically of all, to live in a city.

Jesse was polite enough not to call me a traitor, but I'm sure it crossed his mind. I bribed him with a cup of herbal tea and hoped for his patience. In a city, public transportation, multi-family housing — schools and shopping within walking distance — provide far greater energy efficiencies than our back-to-the-land, four-wheel drive life out at the end of a town-maintained road. Public transportation is so much cheaper and more efficient per rider/mile than driving and maintaining a car. Up in the country, we need at least one vehicle per family, usually two or more. A missing quart of milk can mean a ten-mile drive. The commute to jobs and schools burns up a few tanks of gas every week. Stand-alone, single-family houses are much more expensive to build and maintain than multi-unit complexes. My house, for instance, loses heat from four sides, plus the roof; an apartment may have only one wall exposed to outdoor temperatures. It's ten miles each way to our children's school — and there is no school bus or public transportation to get them there. We own two cars and an old truck because three of us drive to work and school every day, and yet I insist on making my clients' houses as carbon-neutral as possible. Am I irresponsible? Would Jesse be irresponsible if he built his dream house?

Or what about Al Gore? His Academy Award-winning film, *An Inconvenient Truth*, presents a cautionary tale about what will happen to global temperatures if we continue our current rate of carbon dioxide emissions, which comprise over seventy percent of all greenhouse gases. His film has challenged millions of viewers to re-think their carbon-based consumer habits and helped to force policy decisions that will help reduce emissions. But if Al Gore lives in a mansion that uses the same amount of energy as twenty of his less-affluent Tennesseans, must we think of him as ethically compromised? Is the positive impact of the movie offset by his lifestyle choices? Is being Green a pious indulgence reserved for the eco-elite, or can Everyman afford to be part of it?

In Jesse's case, the question was not how Green did he want to be, but how Green could he afford to be. To simplify his range of choices, we discussed three shades of green:

Light Green buildings do as little damage as possible to the local habitat. They include super-high insulation values, efficient heating and cooling strategies, sustainable or recycled building materials, and low maintenance costs. The building must be modest in size. Materials in a Light Green building have a long life-cycle, are biodegradable, and non- toxic. How toxic, for instance, are the off-gassing compounds in certain glues, adhesives, paints, and carpets? Will discarded materials snooze, inert, in a landfill for millennia, or, like natural wood fiber, decompose in a few decades? Which products contain ozone-gobbling HCFCs? What is the cost of eventually decommissioning the building? Did Jesse know that landfill disposal costs for gypsum wallboard scraps (calculated by weight) are close to half the retail cost of the gypsum wallboard itself? Was he ready to interpolate all of this information to his hand-built homestead?

The step to what we might call Medium Green includes the all of the above, plus the integration of renewable energy sources such as solar, wind and water or, better yet, the purchase of carbon credits through a reputable broker. (Assuming that carbon credit accounting and engineering figures are reliable: $30,000 spent on carbon credits will be more effective globally than the same amount spent on personal solutions such as windmills or photovoltaic panels.) The Greenest Green buildings include all of all of the above, plus the dwelling unit would be part of a high-density housing community and participate in the co-housing ideals of cooperative economies, including progressive wastewater treatment, growing fruits and vegetables, and raising animals.

Jesse hadn't bargained for such a flurry of contradictions between his desire to do the right thing, his limited pocketbook, and the imperatives of the marketplace. He hadn't thought through the source-point expenditure of energy (embodied energy) required to produce various products. How many machines burning how much fossil fuel were required to mine, log, mill, extract, melt, grind, reduce, purify, manufacture, shape, and ship a resource from its point of origin to Jesse's building site? What kind of environmental impact on water, soil, air, flora and fauna would be acceptable in the production of his windows, for instance? The silica (sand) from which glass is made is infinitely plentiful, but it involves a high (embodied) use of energy as it is turned into glass. What is the rate at which various building material resources are being exploited? Old-growth California redwood is beautiful, straight-grained and rot-resistant — but is being cut down much faster than it can be replenished. Conversely, plantation-grown southern yellow pine is harvested according to a sustainable yield, like a crop of corn, but has little of the redwood's beauty and durability.

Jesse warmed to the hypothetical prospect of a tree cut down and horse-drawn from the woods to a hydro-powered saw mill where it would be sawed into a 2 x 4s — and dried in a solar-powered kiln next to his building site. Such a 2 x 4 reaches its destination with a lower outlay of energy than a commercially produced 2 x 4 cut from a forest in Oregon and shipped across the country in a boxcar. Shipping aside, the energy required to produce a 2 x 4 is theoretically constant, no matter what method is used, but the source of that energy can make a difference. Theoretically, one John Deere skidder can do the work of twenty horses, but the horses represent a benign sort of embodied energy, and add a little manure to the ground instead of spewing carbon into the air.

In abundantly forested regions, trees are considered by some to be a kind of vegetative produce, to be harvested and replenished cyclically as a crop. Jesse and I had a long conversation about saw-log lumber versus fragmented wood products like chip board, particleboard, waferboard and oriented-strand board. Unlike plywoods, which use large, sound trees for their cross-grained veneers, fragmented wood products utilize limbs, tops, scraps and the edges of sawed logs. This "use-it-all" approach theoretically reduces the number of harvested trees. Paradoxically (Jesse dropped his head into his hands at this point — here we go again!), there is a concern among foresters that the removal of all those tops and limbs and unfit-to-saw logs (biomass) from the forest floor eliminates not only valuable animal habitat, but more importantly, the soil-building nutrients essential to the long-term health of the forest itself.

Ultimately, we specified sawed logs, inch-thick pine boards harvested from Jesse's woods for the sub-floors, and a high-grade chipboard, "Advantech" for the wall and roof sheathing. Jesse's rationale kept the planked, glue-free sub-floors inside the house, and left the glue-rich particleboard outside. Was it a reasonable distinction? For Jesse it was. His choices were now reduced to a balancing act between science, expediency, cost and ethics. It's not easy being Green.

The house Jesse built was ethically Green, aesthetically agreeable, and riddled with the compromises that occur when the purity of an ideal clashes with the messy truths of the marketplace: There were no windmills or photovoltaics, no water turbines or heat pumps. He hired a logger with a horse and cut most of his lumber from his own land. He had no water source for a hydro-powered sawmill, so he had the logs trucked it to a local sawmill. For the longer spans, he used western spruce, and somehow made peace with the idea that sometimes the good is not necessarily the enemy of the best.

The north wall of the lower level of Jesse's two-story house is built into a hill. His windows are triple-glazed, most of which are on the south side. The shell is super-insulated, with values of R=40 in the walls and over R=60 in the roof. He installed a combination wood and oil-fired boiler (Jesse insists he will never use the fuel-oil option), and he uses compact fluorescent lighting throughout. There are no bells and whistles to proclaim solar-age technology, but the house stays toasty throughout -20F winters with less than two cords of firewood, which Jesse cuts himself. Despite its commonplace demeanor, I think of his house as a success. He was happy to discover that the first part of the Green curve is both the steepest and the most rewarding. The extra fifteen percent he budgeted to make the house Green is two or three times as effective as the next fifteen percent of expenditure would have been. I know I didn't deliver the house he initially sought, but given his budget and beliefs, the thoughtful, responsible course he chose was as Green as it could be.

Among my many clients who have wanted to build Green, no two have chosen the same set of rules by which to play. Ellen and Michael Bettmann, for instance, hired my pal Marc Rosenbaum, one of the wisest energy consultants in the country, to work with us on their house in New Hampshire. Following Marc's initiatives, they spent about fifteen percent of their budget on energy-efficient/sustainable strategies. They and their politics are generous, decent and intelligent, and they have passed their values on to their three grown children. Both the Bettmanns' jobs are in the helping professions, and they travel (fly) often, all over the world, to conferences and symposia where they contribute their valuable expertise to good effect. At home, they grow vegetable gardens and use their wood-burning stove often. The house I designed for them is warm and welcoming and often filled with visiting family and friends. It is also about 5,000 square feet and has a lap pool in the basement. Is the house Green? By virtue of its size, it's badly handicapped. By virtue of the remedial efforts we made to assure it was as energy-efficient as possible, I think of it as a success. The Bettmanns were well aware of the ironies inherent in a large Green house, and weighed each decision fully informed of the consequences. Overall, they stuck to their generously proportioned impulses, and then did all they could to make up for them.

I have no idea where the perfect equilibrium lies for anyone but me, but it is clear that there are many ways of measuring one's degree of accountability to the global eco-system. Building Green is one of them, but so are one's choices of daily transportation, jobs, vacation destinations, goods, and services — even diet and politics. For better or for worse, we are born into circumstances that define many of our choices. To live in America in the year 2007, for instance, means that we consume, on average, almost ten times more fuel oil per year than the average Chinese. A Brazilian rainforest Indian uses none. Like it or not, the trend toward consumerism has always been stronger than the trend away from it. If all of Planet Earth were populated with people who lived like Americans, it's been calculated that we would need two more identical planets to maintain a sustainable level of resources. Building Green is a mindful way of acknowledging how high we Americans sit in the chain of material production and consumption, and an important reminder of how precarious that perch may become.

As an observer, participant, and occasional referee, I believe most people are beginning to take their global citizenship duties seriously. We are increasingly aware of the implications of living accountably, despite how easily we become led astray: We "need" a bigger house/TV/hot tub/car because ... because ... because we do. I know the feeling. In sub-freezing weather, for instance, traditional fireplaces are counter-productive as a source of heat. I am quite happy, however, on a cold January evening, to be sitting in front of the flickering flames in my living room. Does watching the blaze connect me to the security and comfort my ancestors must have felt huddled around their humble hearths? Or am I just feeling sleepy and snug from the wine we had with dinner? In either case, mea culpa. I intentionally built the fireplace despite its inherent wastefulness, further proof of how ethically smudged the blueprints for perfection can be. The best I can do is to compensate elsewhere, because in the end, every building we build, every choice we make, has an implicit or explicit impact on the rest of the world. Call it Green, call it responsible, or call it smart; our choices do matter. For, as Jesse said, we alone are the Earth's custodians, and it serves us well to serve it well.

Troppo Molto

The Glenwald Mansion was built at the turn of the century by a lumber baron who made his fortune selling railroad ties to the Boston and Maine railroad. Surrounded by 1,000 acres of steep timberland, the mansion faces south and commands a majestic view of Mt. Washington. In the hundred years since it was built by a virtual army of carpenters and masons, the mansion followed the fortunes and follies of five successive owners and two ruinous vacancies. As an example of non-sustainable excess, the building was the epitome of dead-end architecture. As a repository of beautiful craftsmanship, it was a jewel. When I was called upon to consult on a minor renovation, the current owners, who shall henceforth be known as Mr. and Mrs. Patton, had beautifully restored the house and grounds.

The Pattons led private lives. I knew their first names, but only from their invoice checks, periodically sent by an accounting firm in Chicago. I never met or spoke with Mr. Patton, never saw a photo of him in the house, or the signature symptoms of male occupancy — sports gear, big boots, dirty towels. When his wife called me with questions or instructions, she always referred to herself as Mrs. Patton. Our first of many meetings on the property revealed an attractive, dark-haired woman in her late 30s. Her dress and manner were out of place in the White Mountains of New Hampshire, but so was the Victorian Gothic pretense of the mansion. Mrs. Patton took me for one of her workmen before I introduced myself. Her tone brightened a notch when she realized I was her architect.

My efforts to expand our discussions beyond the professional led nowhere. If she had a career or children, or liked to cook or garden — if she had favorite colors, or finishes, or furniture styles — all of those were categorically kept from me. I never knew what she thought of an architectural idea except as to how it referred to the standard set by Glenwald's anonymous architect, to whose vision she was touchingly loyal. Other matters of taste and practicality were left to me. After working with her for most of a year, all I knew of her personal life was that she was lovingly devoted to her dog, Molto.

The work I did for the Pattons involved the restoration of a circular wine cellar in a sub-basement of the mansion. The cellar's walls were rough-hewn granite, above which was a vaulted ceiling of herringboned brick. The floor was laid with pale marble slabs the size of tombstones; the effect — Mondavi Medieval. A dozen stone alcoves around the perimeter were designed to hold 5,000 bottles, although none were in evidence when we began the restoration, and none added, to my knowledge, after we finished. The work I was asked to do was limited: Aside from having the masonry re-pointed and washed, my principal challenge involved the installation of new lighting fixtures and a humidity/temperature control system designed to keep the wine stable. I was also consulted on the repair of ongoing damages in the house above caused by Molto, a 100-pound pit bull utterly devoid of social skills.

Along with the commission, I inherited a local craftsman named Wade Wentworth. Fifty-ish, lean, and thin-lipped, at first he seemed to resent me, and was reluctant to share his knowledge of the place, as if I might walk off with it and leave him with nothing. Once we got to know one another, he was as forthright and skillful as anyone I could have hoped to work with.

Wade was passionate about the mansion. When he was a boy, his father did maintenance work at Glenwald and told him

stories that seemed like fairy tales — the uniformed servants with
spotless white gloves, the musicians brought up from Boston to
play for dances in the ballroom, elaborate lawn parties that lasted 'til dawn, the crystal chandeliers, and chauffeur-driven lim-
ousines; it was all a world apart from the broken-down hill farm
where Wade lived as a child.

He grew up watching the estate change hands, decline and
prosper and decline again. Before the Pattons bought it, it stood
empty for almost ten years. Wade found himself patrolling the
place off and on, protecting it — not for the anonymous owners
— but out of respect for the buildings themselves and the craftsmanship that went into them. He soon discovered the secrets of
the outbuildings — a trap door in the stables' ceiling that led to
a dusty attic bedroom, the carriage house boiler fitted with
ornate brass control knobs manufactured in England, and the
dank, windowless coke pit beneath the old blacksmith shop.
When a fallen tree branch broke through a window of the big
house, Wade climbed inside and explored every room and sat for
hours studying the workmanship of the coffered ceilings and
parquetry floors. When the Pattons bought the property and
advertised for a caretaker, Wade quit his foreman's job at a local
cabinet shop and signed on. He thought of his new position not
so much as a job, but as his intended destiny.

During one of my visits to Glenwald, Wade asked me to follow him up to the entry hall. We went in the back way, through
the kitchen, butler's pantry and dining room, and as we entered
the two-story hall he motioned me to stop. "The dog," he whispered, glancing over his shoulder at the balcony above the sweeping staircase. "The housekeeper keeps the kitchen door locked
when it comes downstairs."

"What kind of dog?"

"You don't want to know." Wade crossed the hall, knelt down

and ran his hand across the mansion's front door. I could see where the bottom panels and casings had been chewed and shredded. "Mrs. Patton asked me if I couldn't just buy a new one," he said, "Like they keep them in stock on a shelf at Home Depot." Wade stood up and massaged the upper part of the massive door. "This folded linen pattern, these double-reverse moldings — see this grain?"

"English oak," I ventured. "Like iron."

"I've got a source for it in Boston." Wade grinned, despite himself. "I've always wanted a chance to carve a door like this ..."

"You've got one now," I whispered, imagining sharp Sheffield chisels curling up thin slivers of aged amber oak.

"Suits me fine," he said, glancing at the balcony above. "I wouldn't mind if you told her it was a good idea, either — me carving her a new one."

One of the realities of practicing architecture on a small scale is that there is no way to regulate the amount of work coming in, except, of course, to turn down a surplus. Periods of too-much, or not-enough work are not uncommon. Most of the time, we were more than busy and reluctant to take on small, fussy projects like the Glenwald job. I accepted it because we were in a slack period, and was glad I did for reasons other than the satisfaction of working on a unique old structure.

After we'd become more familiar, Wade told me stories of what it was like to work at the mansion. He told them almost furtively, but with a sense of urgency that led me to wonder if he had the opportunity to talk much about his life. As someone who spent all his time working at Glenwald and living in a remote area, he seemed at once stoically independent, and yet I wondered: Was he lonely? He was long-ago divorced and lived alone, but was in daily contact with his widowed daughter, Tina, who lived in a mobile home parked in a field next to his house.

When he pointed out that the Patton's living room was exactly twice the size of Tina's trailer, I wasn't sure if his observation was a matter of precise statistics or social commentary.

Wade's inbred Yankee modesty made it especially difficult for him to discuss complicated personal feelings, but when he opened up to me, I sometimes felt like his makeshift confessor. He told me that once when he was moving a stepladder around Mrs. Patton, his elbow accidentally grazed her. "Right here," he swept his hand across his chest. "I like to died," he blushed, shaking his head side to side. "She didn't seem to care." He said he had never seen her wearing shoes inside the mansion, and he'd noticed she often had two or three toenails painted bright red while the others remained "natural." Usually, he said, she wore her bathrobe indoors all day long — except for the time he accidentally opened the door to the steam room when he shouldn't have. "Oh, my God. Couldn't look her in the eye for months."

Wade gave the impression that he felt disloyal when he talked about Mrs. Patton, but he obviously needed to talk about her — and often. "Sometimes she gets pretty whiney," he said abruptly one day, "Like Tina, when she was a teenager." And then he added, almost as an afterthought, "But that's all right. We get along pretty well, considering ..."

Wade built and carved the new front door in less than two months in his shop at home. Like everything I'd seen Wade build, it was perfect. Most convincing was the way he aged the door to imitate the hundred years of use the original had seen. "Ball peen hammer and a chain will do wonders." He finished it with a mix of turpentine, boiled linseed oil, and apple cider vinegar. A month after it was finished, I got a call.

"This is Mrs. Patton."

I inquired about her health, her dog, the house, and the weather.

After the scantiest of replies — always polite, but equally dissembling — she said, "Wade's been kind of grouchy lately, and I don't know why."

"Doesn't sound like Wade."

"Would you please speak with him?" For the first time since we'd met, I detected a hint of emotion in her voice. "I'm kind of upset by this."

I assured her I would do my best and called Wade that night, before his habitual eight o'clock bedtime. I repeated a literal account of my conversation with Mrs. Patton, assuming there had been an obvious misunderstanding.

"Jeesum. I suppose maybe I was a tad grouchy," he admitted. The next part wasn't easy for Wade, and it took him a few starts before he was able to explain himself. "See, she owes me money," he finally confessed, almost apologetically. "Considerable money." As an old-time Yankee, Wade hated to discuss finances. Men like him would rather eat dirt than have to ask someone for money owed them. To Wade, it seemed like begging. No matter how deserved, how promised, how entitled to every hard-earned penny he might have been, it didn't seem right to have to ask for it. "I billed her for the door material over two months ago," he said, "Paid for it out-of-pocket, and haven't seen a dime back since."

He was talking about real money. Ninety board-feet of imported, antique English oak costs about the same as a weekend for two in Aruba. I asked about his paychecks. They came from Chicago like clockwork, as did mine. The only piece missing was the check for the front door materials, and as I suspected, he had not once asked Mrs. Patton about it.

I called her back the next day.

"That can't be," she insisted. "He's always been paid on time."

I suggested there might have been an unforeseen mix-up on that particular invoice, perhaps it hadn't reached the account-

ant, perhaps the accountant could look for the canceled check —
and that Wade had been covering a large sum of money for several months, hence the reason for his apparent grouchiness.

"I may have to find someone else to do these little odds and
ends if his prices keep coming in so high," she said.

Two days later, Wade had his check, sent priority mail from
Chicago.

When I went over to Glenwald for a site visit in late December,
Wade had been putting up a snow fence all morning, preparing
for the drifts that would soon seek to bury the mile-long driveway. As usual, I was to meet him in the little office he had set up
inside the former tack room of the carriage house. Just as I got to
the door, Mrs. Patton walked out, apparently surprised to see me,
even though we had recently agreed to meet that day. She was
dressed in a huge, hooded overcoat trimmed with fur. We traded
minor pleasantries, and as she hurried across the frozen lawn to
the mansion, I noticed she was wearing house slippers.

Wade was finishing a lunch Mrs. Patton's housekeeper prepared for him each day, and he was happy to see me. As usual, we
began by reviewing his progress, questions, and problems
encountered on the ongoing projects. The wine cellar remodeling
was almost completed, and the front door debacle was well
behind us, but Molto's marauding had continued unchecked and
provided Wade with enough extra repair work to last for months.

"That dog is her baby," Wade said. "She feeds him, washes
him, walks him. For all I know, she sleeps with him. She won't
say anything about her husband, but would you believe he's
never been back here once since they bought the place? Nobody
ever comes to visit, she hardly ever goes out — a little shopping
now and then — just groceries and a few new bottles of toenail
polish." Wade paused, as if to consider apologizing for mentioning something as intimate as toenail polish. "I feel sorry

for her," he continued, "Spending all of her time upstairs with the dog — except when he's chewing the woodwork or jumping through a leaded glass window 'cause he sees a squirrel outside. Anybody comes near her, you could get your throat tore open, but she walks into her bedroom, and he slobbers all over her like a puppy."

A little later, when we walked over to the mansion, he waited until we were almost at the back door when he suddenly said. "I don't think she wears a goddamned stitch under that bathrobe."

The last time I heard from Mrs. Patton was by mail. A month had passed since I'd finished my work for her. It was springtime, and the brooks were running torrents. I'd been paid for my services and was pleased with the work Wade had done. Since I'd had no complaints from Mrs. Patton — or compliments, for that matter — I opened the letter with some curiosity.

Her letter, written on thick, ivory stationary, contained a single sentence:

Many thanks for the beautiful job you and Wade have done. It was signed, Best of luck, Linda Patton.

I was happy to have an excuse to call Wade. When I read him the letter, he let loose a quick burst of laughter at the mention of Linda's name, followed by a long question: "What I don't get is — why'd he move her way up here to a little hick town, where it's ice for nine months, bugs for three, and nobody knows nothing from salt pork and beans?"

Wade continued talking about the Pattons in a way I'd never heard him talk before — speculating on the variety of devious means by which Mr. Patton must have made his fortune, intimating — but never quite asserting — that Mrs. Patton had been cruelly abandoned by "that no-account." And then Wade surprised me with an invitation to meet him the next Saturday in Gorham at his favorite diner — his treat, he insisted, "Anything on the menu." He said he had a story to tell me, but didn't want to talk about it on the phone.

Wade was waiting in a back booth when I walked in at two minutes past noon. He'd already ordered a coke and was unusually courtly when he greeted me. When he teased the veteran waitress about going home with him, she said she'd be waiting for him out back the minute she got off work. She called us both "Hon."

While we waited for our sandwiches, Wade talked about the weather — which brooks were flooding the worst, how many inches of rain had fallen since Tuesday — but once our orders were on the table, he couldn't wait to begin.

"Molto was at it again," he said. "The son-of-a-gun chewed up the newel post at the bottom of the stairs. Unbelievable." Wade explained how the connection between the newel and the rail was dowelled and glued to the bottom tread, but he'd figured a way to disconnect it without harming the stair. "Then I can carve a new newel and save the carved garlands that circle the top, cut off the original section and graft it onto the new. Installation time, painting, and touch-up — I figure two weeks, and I also figure I'll finally ask her if she couldn't do something about the dog. Maybe training would help. I used to train shepherds, you know."

Wade told the rest of the story as seamlessly as his finest piece of carpentry. He must have rehearsed the telling repeatedly in his mind, but I was certain he'd never told it to anyone else before, nor was he likely to repeat it once it was told to me. In any case, I remember it like this:

As he climbs the stairs, Wade hears the sound of a game show on the television in Mrs. Patton's bedroom. When he knocks, Molto hurls himself against the inside of the door, barking and slashing at the same raised panels Wade has twice re-finished in the last six months.

Mrs. Patton locks the dog in her dressing room and opens the door to the hall. Her face looks puffy. She's holding a glass full of ice cubes; her robe is about to fall open. Embarrassed, Wade turns away as he speaks. "Sorry to bother you, but we have a little problem." He points his hammer over the balcony while Molto barks a furious cadence of warnings from the dressing room. Wade raises his voice to be heard over the awful commotion. "Down at the bottom of the stairs." The television is much too loud. How can she stand all this commotion? Mrs. Patton swirls her ice cubes and sips from the glass. Wade looks at her tangled hair and wonders if she's Italian or some other foreign type, and maybe a little bit hard of hearing. "Molto!" he finally shouts, surprising himself and breaking the unspoken rule that forbids him to chastise her dog. Miraculously, the dog falls silent.

She doesn't seem to notice what he's done, nor is she interested in what he is trying to tell her about the damage at the bottom of the stair. "I can't be everywhere at once," she says, vaguely. "How old are you, anyway?"

"Me?" Wade tucks in his jaw.

"Come in," she says, pulling him into the room by his sleeve. "I want to talk to you." She kicks the door closed behind them. "Sit down." The shades are drawn; the room smells peculiar, sweet and sour. "Sit," she says, "sit."

The only available chair in the room has a lacy brassiere draped across it, all frills and bows like Wade has never seen. "That's okay," Wade says. "I'd rather stand."

Molto is barking again, and the game show audience screams in unison. Wade shifts his hammer from one hand to the other. "I didn't mean to bother you."

"You wandering?" she asks, as she lights a cigarette.

"What?" Wade cups his hand to his ear.

"You-want-a-drink?" she repeats, pointing to her glass. Her fingernails are glossy red — except two; her index finger and thumb are unpainted. Just like her toes. Wade wonders how long it would take her to finish painting the last two, or, if she's removing the polish, how long it would take to clean off the remaining eight.

"Bourbon? Scotch and soda?"

Wade shakes his head, "No thanks." He glances around the room; the television screen is at least a yard across. "It's about Molto ..."

The bed is huge, unmade and littered with pillows and magazines. Over by the bathroom door, there's a pile of dog shit on the rug.

Mrs. Patton pours herself another tall drink from one of the decanters on her dressing table. "Here's to living in a fucking wilderness."

Wade can't believe he heard what she just said.

She sips her drink. "A toast." At the sound of her voice, Molto barks ever louder, lunging at the door. "Does he bother you?" she asks.

Wade shrugs. "Hard to hear, what with ..."

"Molto! No!" The beast falls quiet and whimpers. She finds the remote and turns off the TV. The room is suddenly silent and feels very small and hot.

"I just wanted to let you know about the newel post," he says. "I can fix it, if you'd like."

She takes another drink. "You're amazing, you know that? Is there anything you can't fix?"

He tries not to smile. "Not much to it, really."

She cuts a glance at his belt buckle, puts down her glass and begins looking for something.

Wade takes a step towards the door. "Anyway, you can look at it when you get a chance and tell me what you want me to do."

"Wait a minute," she says, "Just a teeny, tiny goddamned minute ..." She opens bureau drawers in a reckless search, pushes aside unfolded clothing and then begins to search through the cartons and shopping bags that clutter the room. The front of her robe falls open as she bends down, but she doesn't pull it closed until she finds what she's been looking for.

"My husband liked me in this one." She holds up a framed photograph of herself in a two-piece bathing suit. Her voice softens. "I was 22. Can you believe it?"

Wade nods politely. She is beautiful. "Nice picture," he says, hoping for the perfect tone. "Very nice."

"It was in New Jersey, at the shore."

Wade mutters, "A day at the beach, all right."

Mrs. Patton caresses the glass with her fingertips. "Nineteen seventy-one." She puts the photograph face down on the bureau and approaches Wade. "I met him at my sister's. She's dead now."

"I'm sorry," Wade says. He has worked for the Pattons for four years and never had a personal conversation with either of them. "Do you have other brothers and sisters?"

She looks at him as if she's just discovered him in her room, and at the very moment Wade thinks he's gone too far, she throws her arms around his shoulders and buries her head in his chest.

They stand like that for several minutes, Wade holding her while she sobs and clutches at his clothing, squeezing him to her with surprising strength, soaking his shirt with her tears. Wade can't think of anything to say or do except to allow her to do what she needs to do. He stands hugging her in much the same way he hugged his daughter Tina when her husband died.

Such was the account of the incident as I remember Wade telling it. When he had finished, he asked me what I thought. I said something inadequate, about how lonely Mrs. Patton must be, how sad for her to be left so isolated. But I could tell it didn't really matter what I thought. The question, as posed, was rhetorical. Wade had obviously come to some conclusions of his own, and I almost expected him to tell me what they were. Once he'd swallowed the last bite of his sandwich, he reached across the table and tugged at my sleeve. "Remember when you read me her letter on the phone last week?" It may have been the first time Wade ever touched me. He pulled me closer. "I already knew her name was Linda."

Six months after my Gorham lunch date with Wade, I received a message on my answering machine from someone who identified himself as Glenwald's new owner. He had found a letter addressed to me, left in Wade's former office. He'd be happy to mail it to me — or I was welcome to pick it up any time. He looked forward to meeting me, he said, and complimented the work I'd done on the wine cellar. I played back the message three times.

The new owners of Glenwald were absent when curiosity took me up there a few days later. The newly hired handyman, Jake Ogden, greeted me with Wade's letter in hand. Jake had often helped Wade when needed, and we'd met several times. He had grown up with Wade, and knew the mansion well.

"So, what happened?" I asked, nodding up toward the mansion, once we'd finished our small talk.

"Her husband divorced her, paid her off, so they say, and she up and moved to Arizona." Jake smiled and gazed off at the season's first dusting of snow on the shoulders of Mt. Washington. "And Wade ..." A grin crinkled the corners of Jake's mouth. "Wade went with her. He don't have to work anywhere from now on."

Was I surprised, or did it all make perfect sense? "Wade and Mrs. — I mean, Wade and Linda — went to Arizona. Together."

There was one more piece, a minor one, but I needed to know. "And the dog?"

Jake laughed. "Molto and Wade, they had to have them a little understanding," he said. "It took about a month, but then, by Jesus, Wade had that puppy laying at his feet like a big old pussycat. Followed him everywhere he went and never chewed on nothing again. Obeyed him perfect. Unbelievable."

I drove home with Wade's letter folded open on the seat beside me — a brief greeting from an address in Tucson, along with a photograph; a smiling Linda Patton with her arm around Wade's waist. They were standing in front of a Ferris wheel, and looked as happy as I'd ever imagined either could ever be. It was signed, "Linda and Wade Wentworth." As I crossed over the mountains, I pictured Wade fixing anything that was broken, touching wood, reaching through the complicated web of money, class and social status, and touching Linda Patton's heart.

Skit

Assimilation is no easy trick in New England's Appalachia. Two and-a-half decades after my arrival, I was still the "Outa state fella that bought Tatt's place up on Pinnacle Road," and as much as I revered my neighbors and the people I worked with, I would always be a nouveau native. I'd spent years trying to emulate their high standards of competence in things manual and mechanical, as well as their stoic ennobling of cold, hard, dirty work, but my good intentions were no substitution for having come to all of that by necessity rather than choice.

We'd all made our choices. Lamar was one of the captains of the SOM team that completed the 660,000-square-foot Rowes Wharf project on Boston's historic waterfront, and he was now a senior partner. Tom Luckey had found his niche and was famously successful as a designer and fabricator of sculptural climbing mazes. These spiraling, floating constellations were being scrambled through and admired in metropolitan children's museums all over the country. Other classmates were trustees of symphony orchestras and chaired professors at places like Harvard and Stanford. We had more slain dragons behind us than ahead, but choices had been made, and the best had been made of those options. I hadn't worn a necktie to work since I moved north, but the social/cultural paradox I was living was still working — mostly. I still believed that worldly achievements were justly admirable, but so was the quotidian triumph of digging a perfect ditch with a shovel. Just when I thought I had it all sorted out, Skit's funeral rattled my perspective.

Skit and his pals started drinking on Saturday afternoon at a hunting camp on Stone House Mountain. Around midnight, he got in his pickup and started home to his wife Rhonda, their twin daughters, Brandi and Brittany. On a sharp curve, he veered off the pavement and struck a roadside boulder so hard that his truck somersaulted down the highway. The engine was ripped off its mounts and pushed up under the dashboard.

A passerby called 911. The Fast Squad brought him back to life twice. He hung on in the hospital for three days surrounded by family. Aside from the injuries sustained by striking the boulder and flipping end-over-end, there was also evidence of a chainsaw hurled loose in the cab of his truck.

Jimmy True once told me that he and Skit spent many a childhood afternoon shooting rats in Skit's kitchen. "Mama weren't much of a housekeeper," he said. He and Skit parted company when Skit dropped out of school halfway through the eighth grade. Later, when Jimmy took over his father's contracting business, he hired Skit on as a carpenter. It amazed him that Skit seemed to know how to do everything without ever having been taught. Jimmy meant it as a compliment when he called him, "A natural born wood butcher."

He got his tattoos in reform school: "Live Free or Die" across one bicep, a blue panther, fangs bared, on the other. Most of Skit's teeth had rotted out before he got his driver's license. He was tall and loose-jointed, with apologetic shoulders and nervous hands. In another family, in another town, he might have stayed in school and been a basketball star. While his former classmates were playing sports and dating girls, Skit was in and out of jail for minor offenses, or working full-time as a logger. At 25, he'd started a beer belly, "My Milwaukee tumor." He liked hunting and fishing with his buddies, and when he worked, he worked hard. Car mechanic, carpenter, house painter, logger, and heavy equipment operator — he'd done it all — just as long as it pleased him. And then, provoked by an insult, real or imagined, or for no apparent reason — he'd disappear for weeks.

Skit first caught my eye when he was 8 or 9. I'd see him on his way to school on winter mornings, riding his bicycle, head down, legs churning through a snowstorm, no hat, no mittens. When I asked a neighbor's daughter about him, she said he was nice, but his daddy was mean, and his mother made him wear smelly clothes.

Skit was always somewhere in my peripheral vision until one summer he came to work for me as a carpenter. I found him to be fully accessible or, alternately, totally closed off to me — I never knew what to expect. He had little photos of his girls taped to the dashboard of his truck. He put himself deep into debt for a better car for his wife, a new stove for his sister, and a pony for his daughters. And he was terribly bright. He quoted statistics verbatim from the New Hampshire Fish and Game annual reports, and was a notoriously shrewd, card-counting poker player. On the job one day, I watched him divide eight feet, nine inches into five equal parts, in his head — in about two seconds.

The night before Skit's funeral, Tom stopped in to see us on this way back from a job interview in Maine. We stayed up late and indulged ourselves in semi-sober soliloquies on life (we were both now north of 50 and every year was better than the last), love (we had both been very lucky), our children (we had both been very, very lucky), and architecture (these goddamned deconstructionist academics were replacing architecture's meat and potatoes with super-sized helpings of verbal salad). The next day, under a gray October sky, Tom and I went to Skit's funeral.

We arrived early and sat in the back. As the pews filled, Tom wanted to know who certain people were, what they did for a living, how I knew them. Skit's cousin Arvin was there in his wheelchair. I whispered to Tom a quick version of the incident that put him there, a teen-aged fight and a fall for which Skit was convicted of assault. I thought I'd know more of the family and friends, but of the several hundred mourners gathered, most were strangers to me.

Skit had lately been driving a big red Mack ten-wheeler for the owner of a local gravel pit. I'd wave when we passed on the road and he'd return an embellished salute from high in the cab, a wry smile on his snuff-stained lips, mock-earnest. In a selfish way, I liked the stories about him, the wilder the better. Maybe it was because his life was so unlike mine, his undomesticated nature in such opposition to the Calvinist virtues with which I'd been burdened. He had no fear of his feral impulses or the consequences of pursuing them. Comparing myself to Skit, I felt boringly diligent and dull. Disappearing without notice for a month, for instance, was for me both impossible to entertain — and outrageously appealing. I'll never know how he felt about me, but I think he would have been surprised to know how much he challenged me to be my more natural self — whoever that was meant to be — instead of the "good" person my education and training suggested I become.

The lady minister called him a trustworthy man and spoke of his friendships, of his love for the lakes and forests and family. I couldn't help but wonder if she'd ever met him, but was grateful, at least, for her generosity. *The Lord is my shepherd* ... As far as I could tell, the psalm offered consolation to no one. *Though I walk in the valley of the shadow of death* ... The sour trace of Budweiser breath seeped through the church. *Thy rod and thy staff* ... A few voices mumbled along with the minister's through the Lord's prayer ... *Forgive us our trespasses, and forgive those who trespass against us* ... It all seemed so irrelevant.

A few years back, Skit stole my chainsaw. I hadn't thought about the old yellow McCullough for a while, but the memory popped up, inappropriately attached to a sad occasion. He'd worked hard that summer on a house that I could afford to build and live in — a dream far beyond his reach. Through no fault or virtue of our own, we'd been dealt different lives, he and I, and both of us knew it. One Monday morning, Skit failed to show up for work, and the chainsaw was missing. When I finally saw him in the general store parking lot three weeks later, he was working for a mason in a nearby town. We spoke briefly about something unimportant; neither of us wanted to discuss his unannounced departure — or the missing saw. As he drove away, I spotted the McCullough in the back of his truck. I never tried to get it back.

It was raining when we left the church for the short walk to the cemetery. A bottle in a brown paper bag was passed around as the hearse crept up the lane. At the gravesite, eight pallbearers shuffled forward, rugged, thick-waisted men embarrassed by the unfamiliar formality of their duties. Their shoes sunk in the puddles as they braced against the wind. Raindrops fell from their forearms and clung to the Formica coffin before slipping down the sides into the sodden mud. Tom and I stood on the periphery, behind Skit's cousin, Arvin, in the wheelchair.

A final prayer was read. Morty's big red ten-wheeler roared by on the highway, its air horn blasting a long salute. A dog barked inside a parked pickup truck behind us. One of Skit's brothers slipped away from the grave. I heard a truck door opened, and a bewildered yelp. When the door slammed shut, Skit's daughters began to wail.

I suddenly felt as if I didn't belong there, as if I understood nothing. What was it about Skit that so reminded me of who I wasn't — and why did I care so much? I stepped back a few yards and stood under a dripping pine as the casket was lowered. Beyond the hollow ring of church comfort, there was nothing much to cling to in the sadness and the rain. Skit would have wandered off altogether, been out in the woods or out on the pond, exempt from social expectations.

The service was over, and as the crowd dispersed, Tom hunkered down in front of Arvin's wheelchair, talking to him at eye-level. They talked until Arvin's father came to fetch him and wheel him out of the rain, into a van. When I asked Tom about their conversation, he said, "The guy is a genius. And funny as hell. He fixes everything from TVs to toasters, self-taught, does it all from his wheelchair, paralyzed from the waist down and he doesn't give a shit about the past; he's all in the moment."

I'd thought about Arvin's plight often. "What would you do if that happened to you?" I asked Tom on the drive home from the cemetery.

"Paralyzed, in a wheel chair?" He squirmed in his seat. "No way would I do electronics." He laughed. "Maybe play air guitar — or be a sit-down comic. Have some fun, that's for sure." Like me, Tom lived largely through his physical capabilities, but he was able to see his life past them, to find a way to fun, despite all obstacles. He didn't ask what I would do if I were confined to a wheelchair, and I wasn't sure I knew the answer, but my physicality was so much a part of my sense of me, I wasn't sure I could ever be as brave and uncomplaining as Arvin — or play air guitar like Tom — or that I wouldn't be inclined to shoot myself.

When Tom left for his cliff-side home in Connecticut that afternoon, he was still talking about Arvin. "What a piece of work," he said. "Next time I come up, I want to see that guy again."

That night I dreamt I was praying — unusual for me, asleep or awake — praying that his Maker would receive Skit well and understand that he didn't steal my chainsaw after all: I wanted him to have it.

The Forest for the Trees

There was something I couldn't quite place about Jim's voice on the phone. He sounded friendly enough, but was he too smooth, too glib — too much of a salesman? I listened carefully as he told me about the 100 acres he'd bought in southern New Hampshire. He wanted me to consult with him on the site work, and possibly later on design a house for him at the top of his hill. "I'm having twenty acres clear-cut now," he said, "and the driveway roughed in. We're going to have killer views all the way up and down the valley."

For most of my life, I've lived in places surrounded by forests. My interest in trees is aesthetic, scientific, and personal. I can smell the difference between oak sawdust and pine, between maple wood and brown ash. I remember certain trees more vividly than I remember certain people. That old denunciation, "He can't see the forest for the trees," describes me perfectly. I see trees as individuals, and in my woods, I regularly appoint myself chief custodian, friend and liberator of All Flora In Need Of Assistance. I also occasionally serve as the requisite assassin.

By the mid-1800s, over eighty percent of the state of New Hampshire's forests had fallen to the interests of dairy and sheep farming. A century and-a-half later, over 80 percent of the state is again forested. Unlike the dry western states' soils, in which most trees wither and a single wagon track may remain visible for decades, New England's turf heals comparatively quickly and provides a fertile environment for rapidly growing vegetation. During the Civil War, Jim's hundred hilltop acres were most probably all pastureland. It would be interesting to see what was growing on his site thirteen decades later.

America's virgin forests, characterized by huge trees spreading a high, dense canopy over a sparsely populated forest floor, are long gone. The pace of transition from species to species in the primeval forest was slow, predictable and measured in centuries. In contrast, the young, explosive second-growth forests of today are a tree-eat-tree battleground. Seedlings sprout inches apart from one another and struggle for sunlight and nutrients. Ten saplings often crowd the space where only one can survive: Half-a-century will sort out the winners and losers.

The clear-cut approach Jim mentioned makes sense in situations where stunted, unwanted or disease-prone species will be replaced with a diverse, healthy stock. I assumed he was cleaning up overgrown pasture, the typical onslaught of white pine, chokecherry, and poplar that overtakes a field within a few years of its abandonment. "Just cutting back the little stuff?" I asked.

"Nothing worth keeping," he said. "Wait 'til you see the views."

We agreed to meet the next day at his site.

Jim's beefy SUV was parked on the side of the road, and as I pulled in behind it, my eye was drawn to the adjacent woods where a broad swath had been cut through the forest for several hundred yards up the hill. It was hard to avoid looking at the carnage while Jim and I exchanged greetings. He was an athletic 55, with a strong handshake, thick gray hair, and a confident manner. What I saw on the hillside behind him looked like a power line right-of-way, an unnatural gash ripped through a healthy stand of hemlock, oak, and beech. Some of the stumps were eighteen inches across — 50- or 60-year-old trees. The natural rolls and dips across the terrain had been ignored, as if the only way up the hill was a straight line. The edges of the cut looked as if they had been precision-cut with a laser.

"That's not even the top of the hill," Jim said proudly. "The driveway is close to half-a-mile. And wait'll you see my vernal pools. You know what they are, right?"

"They're seasonal," I said. "Springtime pools. They sometimes last six weeks if there's been a heavy snow pack.

For the briefest moment, Jim looked puzzled. "There's a lot of water in one of them. It'll probably go all summer."

"Maybe," I said, "But 'vernal' means 'of the spring.'"

"Anyway, I've got my road going right between them. Laid the whole thing out myself."

As we walked up the hill on the road-to-be, Jim explained how he and his wife, Mindy, had in fact already "kind of" designed their house, "But we figured we ought to have an architect check it out," he said. "We ran into trouble squeezing some of the rooms into the floor plan, but we know exactly what we want. Kind of Spanish or Italian, like the villas we saw in Napa Valley. It would be up to you to make sure everything looked good and the roof didn't cave in. Stuff like that."

For me, the first meeting with a potential client is an implicit two-way interview. If our goals seem compatible, we proceed. If one or both of us have reservations, several more sessions may be required to inspire mutual confidence. The more Jim talked, the more I wondered if I would be interested in a second meeting.

At the top of the rise, I looked back down the cut and saw what might be done to remedy the full frontal attack he'd begun. I suggested that by traversing the hill with a few switchbacks, Jim could drive up a gentler grade, avoid erosion problems, and take advantage of the existing contours instead of bulldozing a stripe down the hill. I also suggested he vary the widths of the cut so that they didn't look so unnaturally straight.

"I see your point," he said, a little too quickly, "But that would make my mowing much more difficult." Jim had ordered a big John Deere four-wheel-drive tractor with a five-foot rotary attachment. The dimension of the road cut through the woods was based on the width of the driveway plus exactly six passes with his John Deere on each side.

I had to ask: "You aren't worried it'll seem like an access road?" I stopped short of adding, "... to a regional high school?"

Jim looked at me as if I were to be forgiven for making such a naïve remark — and continued walking. "And right here," he said, gesturing with a salesman's panache, "is my first vernal pool."

Indeed there was a vernal pool on the right side of the roadway, a beautiful plane of clear, cool water. Perhaps thirty feet across and half as wide, its bottom was a collage of sepia-toned oak and beech leaves, flattened as if under glass. Hobblebush, partridgeberry, and ground pine grew around the edges, all prospering in the shade of a huge, ancient hemlock spreading its branches wide overhead. Although it was the first week in June, the pool was still more than a foot deep.

"It's beautiful," I said. "In early spring, you might see spotted salamanders swimming across the bottom. They're mysterious critters. No one seems to know exactly where they go or what they do the rest of the year."

"I thought about digging it out and making it deeper."

I glanced around and saw outcroppings of ledge, a typical sight around vernal pools. In the spring, snowmelt collects in a low spot and is held by impervious soils or bedrock. No permanent watercourse runs in or out. If it weren't for the hemlock's shade, Jim's pool would be already dry. If he tried to dig it deeper, he'd quickly hit ledge, find no more water, and destroy a plant and animal symbiosis that had been years in the making.

I carefully explained all this to Jim, but the way he nodded his head was simply a way of prompting me to finish. The instant I stopped, he pointed to the huge old hemlock and said, "I told my logger to take down that pine."

"That hemlock?" I was astounded — not because he didn't know the difference between a hemlock and a pine, but because he seemed so — oblivious.

"Okay, hemlock." Jim said. "Whatever."

"Take it down," I warned, "And the ecosystem in and around the pool will suffer dramatically when you let in all that light."

"Are the bugs always this ferocious?" Jim swatted at the air around his head."

I hadn't noticed any. "They'll be gone by November," I deadpanned, "But this tree needs to stay."

"It's too close to the road," he said. "Take a lot of time to mow around."

I heard my voice rise uncontrollably, half an octave at least. "What — another two minutes?"

Jim waved regally at his forest. "I've got plenty of trees."

In the little patches of woods I've owned, I've not been concerned about merchantable yields of fruit or lumber. Instead, I've cultivated diversity. I might cut down a dozen overcrowded poplars so that one, slow-growing hawthorn might prosper, or whack a bushy pasture pine because I feel sorry for the struggling mountain ash next door. When I come upon an elm showing signs of Dutch elm disease, I apologize, genuflect, and level it. My system of arboreal triage allows me to pamper the uncommon species — balm of Gilead, the sinewy-trunked blue beech or the pole-tall pignut hickory — and saw down almost anything that interferes with a struggling wild apple. Most wild apples are in fact not wild, but escapees from a nearby orchard, courtesy of a rambling deer or squirrel. I feel triumphant when I'm able to liberate a couple of spindly specimens smothered in a thicket of ambitious young pines. Once I've cleared away the bullies, I prune the leggy apple trees until they're transformed into graceful ballerinas. Sometimes they almost seem to curtsy in the glare of an unaccustomed sun.

I'd seen no sign of apple trees on Jim's property, but the vernal pool hemlock we stood under was easily three feet through and well over a century old. I put my hands against its trunk, and tried one last appeal: "Here's my unequivocal opinion, Jim: I think it would be a terrible mistake to cut this down," I said. "And aside from the beauty of the tree itself, you'll be kissing your vernal pool goodbye."

Either Jim didn't notice my growing irritation, or he was determined to ignore it. "Come on," he said, ever-cheerful, "I'll show you the other pool."

Following Jim along his regrettable road, I resolved to stay calm. It seemed unlikely, but maybe the redeeming chapters to his story were yet to come, maybe the narrative would improve. Another part of me was thinking, and maybe pigs will fly.

The second pool was on the opposite side of the road, in a flat patch of low ledgey ridges and dips. It was only half the size of the first, six inches deep and surrounded by witch hazel bushes. There were no trees standing above it to give it shade. In another week, it would be dry.

"If I can't get more water in this one, I might just fill it in," he said.

Get more water from where? It seemed futile to repeat myself. "Why not wait a few years and see how you like it," I said.

Jim smiled and motioned for me to continue walking. "Let's go," he said. "This is where it gets even better."

After another hundred yards on the gash through the woods, we emerged at the edge of clear-cut hillside. Ten or more acres had been denuded of every upright twig except for a few clusters of oaks. This was no recently overgrown pasture. Big, old stumps were everywhere, oozing sap like watery blood. A century's worth of forest-floor duff lay baking in the sun. As the summer wore on, some of it would turn to dust and blow away. Meanwhile, the skidders had left deep, muddy gouges in the hillside where they'd hauled their hitches to the landing where the logs were loaded onto trucks. What had been a viable forest for the past century suddenly looked like hell on Earth.

"The loggers are about half-done," Jim said brightly, as we began up the final pitch to his site. "Once they get done, my view is going to be fantastic."

I said little as we climbed the low incline toward the top of the hill. Jim talked nonstop about the great split-level house in the suburbs where he had lived all his married life. Now that his children were grown and he had found a buyer for his Laundromat franchise, he and Mindy were looking forward to living "the good life, close to nature, back to the land." As he was busy telling a story making fun of Mindy's fear of mice, I spotted moose tracks in the mud a few yards ahead of us. Jim tramped over them without a glance, eyes fixed on the top of the hill.

"I'm glad you left the oaks," I said on our way past a trio of tall, straight specimens near the top. It felt good finally to be saying something positive.

"Look at that view."

I looked. "You're lucky," I said. "On an open site like this, having these trees in the foreground is a beautiful way to give some scale to the landscape and frame the view."

"I don't have the foggiest why the loggers left them," he said with his unflappable salesman's smile. "This is all going to be my field."

"A few trees won't stop the grass from growing," I ventured, looking up into the treetops. "You've got some beauties here."

"We're going to have a windmill, and live off the grid," Jim said. "Screw the Arabs. Problem is, these trees could block the wind, so they've got to go."

I refrained from asking Jim how many working windmills he'd seen along the Connecticut River corridor, a region notorious for Yankee ingenuity and thrift. (The answer would have been zero.) I wanted to say, yes, windmills are marvelous, but unless your hat is blowing off every other minute, you'd be much wiser to invest your thirty thousand dollars in triple-glazed windows and massive amounts of insulation. I wanted to say that and more, but had increasingly little incentive to do so.

The crest of the hill was a flat plateau, perhaps fifty yards square and tapering off slightly on every side. The loggers had stopped cutting halfway across it, as if a haircut had been interrupted midway through. The red oaks and birches that remained were large and healthy. I might have assumed he was going to leave them around the house, but I would have been wrong.

"These come down next," he said, as if the trees were an eyesore.

I thought about how I would site a house among the trees. I imagined a patio dappled with light filtered through the branches, the driveway sweeping invisibly around the far edge of the field and approaching the house from the north. I imagined a house and gardens that I now knew with certainty I would never design.

"Isn't that the most beautiful view you've ever seen?"

Actually, it wasn't. Not even close. We were on top of a hill to be sure, but it was a wide, flat hilltop with none of the steep drop-offs essential to opening a close valley view. Due to a fluke of topography, most of the hills around it were approximately the same height, and they were arranged so that each obscured most of the next. Sure, I could see the hazy top of a flattish mountain ten or fifteen miles away, but there was no foreground for the first five miles: no valleys, no variety, no passion.

Even if the view had pleased me, I couldn't have concocted a rationalization for the shoddy treatment of the land. Our ideas about views are, after all, personal, and I reminded myself that what Jim saw was what mattered to him. It was his view, not mine. "I think you'd like the view even better if you left some trees around the house," I said.

Jim tapped his temple, as though to remind a first-grader (me) to put on his thinking cap. "The windmill?" he said. "Got to cut the trees to capture the wind?"

My litmus test for a suitable windmill site is simple: it requires six visits to the site — and a hat. If the hat stays on your head for more than half the visits, forget the windmill. The surrounding topography made it clear that Jim's was a safe-hat site. I pictured thirty thousand dollars wasted, a bushel of bills floating lazily to the ground in still air.

"And we're having a walkout basement for our exercise equipment, with the windows pointing south," he said, pointing northeast. "Let the sun heat the room, passive solar."

I couldn't resist. "From the northeast?"

Jim smiled his enigmatic smile. Maybe he felt sorry for me. "Walkout basements save money."

He was right. They do, but Jim's hilltop was flat. Walkout basements are predicated on a sloping site. Ideally, the elevation drops five to seven feet across the depth of the house. "Where were you thinking of siting the house?"

Jim gestured to the middle of the plateau — dead level.

"And pointing south," I said, pointing south.

Jim swung northeast again. "Pointing south. To get the benefits of the sun. It's called passive solar."

I quit.

On the way down the hill, Jim talked about the kitchen appliances they had picked out, the "cool" leather and plaid appliances they had picked out, the "cool" leather and plaid couch they bought on sale, and assorted other pieces of "authentic reproduction antique-type" furniture they knew were exactly right for their house. None of what he said required more than an occasional grunt from me. When I saw a box turtle under a log near the bottom of the hill, I kept the discovery to myself.

In a way, Jim's self-assurance was enviable. He appeared to be truly excited about every aspect of his project, and unflappable in the face of any evidence or opinion contrary to his vision. Whichever version of the Spanish or Italian Napa Valley villa he built, he would probably enjoy it, and for that, he deserved my best wishes. But what he had done to the land, and intended yet to do to secure "his" view was, for me, beyond forgiveness.

Back at our cars, we were suddenly awkward, as if we'd just finished a blind date that had gone really badly. We both knew that I'd told him nothing he wanted to hear, and I knew he'd told me nothing I wanted to hear. We parted with vague, polite allusions to the possibility of definitely maybe there might be a chance of ... something — and he reminded me to send him a bill.

A few weeks passed. I felt odd, billing someone who appeared to have gained nothing from me, and yet it was he who had asked for a consultation and agreed to pay for it. Between travel time and walking the site, I'd spent four billable hours, but I felt tainted: I'd been exposed to something gone wrong, and had no way of stopping it from going further. There were a few times during those few weeks when I was determined to talk to Jim about the responsibility inherent in owning land, that we are only temporary custodians and conservators of a resource much greater than we. I wanted to plead with him to focus more on the needs of his environment instead of his needs for a "killer view" and a big green tractor, but every time I imagined the conversations, I heard his smooth salesman's voice and realized my arguments would be futile.

ERRATUM

Correct text for page 158

couch they bought on sale, and assorted other pieces of "authentic reproduction antique-type" furniture they knew were exactly right for their house. None of what he said required more than an occasional grunt from me. When I saw a box turtle under a log near the bottom of the hill, I kept the discovery to myself.

In a way, Jim's self-assurance was enviable. He appeared to be truly excited about every aspect of his project, and unflappable in the face of any evidence or opinion contrary to his vision. Whichever version of the Spanish or Italian Napa Valley villa he built, he would probably enjoy it, and for that, he deserved my best wishes. But what he had done to the land, and intended yet to do to secure "his" view was, for me, beyond forgiveness.

Back at our cars, we were suddenly awkward, as if we'd just finished a blind date that had gone really badly. We both knew that I'd told him nothing he wanted to hear, and I knew he'd told me nothing I wanted to hear. We parted with vague, polite allusions to the possibility of definitely maybe there might be a chance of ... something — and he reminded me to send him a bill.

A few weeks passed. I felt odd, billing someone who appeared to have gained nothing from me, and yet it was he who had asked for a consultation and agreed to pay for it. Between travel time and walking the site, I'd spent four billable hours, but I felt tainted: I'd been exposed to something gone wrong, and had no way of stopping it from going further. There were a few times during those few weeks when I was determined to talk to Jim about the responsibility inherent in owning land, that we are only temporary custodians and conservators of a resource much greater than we. I wanted to plead with him to focus more on the needs of his environment instead of his needs for a "killer view" and a big green tractor, but every time I imagined the conversations, I heard his smooth salesman's voice and realized my arguments would be futile.

It's true: I can't see the forest for the trees, and for that, I make

ERRATUM
Correct text for page 160

lock by the first vernal pool? Leave it alone, and you can rip up my invoice."

Jim laughed. "What is it with you and my tree? It's going to die anyway."

"Do we have a deal?"

"I'll send you a check for half," he said.

I'm not proud of what I said before I hung up. Calling him names wasn't going to change his approach to nature, nor would it correct his misunderstanding of how architecture — or, more importantly — ecosystems are made. Whatever residual influence I might have had on him was now forever lost.

He eventually sent the check, as promised, for one hour's work, no note enclosed. I countersigned it, mailed it to the Sierra Club, and requested that they add him to their mailing list. I'm still ashamed when I think of the huge old hemlock tree. Of no commercial value as a saw log, ring shake and heart rot would have fated it to be chipped and trucked to a power plant. Incinerated — to make steam to turn a turbine — it might have produced half-a-kilowatt of light shining down on a used car lot in another place where trees once grew limb to limb.

no apologies. For me, the forest and its trees form a church of the sort that doesn't judge virtue or justify war. The forest-tree-church I know is both a reliable refuge and a living university. I treasure the vast variety of leaf patterns, from the thumbnail-sized black locust's leaf to the neatly elliptical shad's, to the striped maple's goose-foot print; each turns in the wind and dapples sunlight to the forest floor in its own distinctive fashion. The long needles and scaly orange bark of a red pine are radically different from the balsam fir's soft, clustered needles and tight shiny bark, and yet the two trees are coniferous cousins. The reductive symmetry of a white spruce's Christmas-tree silhouette contrasted with the wild asymmetry of a lightning-struck hard maple sets them worlds apart. When I look up into the cantilevered limbs of a white oak tree, I see a stunning example of adaptive structural design. For me, the forest is a compelling argument, plain and simple, of a Higher Power — Darwin notwithstanding.

I finally wrote out an invoice for two miserable hours. A few days later, Jim called to discuss the bill: It was too high, he said. He'd be willing to send me half. One hour's worth.

"Including travel, I actually spent considerably more time than what I billed you for," I said.

"But you didn't give me what I wanted," he said, same smooth, friendly voice, same unflappable Jim.

"And that was ...?"

"You know, it just seemed as if you weren't listening to me," he said, "And that's why I hired you, to check out my ideas."

"You mean endorse them."

Jim was not one to argue. "I'll send you half."

"Have the loggers been back?"

"Not since I saw you. The rain, you know, it's been non-stop."

"Then I'll make you a deal," I said. "You know that big hem-

Jim was not one to argue. "I'll send you half."

"Have the loggers been back?"

"Not since I saw you. The rain, you know, it's been non-stop."

"Then I'll make you a deal," I said. "You know that big hemlock by the first vernal pool? Leave it alone, and you can rip up my invoice."

Jim laughed. "What is it with you and my tree? It's going to die anyway."

"Do we have a deal?"

"I'll send you a check for half," he said.

I'm not proud of what I said before I hung up. Calling him names wasn't going to change his approach to nature, nor would it correct his misunderstanding of how architecture — or, more importantly — ecosystems are made. Whatever residual influence I might have had on him was now forever lost.

He eventually sent the check, as promised, for one hour's work, no note enclosed. I countersigned it, mailed it to the Sierra Club, and requested that they add him to their mailing list. I'm still ashamed when I think of the huge old hemlock tree. Of no commercial value as a saw log, ring shake and heart rot would have fated it to be chipped and trucked to a power plant. Incinerated — to make steam to turn a turbine — it might have produced half-a-kilowatt of light shining down on a used car lot in another place where trees once grew limb to limb.

Mississippi Maynard

We met at Logan International Airport, a dozen Habitat for Humanity volunteers lugging our duffel bags to the curbside check in. Thirteen months had passed since the World Trade Center disaster, and it appeared in places that the shoe-sniffing security personnel might well outnumber the passengers. I had a moment imagining my wife Melinda and I handcuffed together in orange prison garb and held incommunicado as our families desperately sought out our whereabouts. Our checked-in luggage contained enough tools to dismantle and rebuild a plane in mid-air, let alone hijack it, and although I knew we were on our way to Mississippi to build houses, I experienced a vague sense of guilt as I watched our carry-on backpacks disappear behind the little black curtains of the X-ray machine — as if we were trying to trick the security people with our decoy changes of socks and toothbrushes while the real weapons of mass construction moved undetected into the baggage bay.

Our plane landed in Memphis under a bright noonday sun, and within half an hour the group was packed into three rented cars and headed south into the state of Mississippi. Our destination was Sherard, a speck on the map in the middle of the so-called Delta, an elongated triangle of rich bottom land between the Mississippi and Yazoo Rivers.

Driving down Route 61, we marveled at the dark tapestries of kudzu vines smothering abandoned barns and trees. Half an hour south of Memphis, the low hills flattened out and gave way to the Delta's deep alluvial soils, flat as pond water. Pecan orchards nudged up against the highway; open fields stretched to the horizon beyond and gaudy casino billboards promised us loose slots, country music stars, and with Lady Luck's blessings, the moon. To the west, we caught glimpses of the levee that follows the Mississippi River southward like a serpentine shadow of swollen earth. The occasional, tiny communities we passed — Lula, Stowall, Farrell — were sun-bleached and half-abandoned relics of a time before mechanization replaced the many hands needed to harvest the Delta's bountiful crops of cotton and soybeans. As we passed the first, huge, dust-encrusted cotton gin, it struck me how far behind we had left the glib sophistications of the east coast megalopolis: we had entered the most southern place on earth.

My work with Habitat for Humanity in the Delta started in 1992, and I've been back many times since. My old friends Ben and Paddy Moore began volunteering there in the late '80s, and it was mostly because of our long-enduring relationship that I first signed on to spend a week with them — but not without reservations. Habitat's mission statement includes some decidedly pro-Christian language, and I had still not quite recovered from my Episcopalian high school regimen with its mandatory chapel services five mornings a week. Those muscular Christian hymns exalting truth and wrath and terrible, swift swords still disturb me. The case for church religion was never made compelling to me, and so it was with a certain degree of foreboding that I joined that first morning prayer in Sherard, Mississippi, presided over by a Catholic nun.

Sister Pat arrived early in a Vikings' cap and spoke in the wide prairie accent of her native Minnesota. In her early 60s and less than five feet tall, Sister Pat had exchanged her wimple and habit for the thrift store work clothes that she wore every day as the local Habitat coordinator. She welcomed the group warmly and asked each of us where we were from and how we had learned about Habitat. After some discussion of the day's building schedule, she asked us to join hands in prayer.

"Dear Lord, there are a lot of good people here today, don'tcha know, they've come down here to build houses for folks who need them so much. We use power tools, Lord, and they can be sharp and dangerous as heck, so we hope You will look down on our efforts and keep an eye out for our safety, eh? And let everyone here have a good time with whatever they're doing, you betcha. In the name of the Father, the Son and the Holy Spirit, amen."

Amen, indeed.

Our week in Mississippi each year is spent pouring slabs, framing walls, hanging sheetrock or doing plumbing and electrical work— whatever is needed to continue the work passed along by the volunteers before us. We never know what we'll be asked to do. When we depart, another group carries on where we left off, and so it goes, until one by one, the houses are completed.

Since I began volunteering, I've seen over a dozen homes completed, signed over, and occupied. The earliest one is as tidy and sound as the day it was finished.

Among those who work on Habitat projects, architectural credentials mean little. Habitat's housing is pre-designed with economy and modesty in mind. Field volunteers with a strong back, true eye and a sharp saw blade are much appreciated, but many come to the work with no particular professional skills, and with minimal leadership, accomplish much. As for the temptation to make "improvements" in Habitat's time-tested designs — move a window here, move a wall there — I force myself to leave all architectural impulses behind and concentrate instead on driving a nail straight and making a square cut.

The Delta's geologic history is made of a thousand years of layer upon layer of soils washed down from the great Midwest drainages. Its layers of social and economic history are equally compelling. As early as two decades before the Civil War, plantation slaves began chopping down, draining and dying in the malarial swamps that became today's immense cotton and soybean farms. Slavery is long gone, but the social hierarchies it engendered still resonate in subtle ways. Although overt acts of racism are rare, assumptions about a child's future are color-coded. Mississippi politics have been good for the few whites who own and manage the croplands, but not so good for the many blacks who plant and harvest them. Poverty, violence, and illiteracy are widespread. The incidences of diabetes and cardiovascular disease rank among the highest in the nation. Jobs are few and low paying, housing is scarce, distances to services are lengthy, and social service programs are almost non-existent. It is in this context that one asks about the relevance of refined aesthetics in Third-World America.

For me, the question is made particularly vivid because of some of the clients I leave at home. The daily decisions I make as a residential architect in prosperous New England fall between the better and the best. If I do my job well, those choices are technically and aesthetically informed, and the client's appetite for a work of unique architecture is satisfied. In contrast, the modesty of design appropriate to Habitat houses is driven by the forces of an economy and culture little known to me as a privileged white northerner.

The day before I last left for Mississippi, a client in Connecticut had narrowed down her kitchen-stove choices between two commercial Vulcans: One cost fifty-five hundred dollars, the other, eight thousand. She was leaning toward the latter, she said, because shipping was available within the week. That she was a self-professed atrocious cook did not enter the equation. Her house would not be occupied for at least another two months, but that stainless steel stove with the big red plastic knobs excited her, and she had to have it. At the same time, she contributes a goodly sum each year to Habitat as well as other good causes. By anyone's standards, she would be considered a kind, generous and loving person. If she can afford the stove, should she buy it? My answer is, "Yes," but the closer I get to the Delta each year, it sounds more like, "Yes, but."

It always seems to me easier to build something for someone else than to build for myself. At home, I typically have a dozen projects waiting, but I find endless reasons to procrastinate — the phone rings, the hike up the mountain beckons, a neighbor stops by, the garden needs weeding — opportunities for disruptions are infinite. In Mississippi, we work a full week with no distractions. Buttressed with Sister Pat's candid morning prayers ("Dear Lord, one of these big galoots dropped a 2 x 12 on his toe yesterday and we sure would appreciate it if You'd keep an eye on him."), Melinda and I spent a week in Mississippi putting the final touches on a house for Delia and Maynard.

Habitat's home-owner selection process is overseen at the local level by volunteer Habitat affiliate committees, which are often church-based. In the small rural communities of Mississippi, everyone knows everyone. Selection criteria are based on need and the proven financial means to cover a monthly mortgage and maintenance costs. Maynard and Delia were among several families who qualified, but their application was among the last to be approved. They'd had to wait in line for three years before their house was begun. Now that it was almost finished — the only big items left were kitchen countertops and the installation of bathrooms sinks and toilets — Maynard was bubbling with enthusiasm.

"Y'all got a lot did today," he said at the end of each afternoon after eagerly assisting us all day. He was twice my size, a grandly gentle figure in his spotless blue overalls and John Deere tractor cap. He hugged us hello and goodbye each day, and when he did, I couldn't stretch my arms all the way around his massive back. He'd fold Melinda into a hug that made her almost disappear. "I thanks the Lord for ever thing y'all got did."

After work one afternoon, Melinda overheard Delia saying she was going to fry chicken that evening. We had tasted Delia's famous cooking at a Habitat potluck a few nights before, and it was dangerously delicious. She told us she had begun frying chicken for her family when her father died and her mother and older siblings had to earn the family's livelihood picking cotton. At nine years old, she worked at the stovetop standing on a stool. When Melinda asked if she could watch the frying and take recipe notes, Delia was graciously amused. How anyone could have grown into adulthood without knowing how to fry chicken?

A few hours later, Melinda was in Delia's old kitchen with Delia and her cousin, Cheresse. Cheresse was a thin cheerful woman in her 50s who had lost a leg above the knee in a cotton gin accident when she was 18. Despite the appearance of an uncomfortable limp, the accident seemed to have done little to quench her high spirits. While the oil in the cast iron pan bubbled and spat chicken grease, the cousins teased each other about bygone romances.

"Be sensible, Cheresse. You know that Charles, he still be sweet on you."

"Old fool is all he is."

"He like the look of you."

"He want some leg?" Cheresse vamped. "I'll show him my special-made — upside his head."

When Cheresse sat down and hitched up her skirt, Melinda saw that the "special made" was fashioned from the bottom half of a wooden crutch screwed to a Maxwell House coffee can. Towels and duct tape, and what looked like straps from a homemade garter belt held the prosthesis in place. We learned later that Cheresse had long ago made the device herself when she despaired of waiting for help from her former employer and the state of Mississippi.

In the tradition of great cooks everywhere, Delia's recipe was a maddeningly vague.

How hot should the oil be?

"Not too hot," Delia cautioned. "But you don't wants it to get too cool, either."

Melinda had heard about the eight-thousand-dollar Vulcan stove in Connecticut, and noted that Delia was cooking on a chipped enamel, two-burner hot top in the decrepit kitchen she and Maynard were about to leave behind.

"What about the batter, Delia?"

"I uses flour and, you know, a little seasoning and spices."

"And, um, which seasoning and spices would those be?"

"Whatever you likes. You know, according to the taste y'all enjoys."

Maynard greeted us every morning with, "All right," intoned to signal a willing agreement with whatever might follow. I noticed other African-American men Maynard's age used the same greeting, which I interpreted as an instinctive survival strategy in an environment where not so long before, a tone less than acquiescent might put them at mortal risk. As I worked with him on his house through the week, I learned that Maynard's thirty-five-year career as a field machinery foreman was preceded by manually picking cotton, beginning at the age of eight. He quit school in the sixth grade to help support his family, and had gratefully worked for the same white man ever since. I never heard a trace of resentment or regret. Maynard's life had been a success. Until the Habitat house, he had lived all his adult life with Delia, their five kids and assorted grandchildren in a sharecropper's cabin owned by his employer. He was deeply religious, and had never been more than fifty miles from his birthplace. Aside from a tattered Bible, Maynard's family does not own a book.

When I was in architecture school, we would have had all kinds of plans for improving Maynard and Delia's lives. Aesthetics, to us, were the natural path to enlightenment. Years later, in Maynard's new Habitat kitchen, I wondered if the better part of enlightenment wasn't coming from Maynard to me. Could it be that my life, so advantaged, so blessed with a kind of affirmative action wholly inaccessible to Maynard, was missing something after all? What Higher Power had I ever thanked for the accident of my good fortune? Maynard, whose life was framed in adversity, was volubly thankful to his Lord for every hour of his life. For him, a thriving row of collard greens was met with humble gratitude. If the car started, if the Social Security check arrived on time, if the sun came up — each of these blessings was gratefully acknowledged. If the car didn't start and the greens withered, Maynard patiently looked to his Lord for guidance, and trusted in His beneficence.

Shortly after we installed his kitchen counters, I saw Maynard caress the imitation-wood-grain laminate as if it were polished alabaster, thanking the Lord with each tender stroke. Later, he stood in his new backyard admiring his shaded back porch, which was suddenly the best back porch in the sovereign state of Mississippi. Maynard's new combination air-conditioner/heater was a marvel, and he eagerly mastered the twenty-four-hour thermostat with its multiple settings. The final touches, the attachment of window curtain rods and the installation of closet shelves were Heaven sent, Amen.

Maynard's life story is every bit as compelling as my client's in Connecticut, but an Architecture of Ideas based on the canon of Euro-centric culture is as useless to him as it is essential to her. To be sure, there is a common need for basic comforts, but the huge differences of culture, education and income vastly separate the two. For both, the bottom line must include what Vitruvius, the Roman architect who served under Julius Caesar called, "commodity, firmness, and delight." Both want each of these virtues, but the tastes by which those terms are defined are measured by differences even greater than the distances between the Delta and the Long Island Sound.

When I think about how the aesthetic coordinates of Maynard's life were met in his Habitat house, and how my Connecticut client's were met in hers, I'm tempted to conclude that the measure of a building depends on its social utility, and that both these examples were candidates for success if we look at them within the context of their respective communities. Habitat provided a great house for Maynard, and the Connecticut client's stove will add yet another layer of panache to her high-ceilinged, cherry wood kitchen. Modernists, postmodernists, traditionalists, and theorists notwithstanding, I can't help but conclude that there is no single standard by which a building can be judged without accounting for where it was built, for whom it was built, and why it took the shape that it did.

Habitat is not alone in providing housing for the economically disadvantaged. The late Samuel Mockbee and his Rural Studio students at Auburn University created a witty, aesthetic alternative that combined youthful whimsy with practical, no-nonsense floor plans. Using recycled car parts and inexpensive, unconventional material such as railroad ties and telephone poles, they built one-off housing in rural Alabama. Much like Habitat, Mockbee's method promoted an architecture of dignity and compassion. Unlike Habitat's, each of his designs are unique commentaries on today's throwaway attitudes and disposable economy. Where Mockbee's approach is individualistic and artistic, Habitat's window widths are doggedly determined by a standard framing layout. Simple standardized trusses form Habitat roofs, and its rooms with plumbing are always laid out back to back. Expressions of individuality are left to Habitat homeowners after they move in, although a rare digression from policy greeted us upon our return to the Delta one year.

On each side of the old church that serves as our Habitat headquarters in Sherard are five Habitat houses. With three or four bedrooms each, they share common rooflines, siding, windows and floor plans. Giant oaks blanket the neighborhood with a generosity of shade. Many of the neighbors are related; cousins play together in the yards, grandmothers watch from the porches. With the houses painted different colors and individualized with modest landscaping and a porch added here and there, the tiny community is house-proud and visually cohesive — with one striking exception.

The story goes that a professor of architecture from a prestigious northern university thought it would be useful to bring his class to Mississippi to work on a Habitat house. Hands-on experience would help the students understand how a building gets built. So far, so good. But when the class realized they would be building just another boring Habitat design that would look like the other nine boring Habitat designs stretched out along the highway, they rebelled. (Or were they encouraged to rebel?) Leaving the floor plan intact — the slab had already been poured by a previous group of volunteers — they redesigned the exterior.

Discarding the standard Habitat, 5/12 roof pitch, they offset the ridgeline, raised one pitch high and dropped the other low. This reconfiguration was apparently intended to justify a row of south-facing, clerestory windows. Clerestory windows are designed to let light and warmth into an interior: They are a practical idea in northern climates, but unconscionable under Mississippi's brutal summer sun. Worse yet, there was no evidence whatsoever of the clerestory windows inside the house. The ceilings were flat, with no vaulted space, no clerestory windows to be seen. Despite what was advertised outside, the interior looked like every other Habitat house on the block. Not only was the clerestory conceit expensive, time-consuming, and regionally inappropriate, the function it claimed to perform was a farce.

This unfortunate example of unabashed form-seeking fostered a polite, but firm resentment in the community; it was an embarrassment. I asked the neighbor next door what she thought of it.

"It's a nice house, inside," she said.

"And the outside?"

Like a child invited to be naughty, she giggled and said, "We calls it, 'The house from hell.'"

"Because of the architecture?"

"Because," she paused to search for the perfect phrase, "Because it look like one thing, and act like another."

Amen.

Habitat for Humanity has a standard procedure for handing over a finished house to its new occupants. The move-in ceremony for Maynard and Delia took place on Friday, at the end of our last day of work. The house was totally finished and mopped clean; furniture would begin to arrive the next day. Circled shoulder to shoulder in the kitchen/dining/living room were the local Habitat representatives, our volunteer group from New England — and in front of the gleaming new stove from Sears, Maynard and Delia stood flanked by their children, grandchildren, nieces and nephews. After a few prayers and some thoughtful remarks from the Habitat officials, Maynard and Delia were given the deed to their new house — and a Bible.

A solemn pause followed, and the Habitat speaker asked if anyone else would like to speak. A few did, and praises flowed in all directions for all the work accomplished. The next-to-the last speaker was Maynard's oldest daughter, who stepped forward and said, "This is the happiest day of my life. Ever since I can remember, I've prayed that someday Mama and Daddy would have their own house, and today, thank the Lord, my prayers have been answered."

A wave of emotion erupted in a round of applause and more than a few tears of happiness. Then Delia gently nudged Maynard forward. He took a few reluctant steps into the center of the room. Everything about the tentative way he held himself, this granite mountain of a humble, decent, loving man suddenly forced to speak to a large group of people about deepest feelings could not have been easy. As he organized his thoughts, the circle around him fell silent. I wanted to save him from the choked-up speech that would surely follow. It was okay to say nothing, I thought. No speeches were needed. He had only to stand mute before his family and friends for every one of us to know the gratitude that overwhelmed him. But Maynard was braver than I.

There is something irreducibly tender about watching a big, strong man speak from his heart with tears running down his cheeks. In a voice so hoarse and deep with feeling as to be almost unrecognizable, Maynard started and stopped twice. On the third try, he continued to the end, thanking, by name, all the Habitat people, all his friends and neighbors, and assuring every member of his assembled family that they would always be welcome in the house that he and Delia could at last call their own. The speech he made was smart, modest, and utterly honest despite the immense struggle each syllable demanded: It was Maynard himself. And when he held up his new Bible and thanked, foremost, the Lord for all his blessings, it seemed that the lump in my throat would stay stuck there forever — and I began to wonder if religion was contagious.

Clarksdale is a small city near our Habitat headquarters. It is the birthplace of more renowned blues musicians than any other place in the world. B.B King, Son House, Muddy Waters, Robert Johnson, and John Lee Hooker are but a few of the many Clarksdale native sons. It also claims more than a hundred churches, some of them huge, some of them drawing fewer than a dozen parishioners. The church we attend during our Habitat days is as dignified and proud as any building in town. With its single-story wings flanking a soaring nave and steeple, its brick facade and crisp ornamental trim speak of a community deeply invested in the business of spiritual belief.

Our little group from Habitat is always warmly greeted at the church and made to feel truly welcome. On this particular Sunday, a very stylish Maynard and Delia waved proudly from their pew. Cheresse, dressed in a bright blue dress and matching hat, sat beside Delia. When a tall man walked down their aisle, I saw them giggle and push against one another. Once again, we were among the few whites in the huge congregation, and I only wished I had brought more respectable clothes.

As the church filled up, I watched the way Maynard watched his neighbors come in and sit down, especially the way he watched the women. Even as an outsider, I'd heard a few stories about Maynard as a younger man, a ladies man with more than a few children outside his marriage. Maynard wasn't perfect, but I liked him better for it, because it would have been a lot easier for him to have taken another road. He'd once served a stint in jail for assault, and I heard he'd treated a brother badly before he died, but Maynard was a man who had decided to win, and he'd defied the region's deadly statistics. Here he was, sitting proudly with his wife in church at 57 years of age, healthy and happy — a homeowner at last. His family and friends conspicuously loved him. His relationship with his Lord was powerful. When the service was over, he would go home to a house with a kitchen counter smooth as polished alabaster.

While the church filled up, a man we'd met on a former trip came over to greet us. Roosevelt was a small, energetic concrete finisher who had generously helped Habitat whenever a new slab was poured. I noticed the edge of a bandage on his wrist and inquired about it. He had burned his arm in a brush fire the summer before, he said, and was still recovering. When I asked if he was under the care of the hospital in Memphis, he shook his head, no.

"They wanted to take me up to the burn unit in a helicopter, soon's it happened," he said. "But I told them, 'No, Sir. I don't fly.'"

When I asked if he'd received good care at the regional hospital, Roosevelt insisted anything was better than flying. "This church," he said, "takes me high as I want to go. Airplanes, helicopters — no sir, uh-uh. If I can't get out and stretch my legs," he said, "I don't go."

Sitting still before the service began, I habitually inspected the interior of the church, played my compulsive game of lining things up, eyeballing proportionate measurements, estimating slopes. As architecture, the building was an ordinary, faux neocolonial outside, gymnasium-plus-amenities inside. Air conditioning ducts hung from the ceiling. Flashy stained glass windows and over-bright lighting detracted from what little effect the space might have attained. But if my hypercritical eye found little to admire in the architecture, my heart soon found much to embrace.

Most of the church's floor plan was covered with rows of oaken pews filled with worshippers. Centered in front of the congregation, a Plexiglas pulpit rose up from a platform. To the left of the pulpit was another platform, raised higher, with a dozen box seats reserved for the distinguished church mothers. These elegant, elderly women were dressed completely in white — white suits, white dresses, and gloves, and elaborate white hats and veils. They held themselves graciously like the pillars of the community they are — and they sang like avenging angels.

Across from the church mothers was another set of box seats for the distinguished fathers of the church. They shared their platform with an organist, drummer, and bassist. Waves of music alternately flooded the church and receded, sometimes in a joyful surf, sometimes with a discreet backwash ripple, but always alive. Behind and above the church mothers and fathers stood the all-male choir, ten resonant voices called upon throughout the two-hour service to raise the rafters unto heaven.

Sacred space encourages its occupants to feel humbled, awed, and redeemed all at once, to feel a compelling sense of connection between themselves and the Almighty. With or without human attendance, the great cathedrals of Europe seem somehow invested with a spirit of divine presence, as if the spaces themselves were ennobled by more than just the architecture. Foremost among the devices used to accomplish this feeling is the use of visual focal points, soaring vertical space and atmospheric light. I've seen it and felt it in grandiose places like the cathedral at Chartres, as well as in whitewashed churches built by the Jesuits in Mexico's remote Sierra Madre Mountains. And now, here in Clarksdale Mississippi, I was to discover how the sacred architecture didn't matter, how the spirit of its occupants could permeate and redefine prosaic space.

In contrast to New England's whispered Congregational piety, the Southern Baptists' link to the Holy Spirit is transmitted through a rollicking performance of music and passionate testimony. The Clarksdale pastor began his sermon by inviting the Lord into His house. Less than halfway through the sermon, the invitation was answered, and His presence became palpable. I listened, amazed, as the sermon rhythmically wove a mesmerizing narrative through the books of the Bible, out into the congregation's lives and back again to the Testaments. The congregation offered shouts of encouragement as the pastor increased the pace of his powerful stride, clapping hands above their heads and shouting, Amen! while the organ, drum and bass noodled in and out of the storyline with perfectly measured passages of restraint and fervor. The pastor spoke often of the gratitude owed for the gifts in our lives, of love and family, of good versus bad and the power of unconditional trust and faith. He spoke of pride and hate and the wages of sin, of forgiveness and redemption, of arrogance and humility. He spoke to everyone in the house, including me. The power of belief had transformed and sanctified a banal piece of architecture into sacred space, a neat trick; I felt blessed to have seen it. When the offering plate came down the aisle, I gratefully emptied my wallet.

Danger Everywhere

My clients mostly come to me by word of mouth — friends of a former client see something I've designed and ask to see more of my work. They are occasionally single, but most often a couple, usually with children still in school, in college or beyond. One spouse may play the leading role in all or some of the choices to be made, or both may be equally involved in every decision. I once had a client's 18-year-old son negotiating all of his family's design issues.

I was referred to Judith by a friend of hers for whom I'd designed a house in the Berkshires. My practice was busy, and my houses were showing up in magazines despite my promotional laziness. I had recently written *Catamount Bridge*, a novel about Vermont twin brothers whose lives are polarized by the Viet Nam war, followed two years later by another novel, *King of the Mountain*. For me, the structural nature of writing fiction was a parallel form of making architecture; in each discipline a structure is built from the ground up, an assemblage of parts, dimensions and textures. Unlike architecture, which rarely proceeds without a sponsor/client, the fiction writer has no client but him/herself, and must personally answer for every choice of character, scene, and line of dialogue. When I worked on Judith's house, my client was someone I never met, a shadow hovering over every move I made, but never quite accountable.

Judith was twenty years my senior, in her early-70s, although she looked many years younger. We were both six-feet tall, but she seemed taller. She was silver maned, widely traveled, and sophisticated far beyond my parochial pretensions to culture. I found myself making mental notes every time she spoke. (What was the name of that palazzo in Florence with the perfectly proportioned library?) She was fluent in five languages, played the piano famously, and was partial to wearing riding boots and jodhpurs, although I never saw her near a horse.

When we met, she had recently bought the old Jasper place, a 100-acre hill farm in a tiny Vermont hill town. Included with the acreage were the Jasper homestead cape and barn, wedged smack against the state highway. Judith's dream was to build a new home high in the meadow, far from the road, and rent out the farmhouse to a caretaker. For the foreseeable future, she envisioned a pied a terre, to which she also might someday retire — alone. "My husband, Sam, is a bit older than I," she said during one of our early conversations. "He detests Vermont, but he's agreed to allow me to indulge my passion for the country on the condition that he'll be exempt from all responsibilities concerning the house." She paused and arched her eyebrows. "Except, of course, to pay for it."

Budget notwithstanding, I encourage my clients to write a "program," a list of everything they've ever dreamed of, with the understanding that although a sequence of surrender may follow, their priorities will eventually emerge. "Shoot for the moon," I tell them. "Tell me every intriguing thought you've ever had about your house-to-be, no matter how unlikely you think it may be to build." Who knows what little extravagance of the subconscious may find its way into the final scheme? Bottom line: I want to know how my clients want to live whether they can afford it or not.

I've received programs including everything from precise dimensions of every room to philosophical musings on the ethos of house-ness. Some incorporate lists of heirloom furniture to be accommodated — grandmother's grand piano or grandfather's eight-foot-tall clock. I commonly hear about preferences for tiled floors, wood-shingled roofs, rough-plastered walls, and a fondness for shades of burnt sienna and ochre. I've had programs left on my answering machine and manuscripts consisting of fifteen, single-spaced typed pages. I once received dueling pleas written by the husband and wife respectively (both lawyers), along with a cover letter explaining that it would be up to me to adjudicate their conflicting desires.

Judith's site was at the edge of the woods in her uppermost meadow. It provided a strong southern exposure and intimate views down the White River Valley. Her program was handwritten on the back of a tattered French library card, and startlingly brief:

"Entry with coats and lav, great room, timbered ceiling, (living/dining/kitchen/ pantry) two bedrooms, bath for each — laundry? Splendid library — books, books, books." In the left hand margin was the cryptic notation, "Guns?"

When I asked her about the reference to guns, she explained she wanted a secure place to store a collection of rare Belgian fowling pieces.

Given what I'd heard about her husband, it was difficult to picture him stalking anything other than a stuffed chicken. "Sam hunts?" I asked.

Judith smiled. "I can assure you, the kinds of things Sam hunts won't be seen down the barrel of a shotgun," she said. "My father taught me to shoot in Scotland when I was a wee lass, and I still enjoy watching a clever bird dog work up a grouse."

In my experience, people build houses in Vermont because they have an affinity with the outdoors. Judith laughed when I asked if Sam was interested in being outdoors.

"You must understand," she said. "The sum total of Sam's experience with the outdoors takes place between the apartment house foyer and the limousine. If he had his way, he'd have the driver pick him up in his bedroom."

After being quite specific about the dimensions of her gun closet, Judith was uncharacteristically vague about her kitchen. Since it was to be located one step up from the east end of the large, rectangular living and dining areas, I proposed a low shelf on top of a peninsular counter, which would help hide the kitchen clutter while allowing the cook to participate in whatever was going on in the rest of the room. That seemed fine to her.

Choosing the types and locations of the appliances was left entirely to me. Judith was also indifferent to the layout of drawers and cabinets. The species of wood was of no concern to her as long as it was darkly antiqued. Her countertop material could be soapstone, granite, tile, or butcher block — it would be my choice. To the exclusion of everything else in the kitchen, the floor and ceiling engaged her interest. For the floor, she wanted handmade terracotta tile, the rougher the better. The ceiling she envisioned was crisscrossed with hand-hewn beams from which would hang wrought-iron racks for copper pots and pans and rows of sausages, bouquets of dried peppers, and braids of onions and shallots. She wanted a rack specifically designed to hold a dozen decorative varieties of olive oil. I pictured floating sprigs of rosemary, red peppers, garlic and olives, the kinds of gift boutique bottles intended more for show than use. Without saying as much, the kitchen Judith coveted was to resemble a rustic Tuscan trattoria. When I remarked that she must be especially partial to Italian cooking, Judith protested that she loved all kinds of food.

"If you were to plan your favorite meal," I asked, "What would you cook?"

The witty ripostes that normally spiced Judith's conversation were suddenly absent, and for the first time since we'd met

I saw a curtain of uncertainty draw across her face. "What would I cook?"

Now I felt as if I were intruding. "If you had your choice."

"In Scotland," she began, "When I was a child, we had Margaret. In Monaco, Fabio. In Mexico City, Constancia — and in New York for the last seven years, my dearest Estella. They've all been terrific, which is no easy feat since Sam is such a fanatic about his health." She took a deep breath. "The truth is, I've been spoiled rotten when it comes to cooking." She paused and looked out the window. "I've begged Estella to move here with me, but, to answer your question, I must confess," Her voice trailed off. "I've never even learned to boil water."

Judith and I met at my office every other week during the design phase of the project. She'd fly up from New York in the morning, I'd pick her up at the airport, and we'd be at my drafting board well before noon. While my partners intercepted my telephone calls, we talked and sketched our way through the details of her house-to-be. She had an astute ability to understand drawings, which allowed her to ask leading questions: Moving the chimney to the west wall, we could have a fireplace in the bedroom as well as in the living room — but then, what a pity — the boiler room is by necessity over there — and it would need its own chimney, wouldn't it? I'd enlarge the dialogue with quick interpretive sketches, lending proof to how our flow of ideas might or might not work out. By the end of the afternoon, exhausted but happy, she'd gather up copies of the latest prints, lavish me with encouragement, and I'd put her on the last flight back to the city.

In the course of our many conversations, Judith taught me much. She was an avid flower gardener with lavish photo albums to prove it. She knew the Latin and common names of every tree, shrub and wildflower in New England. Her references to

European architecture sent me to the library often. She made such common use of phrases like, *quid pro quo, sine qua non,* and *non disputandum est* that I felt alternately more or less adequate according to how well I understood the terms.

Although I heard nothing from Sam during those first few months, Judith's occasional remarks about her husband intrigued me. Sam was orphaned at 6 by the Holocaust, came to the States as a stowaway in his teens, and somehow found some distant relatives in New Jersey. He taught himself English in less than a year, never went to college, but thanks to an uncanny understanding of the futures markets, was a millionaire at 21. The financial world soon bored him, she said. After a near-fatal bout with tuberculosis, he moved into real estate, funded a foundation for low-cost housing, and finally found his calling in international businesses. I learned that he was five-feet, four-inches tall, "skin and bones," neither drank nor smoked, and consumed a fistful of vitamins three times a day. Sam was a worrier, "a bit paranoid," as she put it, who, despite his enormous successes, saw peril lurking everywhere. He was a bachelor until his fiftieth birthday, when he and Judith were married in Monaco — her first marriage as well, for all I knew. Although I'm sure I never learned the full extent of Sam's empire, the impression given was that he presided over at least a dozen companies, foremost of which produced a prominent line of women's lingerie.

By the time we'd finished the design phase of the project, I fancied I knew Sam almost as well as I knew Judith. What I really knew about him was selected by Judith, of course, but every scrap of information I received bolstered the image of a jet-setting international business guru, a Horatio Algeresque self-made man, eccentric genius and unrepentant urbanist.

I finally had the opportunity to test my version one night when the phone rang at half-past eleven. "How you doing, son?"

I was half asleep and didn't recognize the voice, a high-pitched nasal tone of an indeterminate gender. "Son"? It definitely wasn't my mother or my father. "Who is this?" I asked.

"I'm calling from the Miami airport. My jet's held over with something mechanical, so I thought I'd call and say hello." The voice was friendly and relaxed. "It's Sam."

Sam? Didn't he know his voice was all wrong? "Sam?" I sat up in bed and turned on the light, as if to better picture his face. "Nice to hear from you."

"Judith showed me the latest drawings. I've got them right here ..."

I could hear paper rustling. "And what do you think?" I said, when the silence had dragged on too long.

"You're not trying to bankrupt me, are you, son?"

"Excuse me?" While I was wondering if he was being serious — and if bankrupting him was even remotely possible, he said, "Just kidding. You're making my wife very happy, and I've got to admit, the design doesn't look half bad."

"Thanks," I said. "I think we're coming up with something ..."

"One thing," Sam said. "It's about the — what-do-you-call-it — the big room? I'm looking at the dimensions — 36 x 24 — and I'm thinking about the flat roof above it."

I was prepared for the standard suspicions about flat roofs. It was true that in cold climates they often failed dramatically, given the technology used in the 50s and 60s, but it was equally true that a properly engineered flat roof using modern waterproofing systems lasts for years. "I'm specifying a PVC sheet material," I said. " A tough, flexible membrane that expands and contracts with the weather, and ..."

Sam interrupted. "I'm not worried about the weather," he said. "We manufacture PVC roofing at one of our plants in Mexico. It's a good product. I like it. My question is, what about the structure?"

I was glad he asked. My engineer had just sent me structural drawings for review a week before, and the particulars were fresh in my mind. "The roof is spanned side-to-side at the third points with fourteen-inch deep, wide-flange steel beams, thirty-four pounds to the foot." I said, self-inflated with my engineer's expertise. "Between the beams, we've got 2 x 12s running fourteen feet at sixteen inches on center."

Sam said, "What I'm interested in is the loading."

"It's designed for snow, a fifty-five pound live load," I said, "And a ..."

Sam interrupted again. "What happens if an airplane lands on it?"

I'd never been asked that question before. Or since. "On the roof?"

"It could happen."

Our conversation was taking place many years before the events of 911. I thought Sam was joking. "If it's a Piper Cub, we might save our bacon." I said. "If it's a 747, we're toast."

Sam wasn't amused. "I've been sitting here watching the planes come and go, and I can't help thinking about how vulnerable Judith could be up there, all alone in the country."

Did I dare suggest Judith was ten times more vulnerable living under the vast web of flight paths circling Manhattan? Should I offer to check the air routes over her house site (if there was even one, I would have been surprised), or was Sam determined to have something to worry about? "Is there something you'd like me to do about the roof?" I asked.

"Nothing you can do, son" he sighed. "It's just one of those things I was thinking about. Thought I'd call."

"I'm glad you did," I said, glancing at the clock. "Any chance you'll be coming up this way?"

"I'm sure Judith told you. This is her baby. She's the boss. I'm just paying the piper and staying out of it. And hoping she comes to her senses," he added. "She puts her hands in the dirt like a peasant, no gloves, gets horse manure on her skin. All that gardening. For an intelligent woman, it's unbelievable."

"Well, if you're ever inclined, I'd love to show you what we're up to."

"You take vitamins, son?"

"I like spinach," I said.

"I'll send you some multis," Sam said. "And, son?"

"Yes?"

"No need to tell Judith I called. She shouldn't have to worry about airplanes. This little thing about the roof, it's between you and me, you follow?"

A few weeks after we'd poured the foundation, the phone rang after midnight. My wife urged me not to answer, but I suspected who it was, got out of bed and took the call in the living room. "You taking your vitamins, son?"

"Hi, Sam," I said sleepily. I pictured the box of pills I'd received a few weeks before. Sixteen varieties of vitamins and minerals from A to Z. "I'm feeling great, thanks."

"You ever been in Milano in the morning?" Sam described the view from his hotel balcony, the sunrise coming up through the smog. "I had to pull the damn curtains and turn on the TV," he said. "The air these Italians breathe ..."

I breathed in a yawn.

"Judith tells me you've been pouring concrete, and I wanted to make sure about the footing drains before you backfill."

"It's all done," I said, and explained that the house was near the top of the hill, the soils were extremely well-drained, and the grading was such that the house would receive no surface runoff. Although it was unlikely they would ever see a drop of water, I had nonetheless specified four-inch diameter, perforated PVC footing drains around the entire perimeter of the foundation.

"We used twelve-inch drains at our factory in Bogotá," Sam said. "Never had a problem, dry as a bone."

"I'll bet," I said.

"You backfilled yet?"

"Backfilled and rough-graded," I boasted. The job was on schedule. They're starting framing this week."

"Look, son. I need you to do me a favor," Sam said. "I don't want you to pester Judith about any of this, but a building with water eroding it away from underneath — it can lead to disaster. It's dangerous. So this'll just be between you and me, okay?"

I suspected what was coming, and for a moment I thought I should hold my ground and insist he was wasting time and money; but then I thought, if there was no harm being done to the building, and he wanted to pay for it, why argue?

The job foreman, Ellis Judd, frowned when I told him about the change. "I don't know if anybody even sells twelve-inch footing drains around here," he said. "Down at the ball bearing plant, we used six-inch, but that was in a frickin' swamp."

I felt awkward. My responsibility to my client was running entirely counter to common sense. Luckily, Ellis and I had worked together on other jobs, and I liked to think he knew very well I would never have suggested something so daffy. "We can do it," he said gallantly. "And, hey, if we ever want to inspect the footings, we can just crawl through the drains with a flashlight."

Judith happened to have scheduled a trip to the site when the drains were being replaced. The first thing she saw when we drove up the lane was the backhoe at work. "What's all the digging for?" she asked. "I thought the house was backfilled and rough-graded."

I waffled. "Some work on the footing drains." I tried to make it sound casual. "You'll never have a problem with water in the basement," I said. "I can guarantee that."

Judith took in the big stack of twelve-inch pipe and the growing pile of broken four-inch rejects. She turned and leveled a stern gaze at me. "Sam's been calling you, hasn't he?"

"I don't mind."

"In the middle of the night, I'd wager."

"Pretty late," I said, "but not that often."

She walked away muttering, "I knew this would happen."

Whatever else Judith was thinking was kept from me. We discussed many things that afternoon — we alerted Ellis to the placement of an additional window in the bedroom, made plans for a storage room in the basement, paced out her future flower gardens — but Judith never again referred to Sam.

I grew to anticipate Sam's nasal voice the instant the telephone rang late at night. I'd be out of bed and in the living room before the second ring, confoundingly willing to interrupt my sleep and take his calls from all over the globe. As much as I respected Judith, I was also curious about Sam. He had overcome and accomplished so much, but was still at the mercy of childhood demons unimaginable to me. Judith called him paranoid, but he had to be admired for his courage. Who else would I ever meet who had sailed to America hidden in a packing crate?

Another of his frequent late night calls came after the house was almost completely framed.

"Did you get the new shipment of vitamins?" Sam asked.

"They got here safe and sound, thank you." From where I sat slumped in my darkened living room, I could barely make out the cardboard box sitting unopened on top of the first two boxes he'd sent. "All accounted for," I said. "And how are you?"

"I've been thinking about the fan over the kitchen stove," he said. "You know how onions stink when they're cooking?"

Personally, I'd always liked the aroma of sautéed onions, but more to the point, the 750 cfm exhaust fan I'd specified was one of the higher capacity residential units available. I also wondered: Whom did Sam picture cooking onions in Judith's kitchen? "I think we've got the onions covered," I said.

"Fifteen hundred cfm minimum is what we need," Sam said. "In one of my factories, the cooking smells from the cafeteria wafted up into the production area and the workers were salivating for an hour or two before lunch. One of them lost his concentration and cut off a finger," he said. "I won't subject Judith to that kind of danger."

"Of course not," I said. Even half-asleep as I was, it occurred to me that Sam didn't really need my input in our conversations as long as I appeared to agree with him. "Safety first," I said.

"Plus, there's the problem with bacteria."

"Which we should avoid," I said, falling lockstep into Sam's parade.

"Fifteen hundred cfm, son. Suck the eggs right out of the pan."

"No doubt it will."

"And another thing," he said. "About the shut-off valves on the water lines and the hot water heat. My good friend Eric Gustafson runs an R&D lab for NASA. Eric's a National Science Foundation award winner, Nobel candidate, brilliant kid, barely 40-years old. Anyway, he's sending you some shut-off valves for the house, same thing they're using in the space program — high temperature, exotic synthetics, tough as hell. Eighty bucks a whack, but more than worth it if Judith is stranded up there in a five-day howling blizzard. How would we feel if the heat goes off on account of a two-bit valve malfunction, and she freezes to death before anybody can get to her?" Sam answered his question for me. "Terrible."

I might have mentioned that the era of five-day howling blizzards in Vermont had ended with the last ice age, that the valves we typically used cost about ten dollars each and lasted indefinitely, and that plumbers made house calls — but Sam was proud of his NASA connections. Cost was never an issue, and the workings of Mother Nature and manual labor were mysteries beyond his comprehension. Meanwhile, I pictured Eric Gustafson's spaceship valves arriving in an armored car, packed in dry ice. "We've probably got twenty-five of them," I said. "I can count them for you if you'd like."

"We'll send you fifty, just in case you need a spare."

"I'll tell the plumber to expect them," I said. And twenty-five spares.

"And as far as Judith is concerned ..."

This time, it was I who interrupted Sam. "Not a word," I said. "My lips are sealed."

"One more thing, son."

I looked at my watch. Two-thirty in the morning. "Un-huh?"

"What's the well pump made of?"

"Stainless steel and neoprene, I imagine." I didn't really know.

"The impeller, the casing, the couplings?"

I knew it was a Gould pump — a reliable brand, parts available locally, not cheap but not too expensive, either. "I can get a spec sheet if you want. Why do you ask?"

Sam sounded almost nasty for the first time I'd known him. "Copper!" he shouted. "Copper is poison when it's exposed to water for long periods of time, and I will not subject my wife to toxic substances!"

I was wide awake, now. "But Sam," I said, "You do realize that all the water lines are copper."

Something crafty crept into his voice. "Of course they are. I know that. But I've taught Judith to always run the water for two minutes before she uses it."

After a few days of research, I uncovered the only well pump in America with no copper components. It was made by a small company in Ohio. There were no local vendors. The price was twice the price of the Gould. Sam ordered two — one for the well, one as a backup — in case the one in the well failed in the middle of a five-day howling blizzard.

Ellis and his crew worked all through the summer and into the fall. By the end of September, the exterior of the house was completed, and Judith was becoming impatient, even though she knew the completion date was targeted for Christmas. For much of the summer, she stayed in the farmhouse down by the road, and was on the job site every day. When I met her there with Ellis, I often found an uncomfortable awkwardness between them and felt compelled to defend the yeoman against the monarch when her tone became imperious: "This scheduling business is such a nuisance. Why can't you work Saturdays?" I continued to think she was one of the most interesting people I'd ever met, but at the same time I wished she could see that her haughty approach would get her nowhere with Ellis and his Green Mountain boys.

The only personal remark I ever heard Ellis make about Judith was: "She's just not from around here, that's all."

As Sam's late night phone calls continued, the source of the ensuing changes was no longer a mystery. "What's he changed now?" was often the first thing Ellis asked when I arrived at the house. "Bulletproof glass?" The answers Ellis anticipated were as much for his own amusement as for clarification. He was happy enough to carry out Sam's wishes — if only so that he could tell his hunting buddies about the absentee flatlander's latest folly. I knew Ellis had worked with difficult owners before, and his stoic, this-too-shall-pass attitude may well have masked a deeper feeling of contempt. Ellis never said as much, but I suspected he was deeply insulted that Sam had never bothered to visit the site, shake his hand and acknowledge the work.

* * *

In the end, Sam fooled us all and arrived alone and unannounced on a Saturday morning during deer season. He apparently spent a few hours at the house and then stopped at the village Post Office on his way back to the airport. Judith was traveling somewhere, Ellis was off hunting, and I was at home, unaware of Sam's visit.

Surrounded by hardscrabble hill farms and vast stretches of woodlands, Sam and Judith's adopted village consists of a few dozen houses strung out between a two-lane state highway and the West Branch of the White River. Lyman's General store, selling everything from candy to kerosene, is the only commercial establishment within a ten-mile radius. The town's tiny U.S. post office has been located inside the store for at least 100 years, and for more than half of that, its postmistress was Ellis's aunt, Miss Mildred Pritchett. As in many small communities, the comings and goings in and out of the store provide precise updates on every iota of local gossip.

Picture, then, Miss Pritchett, 86-years old, meeting "the fella married to that woman from down country, bought the Jasper farm up on the heights," and try to imagine the lightening speed at which the following account traveled throughout the village:

Sam entered the store, and the dozen or so customers and clerks inside suddenly stopped chattering and watched intently as the stranger walked past the wood stove and up to the post office window. In a too-loud voice, he grandly introduced himself to Miss Pritchett. Overhearing the essentials, the eavesdroppers nodded knowingly and resumed talking. Next, Sam asked to have Judith's mail delivered to the farm as soon as the house was completed. Mildred agreed to take care of his request. She said she understood that Ellis would be needing another four-and-half weeks to finish the house, unless, of course, that terra-cotta tile from Italy was late in arriving, not to mention the nickel-plated sink fixtures the Missus has ordered from — Mildred didn't exactly recall if they were coming from France or Germany — on account of which Ellis might not make the Christmas deadline, but he was doing the best he could under the circumstances, now wasn't he?

Blame Sam's bigheartedness for what happened next. Corporate giant, self-made man, maker of a famous line of women's lingerie that he was, I also knew firsthand he was impulsively generous. I'd heard stories from Judith about his many charities, and aside from crates of vitamins, he'd also sent me wool socks, a winter coat, a Cross pen and pencil set, and dozens of health magazines. As odd and sometimes irritating as his late night calls might have been, I knew him to be utterly sincere.

Unfortunately, Mildred didn't know any of that when she asked if she could help him with anything else.

Looking her straight in the eye, he asked, "What size bra do you wear?"

"Beg your pardon?"

Some say that the clock above the wood stove stopped ticking; water pipes froze, dogs stopped barking, light bulbs blinked and dimmed. Half-spoken words halted on the tips of unbelieving tongues. Lyman's General Store had never suffered such a grievous stillness.

"Cup size?"

"That's quite enough, now."

Before Sam could add that he wanted to send her a dozen bras in whatever color she desired, Mildred Pritchett reached up for the roll-down window and slammed it shut in his face.

By Monday, when I was told the sordid tale for the first time, it was already old news. I heard variations of it for years afterwards, from real estate salesmen, tree surgeons, and plumbers many miles away. No one knew or cared that the house was an architectural success, that Judith convinced Estella to come and cook in a kitchen draped with hanging meats and vegetables, or that airplanes continued to ignore the hilltop in favor of more populated targets. On that project, I'll be less remembered as the architect than as the guy whose flatlander client asked the spinster postmistress to tell him about her underwear.

All Kinds of Houses

Architecture isn't created in a vacuum, nor are its composite parts. An element as simple as a window or a door is devised of a material, a shape, a color, texture, finish, weight, and style that altogether represent a cultural continuum. Because the world is large and the human race ingenious — and because each culture is driven by a mishmash of ethnic, political, religious, aesthetic, climatic, and economic forces — the variations of architectural expression are virtually infinite. Architecture signals who we are and where we came from. As a designer, I need to keep those signals clear, and in order to keep them clear, I need to know something about history.

A mile down the dirt road from my place, an abandoned hillside farm is being slowly reclaimed by nature. The house caved in some years ago; its cellar hole is still humped full of the rotting timber and scrap metal residue of a structure long forgotten. Across the road, a barn foundation lies wide open, home to raspberry canes and staghorn sumac. The only building left standing is a tiny 6 x 8 foot structure once used to store milk until it was carted to the local creamery.

A few years ago, the giant maple growing next to the milk shed dropped a dead limb through the roof. The building is tipped now; the door is askew on its hinges and the single window's sash is without glass, but considering the milk house probably dates back to the late 1800s, it still stands remarkably true. More than likely, it was built by the same farmer who milked the cows. Much of my affection for the region's self-reliant values could be summed up in the heritage encoded in this little jewel of a building. I never pass it without a fond nod of respect.

That long-departed farmer no doubt worked like hell eight days a week. As a farmer, he was typically also a farrier, blacksmith, mechanic, veterinarian, herdsman, lumberjack, harness maker, cooper, gardener, carpenter, engineer, businessman, husband, and father, bound by both inclination and necessity to master a full range of skills — but he still found time to fuss over his milk house in the Greek revival style, complete with a molded frieze and deep cornice line under the double pitch roof. Despite the building's diminutive size, he embellished the corners with pilasters, completed with a modest capital and base. The single window is framed with molded side casings and a double-capped crown. What could have been a rude shanty elsewhere became, in rural New Hampshire, a miniature Temple to Milk.

For me, one of the most appealing aspects of New England's rural landscape is its wealth of dignified architecture, most of it imported from Old England. Variations of Georgian and Federal styles in houses, barns and outbuildings appear in even the remotest early settlements from Maine to Georgia, but New England got more than its fair share. Transcending the merely utilitarian, Great Britain's legacy took root and thrived handsomely through more than two centuries of use and abuse all over New England. Was it nostalgia for Old England that prompted such wholesale imitation, or was it too early for America to find a voice of its own?

Traveling through Quebec and Canada's Maritime Provinces, I've been struck by the notable absence of derivative, historic architecture. It seems that anything built since WWII is aesthetically off-key. Why, one wonders, did Canada's immigrants ignore their legacy and build awkward, graceless buildings while contemporaneous immigrants to their south were loyally reproducing the best of what they'd left at home? In either case, the answer may be that it takes centuries to establish an indigenous vernacular. Most of the New World was still too new to produce its own, and perhaps Canada simply made the mistake of trying to create one too soon, or didn't try at all.

As architecture without architects, indigenous housing is by necessity wise in the ways of how to live simply but well. Walking through a whitewashed Aegean fishing village or through the lanes and backyards of colonial Williamstown teaches us most of what we need to know about human-proportioned design and neighborly accommodation. These home-grown solutions mirror the historical culture from which they're derived and exploit the natural materials of the local environment.

Most Old World housing is surrounded by courtyard walls, but house-proud Americans spend considerable money and effort to show their neighbors how well they live. Since Americans seem particularly concerned with the "front" of the house, most suburban development homes are sited with their best face toward the public — without regard to the sources of sun, view, wind or topography. Whether it points north or south, uphill or down, the welcoming front façade and landscaped lawn apparently must face the street, as if a failure to do so would impugn the owner's right to a claim of good citizenship.

The most peculiar part of this best-face-forward custom is the vestigial front door. Because so much of America's architectural DNA can be traced back to the Georgian and Federal styles, the predominant façade is most often based on a five-bay pattern — a pair of windows symmetrically flanking a center-hall door — which is rarely used. Our reliance on the automobile has meant that one end of a house is typically connected to a garage, and because it is convenient to do so, we go from the garage into the house by means of a secondary door — most often through the kitchen. In a triumph of symbolism over reality, the street facade continues to suggest an interior logic that no longer exists. Often painted an accent color, the front door persists as an acceptable icon; functional or not, the classic five-bay composition, with the door in the middle, gratifies an atavistic image of what an American house is supposed to look like.

If the front facade of the American developer's house is stylistically sacrosanct, the back is just as often a hodge-podge of add-on compromises. For example, the added-on shed dormer that expands the attic of a (potentially) perfectly proportioned cape into livable space is always at the back of the house where it sabotages the proportions, but won't be seen. Hundreds of thousands of new houses are built each year with the compromise dormer already built in. From an architect's point of view, the front-side, back-side, double standard is a shaky proposition; we like to think that every part of a building is entitled to equal rights. Rear-facade additions are often the most utilized spaces in the house, and yet they are held to a much lower standard of design. Colliding vocabularies of incompatible window types, awkward dormers, porches, and walk-out basement doors are allowed to totally contradict the stylistic discipline of the street façade. Describing one's house as, "Williamsburg colonial in the front and sort of contemporary in the back," is another way of saying coherent design sort of matters. And let's face it: God sees the back of the house. Prettifying the front while the backside resembles a train wreck is like putting lipstick on a pig.

Some clients come to a residential architect with a specific style in mind; others arrive open-minded, trusting that an appropriate style will emerge. I'm sometimes asked to suggest a style I think best suits my client's wishes, but I've also agreed to design in the styles of Greek revival, Craftsman, Shingle Style, Georgian, Federal, Modern, Adirondack and even a version of Edward

Lutyns' Irish manor houses. I've never been asked to build in the style of Victorian Gothic or Beaux Arts — for which I give thanks every day. Given free reign, my preference gravitates towards the regional vernacular in which the project will be built. Since most of my projects are in rural New England, my buildings instinctively tend toward some variation on the New England vocabulary of steep roof pitches, clapboard or shingle siding, multipaned, double-hung sash and two-story floor plans.

The seminal styles to which I'm drawn reached America's east coast with the early English colonists. To begin with, Georgian architecture, exemplified by the designs of Inigo Jones, Christopher Wren, and James Gibbs, was spread throughout the colonies from the late 1600s until after the Revolutionary war, especially in those seaport cities trading heavily with England. Design particulars were disseminated by means of inexpensive pattern books specializing in the intricacies of cornice, stairway, door and window details; a carpenter in the farthest reaches of the frontier had access to the most sophisticated architecture of the times.

Federal, or English Adam style, as practiced by Charles Bulfinch, William Jay, Benjamin Latrobe and others, became popular between 1780 and 1820. Once again, the design antecedents were of Greek and Roman origin, but in this case derived from original examples rather than from the Renaissance interpretations that inspired the Georgian style. For most North Americans, the forms, scale and detail of the Georgian and Federal periods encompass the DNA code of the most stylistically common American house.

What follows the Georgian/Federal/colonial period is a century of increasingly mannered, derivative — and clumsy revivals — a zigzag history of neo-classical musical chairs as America searched for an architectural identity of her own.

Brief and irreverent, the sequence goes something like this:

First of all, Classical Revival and Greek revival styles maintained a familiar genetic relationship with their predecessors. They are indisputably handsome, sturdy-looking houses. We still like them.

Next comes the Gothic revival style: Picture the little house behind the pitchfork-wielding farm couple in Grant Wood's iconic painting. It's cute, ornamental, informal, and storybook rustic — not a style likely to be coveted by the McMansionists.

The Romantic, Italianate, Victorian and Second Empire styles are architecturally akin to awkward step-children who eat too much at family picnics: You want to admire them, but there is so much food stuck to their faces, you can't.

By the 1870s, America was finally sure enough of its identity to find its architectural voice. One of the first truly American idioms began with Frank Furness and continued into the turn of the century with the work of Louis Sullivan and Henry Hobson Richardson. Working with the ancient elements of arches, pediments, lintels, and columns, they broke away from archaic assumptions and put these elements together in an unprecedented anatomical order. Without knowing what was to follow, they were, in fact, laying the early foundation for modernism: the weight of history was finally driving original architectural design in the colonies.

Also developing at the turn of the century, among others, was the work of Frank Lloyd Wright, the most singularly all-American architect of his time. Popular through WWI, his Prairie Style houses featured low-pitched, hipped roofs, wide overhangs, Italianate-Mission style detailing and an emphasis on horizontal massing.

In Pasadena, California, Charles and Henry Greene popularized the Craftsman Style (1905-1930), characterized by low-pitched gabled roofs with wide over hangs, exposed rafter tails and a celebration of woodcraft and joinery. Craftsman was also identifiable with the emerging hand-built look of the Arts and Crafts and Cottage styles.

And on the east coast, America's summer seashore elite was drawn to the Shingle style of McKim, Mead and White. Bernard Maybeck, Gustav Stickley and George Howe also contributed to various other threads of the emerging vernaculars. While Gershwin brought America to a new, sophisticated sound called jazz, America began to sing a song of architecture all her own.

But it wasn't to last. From the mid-1920s into the mid-1960s, our newfound pride in American-born architecture was losing ground to Europe's hymn to technology, the Bauhaus-inspired Modern (International) style. Although modernism was equated with moral depravity and Communism by America's fundamentalist clergy and teetotaler bourgeoisie, its architectural expression — flat roofs, hard geometries, smooth, taut facades, glass curtain walls, and contempt for ornament of any kind — captivated the imaginations of America's avant garde and became an indispensable American icon — until the Viet Nam war.

By the mid 1970s, modernist architecture was increasingly regarded as visually bankrupt and philosophically ruthless. For me, as a young architect, its failure lay in its objectivist dogma, aversion to ornament, and most critically, its inability to adapt to the needs of its occupants. The modernist vocabulary did not include the words "humanist" or "neighborhood friendly" — or the notion that human-scaled, mixed-use communities produced a human vitality and integrity impossible to imitate with high rises and highways. New Haven, Chicago. and St. Louis were devastated by modernist city planners who ripped the guts out of the inner cities in the name of urban renewal. By the mid-1980s, when the last of the corner grocery stores, neighborhood druggists, and barbershops were emptied and replaced with big-box conglomerates in far-off malls, the inner cities' streets became hostile to all but the automobile.

If we fast-forward to the present and look back, we see that the unprecedented freedoms unleashed by the Age of Aquarius, combined with the upsurge of millennial prosperity, has turned architecture into a big-tent, postmodern, Wild West, eclectic circus. Rich with references to historical precedents, dedicated to physical comfort, enamored of color, texture, technology, and spatial informality, the postmodern movement embraces everything from LEED-certified office towers to Frank Gehry's titillating, titanium sculpture/buildings.

Size does matter, but despite our nation's ostensible energy-conscious mindset, and knowing that bigger buildings mean bigger energy footprints, Americans continue to build ever-bigger houses. Huge rooms may be appropriate for an Elks Club gathering, but for a spouse and a couple of kids, it's difficult to rationalize cavernous halls and tree-top-tall ceilings. With audio-video temptations and computer screens beckoning from every corner, the likelihood of family intimacy becomes proportionately inverse to the size and technical supremacy of the house. This kind of architectural obesity sadly confuses size with quality. When I see these huge emblems of entitlement built cheek-to-jowl in the latest Ocean View Estates development, I root for the termites.

As if to mimic the wretched excess of the super-sized McMansions, a few scholarly architect/philosophers have invented another sort of wretched excess: architectural theory.

When there's a problem to be solved, my Yankee neighbors don't put much faith in words. For them, watching and listening are twice as useful, "... which is why God gave us two eyes, two ears, and only one mouth." I can't help but think of them when

I read what our theorists write about architecture.

Expecting an architectural theorist to build real architecture is akin to asking a conceptual artist to paint a duck: it's not what they do. Architectural theory is, by its very nature, abstract; its practitioners have no choice but to build in words. Fair enough. The problem is, their constructions are intolerably complex, as if mountains of verbiage will automatically elevate any old molehill of an idea. Theorists are loathe to use prosaic terms. In theory-speak, "floor level," translates to, "datum plane." A straight-forward term like "symmetrical elements" (two windows centered on a door) becomes "isostatic lines." Sentences and paragraphs become syntactical nightmares, the rhetoric so obstinately esoteric that it smacks of literary narcissism — which is annoying to anyone who prefers to call a brick a brick, and put one on top of another. Accessible to few, and satisfying to none but the theorists themselves, theory's paper-architect practitioners invariably chew far more than they bite off.

Architect Peter Eisenman, for example, has few buildings to his credit, but prevails as one of our foremost architectural theorists. He candidly describes himself as "a bad writer, completely tone deaf," — which is one of the few things on which he and I agree. When he (admirably) admits his prose is "exhausting reading, like root canal," one wishes he'd either enroll in composition 101 or examine his need to seek so much attention.

Here he is in a letter to the late, and equally opaque, French philosopher Jacques Derrida:

"Architecture requires one to detach the signified not only from its signifier but also from its condition as presence. For example, a hole in a plane, or a vertical element, must be detached not only from its signifier — a window or a column — but also from its condition of presence — that is, as a sign of the possibility of light and air or of structure — without, at the same time, causing the room to be dark or the building to fall down."

I'm not making this up. Another example, in a published dia-logue between himself and Derrida, Eisenman, treats the reader to the following:

"The discourse, like the relation to that which is in general, is qualified or disqualified by what it relates to. On the other hand, the metonymy is authorized by a passing through genre, from one genre to another, from the question of the genres/types of being to the question of the types of discourse."

If you're anything like me, you probably weren't aware of that, although Daniel Liebskind may be. Theorist and putative architect of the Freedom Towers, he leveraged his fifteen weeks of fame with the observation that *"Architecture has no history. Architecture has no fate."*

Remind me to stay out of his elevators.

I grumble because I want these smarty-pants theorists to improve my understanding of their ideas instead of tossing about "metonymies" and substituting the word "signifier" for "window" And perhaps I grumble most of all because I don't understand why I don't understand what they're up to.

Lamar enjoys watching my blood pressure rise when we talk about theory. He thinks the study of theory is "interesting," a part of the big-picture. He's right, I suppose, and I admire his intellectual curiosity, but I carry on like a crusty schoolmaster when we argue our positions: "We need lucid language," I grumble. "Why should we dignify such a self-referential, eso-teric, narcissistic, incestuous pseudo-language?" I begin to sound like a theorist.

I agree: architecture means many things to many people, and theorists have just as much right to interpret its meaning as any-one else. But for me, as a practicing architect, theory is no more than a side bet on the main event, a parasite harmless to its host. For me, good architecture has always been able to tell its own

For me, good architecture has always been able to tell its own story — form, space and light — brick by brick; it needs no obscure theories to explain its meaning — and that's all I have to say about that.

Lastly, this: In the era of Mark Twain's rural America, a proper neighborhood family home had a wide front porch from which the adult occupants could sip iced tea in their rockers and converse while their children ran happily through adjoining lawns in the lingering summer twilight. And in this manner, people, places and things were woven together in harmony. Sometime after the '50s, the sitting porch disappeared and the would-be Tom Sawyers and Beckys of the world were forced to come inside and play in front of a flickering screen. As neighborhood activities drew increasingly inward, life became increasingly dangerous outside. Both parents worked and came home late, and TV held the promise of Cocoa Puffs for breakfast. Before long, entire communities were designed without sitting porches, lawns or sidewalks, and the comforting connections between people, places and things were lost.

I think we missed the boat when we stopped building (the equivalent of) big fat front porches and skinny little milk houses detailed in the manner of Greek temples. We enhance our lives by paying attention to history and making buildings that pay attention to who we were then, and who we could be now. My theory is that we can gain a lot by studying how the buildings in Tom Sawyer's neighborhood knit his community together, how content trumps size, and how the things that draw us together mean so much more than the things that hold us apart.

Chucking the Puppy

It was quitting time, a snowy Friday afternoon in March, and Dawson Tuttle's truck was the only one left in the driveway outside Martin Wallin's house. I had designed the project with some concern — Martin and I had never quite clicked — but I liked how the house fit into the wooded hillside, how its rooms seemed to interlock with one another without effort. The project was currently two-thirds finished, still on schedule, and almost on budget. Just the day before, Giovanni Todi and his troupe of singing plasterers had left for home before the snow began, driving down I-93 to Boston's North End. Wherever they worked, they listened to Puccini, Bellini, and Verdi, played at full volume. None of the busy, six-man crew was ever reluctant to add his voice to an aria. I liked Giovanni's plastering crew foremost because the work they did was always perfect — and incidentally for the music that I imagined frescoed into the wet, impressionable plaster. My exposure to people in the building trades had long ago disproved the idea that culture and intelligence were confined to college graduates. Who else but Giovanni had a photo of Pavarotti taped to his lunchbox? The crew's typical daily lunch break took a full hour and involved serious appreciation of Parma prosciuto panini and handmade fungi tortellini heated in Giovanni's plaster-spattered portable microwave. A day after they left the house, I could still smell garlic and oregano tomato sauce, and it seemed as though I could hear echoes of La Boheme in the gleaming blue-white walls, base notes lingering in the milky chill of the fading light.

Part of my job as an architect is to inspect my buildings as they are being built, check to see that my client's and my interests are being served, that the materials and methods I've specified are installed and performed in a professional and timely manner. I like this phase of the job, but contrary to the check-a-box assistance offered by several A.I.A. Site Inspection Forms, I work more by instinct than rote. Yes, I notice the nuances of the carpentry and mechanical trades, but I also take note of how clean a jobsite is kept, how materials are stored, what's on the radio (and how loudly it's played). Over the years, I've been sensitized to attitude and ethos, good and bad, including bumper stickers on the trucks, *Earth First — Then We'll Log the Moon.* I learned to listen to the tone of conversations, watch for who breaks early for mid-morning coffee and who lingers late to complete a job that could just as easily be completed the next day. The prevailing workplace attitude is instructive, and if it is positive, I favor that contractor when the next project is let out to bid.

I could hear Tut running a machine inside the garage, and, as always, looked forward to seeing him. But first, I made a quick tour through the house, noting the changes since the prior week's visit — the temporary heat in each room, windows left slightly ajar to let the moisture escape as the plaster cured — rough plumbing stubbed in, junction boxes sprouting capped-off wires, fixtures and fittings in cardboard boxes ready for installation. The newly troweled plaster smelled chalky and clean. The sub-floors were scraped raw, sluiced white with plaster residue, as if imitating the snow outside. Walking from room to room, I ran my hand along the white-flanked walls, taking pleasure in the smoothness. Martin was due to arrive soon and, as I finished my tour, I was pleased. Now that the rooms could be seen in their purest, most abstract form, they seemed graciously endowed, each space inviting the next — tall ceilings, balanced light, a curve here, an angled wall there. My reaction, as always, was part gratitude and part surprise; everything looked at least as good as it had on paper.

Tut had set up shop in the attached, four-car garage, and when I walked in, he was milling out molding stock. I watched as a twelve-foot length of square-cornered pine was remade into curved surfaces, newly naked beneath the high-speed whine of the shaper's cutting heads. He shut down the machine when he saw me.

"No rest for the wicked." I said.

Tut brushed sawdust out of his gray-flecked beard. "Still snowing?"

He looked tired. I'd known him for years, worked with him on too many jobs to count, and I could tell by his voice, by his unsteadiness as he sat down on a sawhorse, that something wasn't right.

"You feeling okay?"

Tut glanced at the neat stack of moldings he'd created, looked at his watch, and shrugged. Tut was measuring the hour against what he'd achieved, and it was obvious to both of us that he was, as usual, way ahead of any clock-imposed schedule. "Twelve hundred feet of crown," he allowed. "Decent batch of pine for a change."

When I asked again how he'd been feeling, he hesitated, ashamed of his mortality. By Tut's reckoning, his poor health diminished him solely because it diminished the amount of work he could produce.

"They had me on three pills, two little red ones for the infection and a big white one for I don't know what," he said, "and I was doing okay. Then last week, this new doctor — looks about 15-years old, you ask me — this boy doctor says I don't have to take the white one, don't need it, and besides, that's the one that costs me over four thousand dollars a year and the insurance won't pay on it. So I stopped." Tut's eyes flickered across the garage, focused on a window, and blinked half a dozen times. "Now, I see double and trip over my frickin' feet."

Tut's troubles had started six months before, just as he turned 50, when a long, slow decline into fatigue was finally diagnosed as a malfunctioning heart valve. Corrective surgery was successful, but weeks later, an infection set in.

"Any of the white ones left?" I asked.

"Gone," he said, "History." A diversionary pause. "Drawing any more houses?"

"I'd like to talk to that doctor," I said.

"Four thousand dollars a year for pills," he said. "Just for the white one. Debbie's lost her shift at Kedco, and, I don't know ... I imagine we'll get used to it." Tut looked out the window, as if to find solace in the falling snow. "How come they cost so much?"

It was exactly the kind of question Tut had always asked — innocent, ingenuous, and frank — he was incapable of cynicism. Calculating the grain in a piece of pine came naturally, but economics and world affairs puzzled him. What are they fighting about over there? Science was a mystery. So, what's this thing about the planet warming up? He felt free to ask me anything about anything, and accepted my explanations — if I had any — without question.

About the origins of architectural design, Tut was downright confounded. "How in hell do you think up this stuff?" he asked one day when he was building an elaborate curved counter I'd designed. "I mean, do you lay awake nights dreaming about it?" Tut supposed you could make yourself have an idea. He had built everything from roll-top desks to violins in the little shop behind his house, but he built them according to someone else's blueprints, down to the millimeter. Scribing a baseboard to an uneven floor, building a winding staircase — those were learnable skills he could teach himself, step by step, and he was a brilliant student. But the concept of original ideation baffled him. Where do ideas come from? I could never quite convince Tut I didn't have a clue.

For example, I once designed a car garage/museum to house Peter Williamson's collection of antique Bugattis. The building was a practical, handsome-enough facility when completed, but my real reward was being able to spend hours in the presence of his gorgeous, hand-crafted vehicles. You could know nothing about cars and still be dazzled by a majestic Baby Royale Sedan, or the open wheeled, vintage 1927 type 35-C racer (which Peter trusted my lead-footed partner Geoffrey to drive at speeds of over 100 mph.) Bugattis are part sculpture, part fine furniture; speed, power, and elegance infused with poetry. The rarest of the rare in Peter's collection is a type 57-SC Atlantique coupe, an object as beautiful as anything I have ever seen.

Why am I swooning about these cars? Because some years later, when I was drawing up a fireplace and mantle for a particularly sculptural house, my hand was subconsciously guided by memories of the sensuous lines of Ettore Bugatti's Atlantique fenders. Would the connection between a fender and a fireplace make sense to Tut? It made no more sense to me than the cost of Tut's drugs.

"Goddamned health insurance is a disgrace ..." I began.

"'Bout as useful as tits on a mule ..." As if to change the subject, Tut slowly unscrewed his coffee thermos, pouring the last of its contents into his cup. The two middle fingers on his right hand were shortened to the second knuckle, lost years before to a jointer. Part of his thumb and parts of two more fingers on his left hand had also been claimed by his work. I remembered one of the incidents — a perfect stripe of blood on the ceiling above the table saw, a fainted co-worker on the floor, Tut stoic on the way to the hospital, curious about how they might reattach the severed finger — which he had wrapped in his handkerchief and stuffed in his shirt pocket. And now, outrageous prescription costs, loss of balance, dizziness, and seeing double. And all the hours Tut still spent close to sharp things spinning fast ...

Martin flung open the outside door and came in stamping snow from his boots. A trial lawyer and bachelor, he was wearing a stylish down parka and a Russian lamb's wool hat. He was tall and tensely thin, with thick, graying hair and deep-set Mediterranean eyes. In the year since we first started designing his house, I had never seen Martin look happy or sad or remotely emotional about anything. But there was a loneliness to his energies, a vacancy beneath the incessant phone calls, meetings, and travels that always kept him at a distance. Once, when he talked about his late mother, I saw another side. In a few short sentences, he'd told me how he moved her into his apartment and cared for her, alone, in the weeks before her death. He told me how empty he'd felt when she was gone, how he wandered his rooms expecting at any moment to find her. I was still caught in his tender story when he flipped an emotional switch and began talking about his new, seventeenth story, corner office, his forty-foot sailboat in Florida, and a fund drive he had chaired which broke all previous records. And now, it appeared that part of his search for that elusive something would also include this four-bedroom, three-bathroom house in Vermont.

I asked about the road conditions on his drive up from Connecticut, and he replied, "Seems every time I come up here, it's snowing." The tone suggested that Tut and I had somehow prearranged the weather.

"Should of built down in Florida, you don't like snow," Tut mumbled.

"So, where are we?" Martin wanted to know — meaning, are we on schedule? Schedule, size, and cost, in that order, were his principal concerns. Design was not high on the list — unless it was driven by size — in which case bigger was always better. But above all, schedule ruled. In order to avoid a capital-gains tax on the huge house he'd sold in Greenwich, he had to be in his new house by the first day of June, and the house had to cost a lot — lest he pay Uncle Sam on the gains — but not cost too much, either. The general contractor and I had assured him he would be in on time, but that didn't stop him from worrying.

"The plasterers are finished," I said. "As you'll see, it's looking good."

"Okay then, what's next?" His speaking style was perfectly attuned to the techniques of cross-examination. Overall, he gave an impression of impatience, and I wondered how he would adapt to the deliberate pace of Vermont's intransigent weather, mud season, and black flies.

Tut turned away from us, unplugged the shaper, and wound the power cord into a coil.

"They'll start trimming on Monday," I gestured to the freshly milled molding and turned toward Tut. "Tut's been working late to make sure it's all ..."

"When's the tile setter get here?" Martin interrupted.

Tut ignored the snub. I tried to do the same while I reviewed the next few weeks' schedule. As I spoke, I watched Tut put away his tools and pull on an extra flannel shirt. Winter coats are for flatlanders and little girls. Real men in New Hampshire wear layers of thick flannel shirts, untucked. I've never known Tut to wear a coat, even at twenty below.

Tut paused at the glass-paneled door before leaving. There

was something poignant about the way he stood there, motionless, staring down the hill. Maybe it was the unsteadiness of his hand on the knob, or the blurred images I imagined he must have endured seeing double. Or maybe it was because I knew he and I were no longer as young and invulnerable as we once were.

On his way out, Tut stopped, caught Martin's eye and asked, "That your Grand Cherokee?"

Barely glancing at Tut, Martin answered that it had only 10,000 miles on it, had all the options, a five-speed gearbox, high range, low range — and a good thing, too, considering the crummy weather. It was the kind of answer that invited no response, and Tut, accordingly, offered none. But he knew something I didn't, and I was left puzzled by his impish grin as he gently closed the door behind him.

Starting in the basement-level mechanical room, I took Martin through his house room by room, assuring him that the spongy plywood stair treads were temporary, explaining the difference between the low voltage thermostat wire and 120 volt three-wire cable, admitting I didn't know why three parallel water lines led to the master bath — until I remembered he had asked for a continuously circulating hot water loop — a feed and return — plus the cold feed made three — so that he'd have instantly hot water when he turned on the tap.

We ended our tour in the master suite and its temple to high-country hygiene. With its twin lavatories, drive-in shower, and modestly sequestered bidet and toilet, the space suggested a level of connubial intimacy that I could only wish for this childless, never-married bachelor. A four-person Jacuzzi dominated the room from its multi-stepped altar, surrounded on three pearly white sides by high, transomed windows looking out over postcard-perfect woods and fields. Tut called the tub "Lake Champlain"

"How much would it cost," Martin asked, knocking the side

of the tub with his knuckles, "To chuck this puppy and put in a big one?"

"This little one ..." I silently reproached myself for sounding reproachful, "seats four."

"Guy I know has one, seats eight."

I almost asked if it came with a diving board. But enough of that. I was losing my objectivity and resolved to shut up and estimate how much would it cost. The entire room was both figuratively and literally built around the tub, not to mention the added floor structure required to keep 150 gallons of water aloft. We'd have to move two walls — and all the plumbing in them — replace the huge custom windows and reconfigure the roof above them, redo the shower and possibly saw a hole in the side of the house — if not to get the existing tub out, then definitely to get the new one in. We would be easily adding tens of thousands to the multiple hundreds of thousands already spent on the house.

Martin stood in the unfinished shower stall, waiting for my answer. He had his lamb's wool hat pushed down to the bridge of his nose, as if to blind himself from my estimate. I couldn't see his face when I said, "Forty, fifty grand." I kept mentally counting. "Probably more. And it would add at least a month to your schedule."

He stepped from the shower and wearily pushed his hat back up on his head. "Fifty grand, huh?"

"I can talk to the G.C. and the plumber and get tighter numbers," I said. "But we're talking real money."

A long, prickly silence.

I looked out the window, imagining the tedious setbacks replacing the tub would entail, not to mention the absurdity of it all. The day had faded into a freezing dusk, draining light from a thin, snowy sky. Directly below, the circular driveway wrapped around a huge, bare-branched sugar maple before it sloped away, steeply southward along a stone wall. The tracks I'd left were all but erased by snow and wind. The fresh tracks left by Tut's departing pickup cut graceful parallel arcs in the snow and continued straight down the hill. I noticed the pattern they made as they crossed the tracks left by Martin's new Grand Cherokee — the tracks made when he had driven it up to the house — and the later set made after he had apparently left the Cherokee in neutral with no handbrake on, and it had rolled back down the hill in the dark, all by itself, gathering speed before it left the road and crashed blindly backwards into the stone wall and rolled over on its side.

"Anything that's worth anything, it costs a lot of money," Martin said.

"I've got some bad news," I said, still focused down the driveway.

"I know, I know. It would screw up my schedule," Martin called out as he wandered into the adjacent bedroom.

"Worse than that ..." I called after him.

"This bedroom looks smaller than I imagined," he said.

I stayed by the window and wondered about the ways in which Martin expected to enjoy his new house, tried to imagine which parts of it would give him peace and pleasure — and if he would always live in it alone. Could the architecture I'd created fulfill a dream I had so little hope of comprehending? I didn't know; I still don't. I found myself looking for an answer in the tire tracks down the driveway, Tut's and Martin's, intersecting one another. Mine would be the next alongside theirs, over and under, opposites and parallels, running together, veering apart. We were all connected, but the links between us were not so easy to define. And if we ever could truly connect — Tut, Martin and I — which of our many differences would need to change, and which would survive?

Busy

Residential projects generally require four to eight months for the design and working drawing phase, and ten months to a year to complete the building itself. Two years from start to finish is not uncommon; less than a year is unusual. The pace at which a project advances mostly depends on the availability and diligence of both the architect and the client. Except for the rare cases in which a client gives the architect complete carte blanche, neither can take the next step without the other.

My clients, Arthur and Peggy Tilden, ran a successful exotic foods import business they built from scratch. Peggy was a great cook and smart businesswoman, especially shrewd at anticipating trends in the international gourmet markets. Arthur was the artistic force behind the company, and in his spare time, a gifted painter. With their children grown, they spent months of the year meeting with their suppliers all over the world, and another few months at gourmet food shows across the United States.

No thanks to my Teutonic ancestry, I am congenitally punctual, as if being five minutes late might mean I will be forever labeled unreliable. If I promise a drawing by Wednesday, I feel better finishing it on Tuesday. The Tilden's punctuality genes flowed from a more forgiving pool. From their point of view, schedules were more like approximations, or flexible estimates. When we were able to arrange a meeting, it was often wedged between a fourteen-hour flight from Bombay and a packaging convention in Atlanta — or after the trip to Atlanta, but just before the vacation in Vail, depending on the weather. If it was up to me to send them a drawing, they insisted I send it FedEx, next-morning delivery. Letting me know they'd received it, however, might take a month, and even then, addressing the issues the drawing explored might take a month or two more — as soon as they had a free minute. (Why did I send it FedEx?) While my father might have taught me the meaning of "Hurry up," the Tilden's taught me the meaning of "Hurry up, and wait."

The promise of the Tilden's project was an architect's dream. To begin with, the site was in a secluded valley near the headwaters of the Housatonic River in western Massachusetts. The property included a rushing trout stream and a deep pond surrounded by acres of fertile rolling pastureland and hillside forests thick with oak and hickory. Arthur and Peggy's programmatic requirements included graciously proportioned rooms, high ceilings, three fireplaces, a huge library for their collection of rare editions, a guest wing, painting studio, wine cellar, and a greenhouse. For the exterior, they imagined field stone walls, slate roofs and immediate access from the house to its multiple patios and gardens. Their taste was both sophisticated and casually eclectic, and there seemed to be no limit to their budget. Was there anything not to love?

Our honeymoon was terrific. Lots of fax, FedEx and phone, as well as meetings at the site and in my office. I had their undivided attention and took full advantage of it, nudging my other projects aside and making promises to my other clients I would somehow find a way to keep. The Tilden's Christmas gift catalog was thankfully off to the printers, and we had exactly three weeks before the next scramble of flights to Asia and emergency meetings at the Hoboken docks. If there was such a thing as design heaven, this had to be it.

We began and ended each session with grand ideas. I had rarely made so much progress with a client so quickly — partially because there were no apparent budget constraints, but also because the Tildens seemed to know what they wanted. Each time they had to choose between the high road and the low, they chose gallantly, and without hesitation. What few differences we had were settled in a rational, win-win manner. My only concern was that Peggy couldn't visualize the three-dimensional spaces implied by the lines on my two-dimensional drawings.

I sympathize with anyone who can't read plans. If ever I'm tempted to become impatient, I have only to remind myself how lost I become trying to decipher an error warning on my computer screen.

"Don't we need a coat closet by the door to the garage?" Peggy asked one day.

Arthur said, "There is one, honey."

I casually drew my finger across the blueprint to the dark lines that represented the coat closet walls, the dotted line representing the hanging rod, and the arcs of two closet door swings. "It's about ten feet of hanging space," I said. "Is the size okay?"

"Sure," Peggy said. "But, is that the garage? Way over there?"

Arthur glanced at me, and shrugged.

Peggy laughed at herself. "I thought it was over here." She pointed to the fireplace in the master bedroom. "Is this drawing upside down?"

And on and on, like that.

As the plans evolved, it became evident that house they'd imagined two years before was but a pale version of what they really needed. Their art collection included a number of pieces requiring huge amounts of wall and floor space. Each time I sketched out a plan, they seemed to want each room to be "just a little bit bigger." We needed to make space for a concert grand piano they'd forgotten to mention. They brought back a massive pair of carved doors from one of their trips to Thailand, hoping to incorporate them into the plan. When I took the measurements, we had to double the proportions of the entrance hall. Two guest rooms turned into three, a pantry became a second kitchen, and a two-car garage was enlarged to make room for four cars. All of this in the first ten days of design.

When I saw how much bigger the building was going be, I began rearranging the floor plan into a U-shape around a court-yard. The wing to the west of the courtyard was dedicated to the guest quarters, painting studio and garages. Opposite it, by a dis-tance of over seventy feet, the east wing housed the greenhouse, master bedroom suite, and kitchen. Connecting the two wings on their southerly ends were the entry foyer, great hall, library, second kitchen and dining room. Except for two guest suites above the garage, all the rooms were at ground level. "In case we ever get old," Peggy said. "No steps."

Piece by piece, the three-sided courtyard and axial nature of the design began to reflect the attributes of a French country manor, which pleased the Tildens, despite their Berkshires address and penchant for Australian wines. The north-entry foyer led to a great hall, thirty feet deep by forty feet wide, with a walk-in fireplace dominating the east wall. French doors at the center of the heavi-ly fenestrated south wall opened under a pergola, from which a path would extend axially through a garden's gated hedge and fol-low an *allee* of lindens to a nearby horizon, where it would termi-nate at a semi-circular pool and fountain. We were on a roll. From the entry door to the fountain, the house and gardens were designed to provide pause, surprise and delight along an axis link-ing the inside to the outside, the manmade to the natural.

Once the French connection appeared to have seized our imaginations, I began to reconsider how the driveway would approach the courtyard. "We have two choices," I said. "Either we approach and enter the open end of the courtyard from the north — which would point us straight at the front door — or we extend the west wing northward about sixteen feet, and drive into the courtyard through an archway between the garage and studio."

Surprise and discovery equal pleasure. The notion of driving through a building into a courtyard was suddenly irresistible. The west side of the house was to be mostly garage and studio space anyway, and it naturally lent itself to an informal vocabulary of windows and doors. Coming up the lane toward the house, one would see light through an arched tunnel punched through a barn-like façade. Once inside the cobbled courtyard, the visitor would have a coherent sense of the entrance to the house, the visitor parking spaces, and the garages. Our design was beginning to take on a life of its own, and we were mighty pleased with what we saw.

Then, as suddenly as it had begun, the honeymoon was over. My would-be partners were off on a long buying trip to Indonesia, and I was left abandoned in the foothills of New Hampshire. They said they wouldn't be able to concentrate on the house again for at least three months, unless I could drive to Montreal and catch them on a three-hour layover on their way to Seattle.

It took a few days to adjust to the more prosaic challenges of my practice. The work I had re-scheduled for my other clients needed immediate attention. It was interesting enough, but switching my mindset from a vast, no-budget French country manor to a frugal New England cape required a few deep breaths and a hefty dose of humility. When the Tildens returned, I planned to have a substantial set of drawings against which to test our premises. Changes would continue to occur after every meeting, but I welcomed them as an affirmation of architecture's Darwinian nature.

According to my calendar, The Tildens were due home on the twelfth of August. I thought perhaps they would call once they were settled. On the eighteenth, I finally phoned their office, spoke to Peggy, asked about their trip and their upcoming schedule. She sounded tired and preoccupied.

"The drawings are looking good," I said.

"You wouldn't believe what these idiot printers did to our catalogue," she said. "Does anyone know how to think anymore?"

I was once again reminded that my enthusiasm for someone else's project doesn't necessarily coincide with theirs, and asked about arranging a meeting.

"Let me look at this crazy calendar," Peggy said. I could hear an angry flipping of pages. "Atlanta again," she grumbled. "Miami, Miami, oh, Jesus, Houston. And then, let's see. No, that's not 'til December. Taiwan again on the fourth, fly back through San Francisco. Damn, I forgot to reserve our booth at ..."

I heard what sounded like a book slammed down on a desktop.

"Can I have Arthur call you right back?"

Arthur called right back — three weeks later. When I first heard his voice, I mistook him for another client whose house I had just begun. "We've got some time near the end of October," he said. "How about you come down to see us, around noon on the twenty-first?"

It was a three-hour drive, but I was excited to get the project moving again. The last of the foliage was still bright in the valleys. Higher up, the flanks of the Berkshires were gray and bare. Another month would bring the first snows. For me, winter is the natural season for preparing working drawings, spring, summer and fall the natural seasons for building — and playing hooky. So, let it snow. I was looking forward to beginning the Tilden's final drawings as soon as we had solidified the design. To be sure, we hadn't yet nailed down a specific schedule, but I was assuming we'd start building sometime that next summer.

When I pulled into their driveway at a few minutes before noon, there were no cars in sight. I walked up onto the porch and tried the doorbell. Didnt Arthur say the twenty-first? I got back in my car and opened *Looking For Trouble*, Leslie Cockburn's mesmerizing chronicle of her adventures in international journalism.

Two hair-raising chapters later, the Tilden's Saab station wagon edged up beside me. I had just finished a chilling account of an interview with the Medellin drug czar, Don Pablo Escobar. As I put my book away and got out to greet my clients, I half-expected to see circling helicopters and armed DEA agents. Instead, two dogs hurtled out of the Saab and tried to knock me down with their frenzied welcome. They each held a pair of tennis balls in their mouths, to show me exactly how clever they were. Arthur and Peggy were apologizing profusely for being late. Their warehouse manager was sick. There was a leak in the roof, a foreman had quit, one of the secretaries was having a baby, a computer had crashed, and a shipment was overdue to arrive. The dogs leapt around us in a furry flurry of inexplicable joy as we went into the house.

Dogs seem to like me. Peggy's golden retrievers, a breed inclined to bestow indiscriminate affection on saints and sinners alike, liked me excessively. When we sat down to look at the drawings, I gave them a little attention and thought that would be the end of it. Half an hour later, after I'd devoted at least twenty minutes fending off their slobbering muzzles and imploring paws, I asked Peggy if she might have another place for them to play. When she apologized and led them out onto the porch, I thought we'd at last get some work done.

The dogs barked in tandem while I tried to explain how I'd moved a wall here, shortened a hallway there. Their barking was accompanied by frantic scratching at the door. I pictured shredded paneling and imagined them performing their let-me-in-immediately! routine at the new house, destroying the carved doors from Thailand. After ten minutes of canine cacophony, Arthur's cell phone rang, and he excused himself from the table, saying he'd be just a second; it must be the warehouse calling about the delivery. Go ahead without him. For the next half hour, I was alone with Peggy, whose enthusiastic interest in the drawings she couldn't read was vastly exceeded by my inability to concentrate.

The howling on the porch never stopped. Not for a moment. Peggy was blissfully deaf to it, and Arthur must have been, too, because despite my fervid prayers, I heard nothing to indicate he'd tried to stop it. I couldn't focus on what we were doing. If the barking didn't stop, I was going to have to kill them or strap myself into a strait jacket and pray for oblivion. "Maybe the dogs would prefer," (Was my voice really shaking?) "To be in here with us?"

Peggy looked up from the inscrutable drawings, blinked a few times, and said, "What?"

I nodded toward the porch. "The dogs?"

"I'd forgotten all about them," she said, getting up from the table.

As I began the drive back to New Hampshire, I took an inventory of the day: If I disregarded the time spent driving and waiting for the Tildens to appear, and calculated the time spent enduring the pawing and yowling and distracting phone calls (there were two more for Arthur and one for Peggy), we probably spent less than a total of twenty-five minutes together in productive discussions all day. In fact, the meeting had ended prematurely when the last phone call alerted them to another emergency at the warehouse.

Looking For Trouble, on the other hand, is a great book.

I don't expect my clients to put their lives on hold while I design their houses, nor do I expect them to be as absorbed in the process as I am. The Tildens were busy running a successful, complicated business, which required their constant attention. But they also wanted to build a successful, complicated house, and if it were ever to happen, it had to become, at the minimum, an occasional priority. The speed and clarity with which we had initially developed the plans had been replaced with endemic attention deficit disorder. If the chaotic afternoon was any indication of our future rate of progress, we would need the next couple of decades to sort out the cavalcade of decisions yet to come.

A few weeks after our second meeting, I agreed to take on a house commission for my old friends, the Jessups. I explained that the Tilden's project and two other smaller jobs in the office would have priority, but if the Jessups were willing to queue up, I would be happy to work with them. We met once a week for two months with no distractions. Meanwhile, I had mailed revised drawings to the Tildens and heard nothing in response. My phone calls went unanswered. If I had been idle, I would have been offended and pressed harder, but the days were full of projects in progress, and at times I forgot all about the Tildens.

Most importantly, my wife Melinda and I were living a dynamic partnership, integrating less work with more play, designing projects together, playing music and visiting her student-day haunts in Paris. I was finding parts of myself that owed nothing to the Gods of Accomplishment. I made up for lost time with my grown children and finally realized I could never be Skit or Lamar or Tom or my talented Yankee neighbors — just as they could have never been me. But I could, and would admire them eternally.

The Jessup project was a quarter the size and ambition of the Tilden's, but challenging and fulfilling. The design phase was completed and the working drawings begun when I finally heard from Arthur.

"We're really excited about getting back to the house," he said, as if we had spoken just yesterday. It was the middle of February.

"Me, too," I said, flipping through the previous year's calendar to check the date of our last meeting — the end of October. "When's good for you?"

"It's been really busy around here with this new line of Japanese cookware we're promoting."

Our third meeting took place — after two cancellations — in late March, at my office. The dogs were left at home, and thanks to a hill between my office and the nearest cell tower, Arthur's phone never rang. But even without those distractions, we made little progress. Peggy appeared to have lost sight of the big picture and began focusing on odd little details. "I just don't like windowsills." Arthur would sail off on travel brochure tangents: "We saw the most fantastic thatched roofs in Laos ..." without coming back to address the unresolved issues concerning the un-thatched roof on his house. Despite the time and money spent on design so far, we were stuck, and I had no way of moving us forward until they were ready. When they left my office, I was exhausted.

Lamar had been talking about being exhausted for the last several years. When we'd met for lunch recently, I was struck by how old he looked. Okay, we were thirty-some years out of school, but he looked beat. The wry wit was still there, but it seemed more of a burden now, as if it were obligatory. For most of the past decade, he'd been working on a high-rise project in Seoul, Korea, flying back and forth twice a month with no more than a one or two-day layover.

"Samsung took a big chunk out of my life," he said. "I can't say they stole it, because I willingly volunteered, and I've been compensated more than fairly. But I don't see Simone half enough, and my grandkids hardly know me."

Thinking about what he and I had done since we first met in New Haven, it was clear to anyone that the train he'd jumped on was a bullet compared to the pokey milk train I'd hopped. I could hang the "Gone Fishing" sign on my office door most any time I chose, and did so with more frequency and willingness with each birthday, but Lamar's world provided him with no such luxury. He'd been personally responsible for the design and construction of six immense projects during his career. Their positive impact on cityscapes and the lives of untold thousands of people would be measured for decades to come. His prize-winning work was featured in international professional journals and might someday have a place in the history of important architecture. Lamar was definitely a "success" in the traditional sense of the word.

The combined costs of all the houses I'd ever designed couldn't buy the first two floors of one of his giant creations: By volume, my entire oeuvre could be stuffed in one of his convention halls. Ninety percent of what I'd built was within a three-hour drive from my office. I'd never had an expense account, a secretary, a rack of bespoke suits, or been to Seoul. Unlike Lamar, I'd never had the confidence to share big decisions with others, and consequentially never been in a position to make decisions of any great magnitude. He was a brilliantly charming, social animal; I preferred to work alone in relative solitude.

"I'm weary of it all," he said. "And I'm thinking about retiring in June. Do some sailing, take long walks in the woods with my grandson." He cocked an eyebrow to let me know what was coming. "Be kind of a professional bum, like you."

"Careful of what you wish for," I said. "I've got some clients in the Berkshires who would drive you back to your sixty-hour workweeks in a heartbeat." But we both knew it wasn't true: the stress he'd endured over the course of his career was a mountain compared to my occasional molehill.

The idea of retiring was foreign to me. I still loved drawing lines on a blank page and making something happen that had never happened before, even if it was only somebody's back porch. I'd given up wondering if "I could have been a contender." For me, architecture was inseparable from life, and both were becoming more and more about the journey and less and less about the destination.

"Seriously," Lamar said. "Simone and I are thinking of buying a house in western Connecticut and seeing what it's like to stay put for a while."

Lamar Finch with dirty hands and wearing muddy boots? "Why not?"

"I'd like to grow a big vegetable garden and wake up to warblers singing in the trees outside my window. Buy a hammer and saw, maybe build a birdhouse or two."

How odd and wonderful it was for me to hear him talking like that. "Do it," I said. "Please. Just do it."

My next get-together with the Tildens took place on the day before they left for China, twenty-two months after our first meeting. Once again, the meeting felt rushed and fragmented, and we resolved almost nothing. I began to wonder: Was their marriage on the rocks? Were they having financial troubles, health concerns, drinking problems, legal woes? I looked for clues and found none, except that I thought perhaps their constant courtship of chaos was not so much a renunciation of order as a means of staving off boredom. Could it be that this conspicuously solid house plan was a periodic, metaphoric substitute for the tranquility they wanted but feared?

By the summer of year four, very little had changed from our original plans. Arthur wanted to store cars in the basement by means of an outside elevator (an idea I tried to discourage), and Peggy was prematurely focused on kitchen cabinet knobs. These issues aside, it seemed to me that the basic layout was still in need of fine-tuning. At the end of our August meeting I suggested we build a model of the house at a quarter-inch scale so they could see it all clearly.

"You think we're far enough along?" Arthur asked. "No point doing it if we're going to change things around."

Peggy wanted to know if I could have it done before they left for New Orleans, less than a week away. When my old friend Tut agreed to build the model, he asked how soon I wanted it done.

I told him to take all the time he needed.

Tut shaped the pieces from solid wood instead of using the traditional chipboard and glue favored by most model makers. To indicate windows, doors and exterior trim, I cut out drawings of the elevations and glued them to the corresponding surfaces. At quarter-scale, the perimeter dimensions of the house were roughly two feet per side. In order to show parts of the gardens and driveway around the house, the plywood base was four feet square. All assembled, the model weighed about twenty pounds and barely fit in my car.

A few months after their trip to New Orleans, we scheduled a meeting at their site. Peggy was ecstatic to hear I'd be bringing the model. I wanted us all to look at it on the site so that we could confirm our orientations and sight lines.

I arrived at the appointed hour and, as expected, was mugged by the dogs. Luckily, it was a warm September day, and the dogs were happy to chase each other through the fields. Peggy played with them as we strolled around and revisited our understanding of the driveway's approach, the sun's seasonal paths and the views available to various rooms. All the while, I was itching to show off what was wedged into the back of my car.

After an hour of touring the site, I couldn't wait any longer. "I've got the model," I said.

"Of the house?" Peggy asked.

(Was she expecting Naomi Watts?)

"Shall we have our picnic first?" Arthur said.

The model had cost well over three thousand dollars to build. We were four years out of the starting gate, and there was still no commitment to finalizing the design and moving into working drawings. I'd become desensitized to being periodically abandoned in the Tilden's long-term parking lot, but as I watched Peggy play with her dogs, it struck me that what we had done so far was actually the easy part. The first two hundred questions we had (more or less) settled in the design phase were nothing compared to the two thousand yet to be answered. Once the tsunami of construction schedules was set in motion, the lack of timely answers demanded by a huge and complicated house could only lead to a level-five disaster.

They loved the model. The design finally came alive for Peggy, and I was convinced we'd get rolling now that she could see what everything looked like.

For most of the afternoon, we staked out the house — the front door here, the bedroom windows looking out toward the meadow over there. For a moment or two, I dared to be optimistic about the prospect of seeing the house built. We talked about schedules and interviewing builders as if a few years of avoiding those subjects had never occurred. The day was a great success, and I believed we were back on track.

It would be ten months before I heard from the Tildens again.

The last time I went back to the site, I couldn't find the stakes. The house had a total of thirty-six corners, and we had painfully laid it out twice — once on that sunny September afternoon in year four, and again the next August — the year the dogs died of old age. Now it was May again, the grass was knee-high, and the few stakes remaining were rotting on the ground.

We went through the motions one more time, north corner here, south corner there, but this time, it was I who was distracted. What was I doing? How many more times could I endorse this make-believe project? Since they'd first hired me, they had probably flown around the globe twenty-seven times, and I had completed nine other houses. I was happy to have built what I had built, and the Tildens were apparently happy with what they could pretend to have built. Aside from hammering corner stakes into a field, the sixth anniversary of our architectural romance had passed without our having built a single thing together.

When we went back to their station wagon — the third they'd owned since we'd first met — I saw Tut's model shoved lopsided into the cargo space. It was filthy with dust, and the west wing looked as if it had been damaged by a hurricane.

We remained friends, the Tildens and I, but we lived many hours apart. Talk of the house tapered off to a trickle, and finally stopped. Eight years after we first met, there was still no building, but I still hope there will be someday — with someone wiser and more patient than I supervising the project. Sometimes I imagine I'll get an invitation to the housewarming party, and take Melinda to see how it all turned out. We'll drive up the lane and into the cobbled courtyard. The house will look better than I had imagined. We'll notice the crisp roof fascia details and the tapered granite lintels above the windows. Peggy will greet us at the huge, carved front doors, and Arthur will be showing his admiring guests around his painting studio. Standing in the great hall, I'll look southward through the French doors, past the garden gate and down the long *allee* to a fountain sparkling in the afternoon sun. Sometimes, I imagine it all could have turned out just like that.

Lions and Tigresses

Melinda had just dropped into the office to rescue me for lunch when the phone rang. I excused myself and took the call. To Melinda, my end of the conversation sounded like this: "Who? ... Oh. What a surprise. ... Sorry, but I'm afraid I can't do that."

The tone of my voice told Melinda this was not a friendly call. She raised an eyebrow. Who is it?

I held up my hand. — just a minute — this won't take long. "I'd be happy to send you copies of the drawings," I said to my caller, "But before I do, I'll need to have a check from you for my last invoice." A long pause ensued. "I understand, but that's my position." I hung up the phone gently and said, "Amazing."

The standard form of agreement between architect and owner states that the architect owns the original drawings of the client's building. The client has access to the drawings, but cannot reproduce them for uses other than the initial purpose.

My caller was one of three clients who have refused to pay for my services. After almost four decades of practice and hundreds of projects, I enjoy lasting, genuine friendships with the vast majority of my clients; my fees were never an issue for them. The few exceptions feel more like disappointments than financial burdens. Despite never having paid me in full, my caller wanted me to send her copies of working drawings I'd done for her years before, when I was a divorcee bachelor, several years before Melinda and I met.

Over lunch, I unfolded the saga behind my design of the caller's building — a good one — and my not-so-good experience along the sticky border between professionalism and unwanted romance.

When Lamar or Tom were asked to design someone's house, they often recommended their potential clients to me. For Lamar, the idea of single-family house design was horrifying. "Much too personal, much too finicky," he'd say. "I don't even want to know my friends that closely, let alone a paying client — and furthermore, there's nothing remotely similar between house construction and the kinds of buildings we do at SOM." Tom added onto his Branford house more times than the local building inspector would ever know — a cello practice room for Ettie, a tiny guest house dubbed "The Love Shack," and a loft for Spencer high above the cliff-sided room — but being a full-time residential architect was too predictable, too constrained for Tom's spontaneous energies.

I had often heard Lamar speak of a past girlfriend, a woman I shall call "Sara." Long before I met her, I knew she'd lived variously in Marin County and Palm Beach prior to moving to New England, and like most of Lamar's ex-girlfriends, she was wealthy, blond, petite, good-looking, and self-possessed. Within a few years of her arrival in New Hampshire, she had earned a reputation for hosting snazzy dinner parties at her "farm" in the Lakes Region. A friend of Lamar's once told me about a skinny dipping party in her pond, with Sara audaciously afloat on alcohol and designer pharmaceuticals.

The project Sara had in mind for me was for an indoor lap pool. "I've decided swimming would be the easiest way for me to stay beautiful," she said, as we sat in her living room overlooking the sheep-sheared meadow across the valley. "I hate exercise, but I just turned 40, and ..." She stopped and assessed me from head to toe. "How old are you?"

I had turned 40 some years before, but was still a wanna-be athlete and worked hard to convince my doubting body that I was still 29. "I'm old," I said, hoping she would protest vehemently — which, alas, she failed to do.

As our discussion of her project proceeded, it became clear that I was being interviewed, one of several architects being considered. The pool she wanted was to be seventy-five-feet long and ten- feet wide, which meant the building would measure at least ninety-feet long and twenty-five-feet wide. It would need to be housed in a separate building; the sloping terrain around her house was not suitable for such a large addition. Budget, she insisted, was not an issue. Thank you, Lamar.

Indoor pool water is typically heated from +82F to +84 F, and because the water is warmer than the ambient air, large quantities of vapor are produced. I described some of the badly ventilated indoor pool buildings I'd seen, the soaking wet, rotted-out walls, and dangerously compromised roof systems. During cold weather, when vapor finds its way into the building shell, it eventually meets the dew point and turns to water, then ice. The worst examples, I explained, occur in extreme climates, like ours, when the vapor-turned-to-water builds up compound layers of ice. Sara's eyes began to flit around the room, signaling that she'd had enough dire tech-talk. I cut to the chase and assured her that I'd designed three successful indoor pool projects, and that licensed, consulting engineers would guarantee the building's air-handling and humidity controls.

I had apparently survived the first part of the interview; she invited me to return that evening for dinner. "Nothing fancy," she said. "Some friends are coming over. I'd like them to meet you." Part two of the interview, no doubt. Since my relationship to food was opportunistic, indiscriminate, and omnivorous, and I would otherwise be left alone to forage on my own, I accepted.

"I'd like to meet them, too," I said, but I was thinking more about satisfying my incessant metabolism than my need for company.

Her friends, Blair and Cathy, met me with stiff Anglo-Saxon

handshakes and perfectly toothed smiles. Cathy was the kind of darkly beautiful woman who gathers her power with silence. Blair was reddishly plumed, large in voice and stature, and enjoyed being in the spotlight. He quickly established their bona fides with Sara by way of fond references to holidays past and a former husband of Sara's who had recently married a "peasant." Then it was on to me: where had I gone to school, with whom did I study, what did I think of Richard Meier — and how the hell was Lamar?

My answers were brief and perhaps even satisfactory. Halfway through the osso buco, Blair launched a soliloquy about his role in the acquisitions and mergers of a string of sportswear manufacturers. I tried my best to look interested while Cathy made no effort whatsoever. She and Sara said nothing during the conversation, as if interrupting the garrulous Blair was not worth the effort. Instead, they watched the evening's events with the cool detachment of twin clinicians observing laboratory rats. I left at midnight, well fed, but uncertain of my future as Sara's architect. On the drive home, I wondered if I had used the correct fork with my salad.

Sara called the next day. "Cathy liked you, a lot. So did Blair."

I'd apparently passed two thirds of the audition. "He sure knows his sportswear mergers," I said.

"Blair can be tedious," she said, and paused. "But you're not." The project, she said, was mine, and she wanted to begin at once. "And the blue shirt you wore matched your eyes perfectly," she said. "You should always wear blue."

Designing the building around the pool posed the challenge of how to enclose the pool's long, narrow shape with an envelope other than a long, narrow shape. Except for a small seating area, Sara had no programmatic needs that would justify much floor space wider than a walkway along the long sides of the pool. We both knew the room would look institutional and barren with nothing in it, so what could be done? I sketched a curvy scheme that would add enough space for plants and rock gardens and a trickling waterfall. Bingo.

The building form that evolved resembled the outline of a long, thin violin with squared-off ends. (I wouldn't dare try to explain its evolution to my carpenter friend, Tut.) The outside curves were mostly glass, which brought natural light to the groves of potted-plants divided by the violin's waist. At the pool's shallow end, a fountain would spill from the top of a moss-covered stonewall. As the plants matured, Sara could swim under leaves and branches draped over the edge of the pool. She was delighted with the idea of being inside a lush, green environment in the middle of winter, and she admired how the violin shape fit into the landscape, despite the difficult terrain. "It resembles the curves of a woman's naked body," she remarked one day. "Is that what you were thinking of?"

It seemed to me I was mostly trying to keep it from looking like a bowling alley stuck in a hotel corridor.

Details about the air handling and heating strategies — air-to-air heat exchangers, negative pool room pressure and radiant floor heating — seemed all but supernatural to her. I was uncomfortable when she said I was a genius (which I would hate to be, given the evidence of how difficult life can be for those thusly accursed), but I also admit I looked forward to hearing her call me a genius again.

When preliminary budget figures came in, I was dismayed at the projected costs, but Sara soldiered on, even when the estimates were double the amount she initially intended to spend. I suggested ways to cut costs while she picked out decorative tiles that drove the costs even higher. It was easy for me to convince her of what I thought were good design ideas, but nearly impossible for her to assign those ideas with proportionate dollar values. Everything I suggested was as equally fabulous. I almost believed it myself at times. We joked a lot and occasionally talked about our personal lives. She had a lewd sense of humor, and occasionally she'd tell a joke so transparently suggestive that it made me squirm.

Overall, the project began eerily smoothly. When I sent Sara an invoice, a check appeared by return mail. If I called with a question, she did her best to answer it promptly — although she usually asked what I thought she should do, and invariably followed my lead. At her request, our meetings took place in her dining room, mostly at the end of the day.

In December, about two months into the project, we'd just finished discussing a list of items that needed attention when Sara handed me a corkscrew and a bottle of Merlot. "Have a glass before you go?"

I almost said no thanks, but didn't.

"Shall we go into the living room?"

Flames were flickering in the fireplace, and Miles Davis was blowing softly on the stereo. Sara excused herself, and reappeared a few minutes later in a quick change of clothes — bare feet, linen slacks, and a lavender silk blouse with one-button-too-few buttoned up — and, was that perfume? I smelled trouble. It wasn't the first time that Sara had made an effort to appear as the attractive woman she was. Unfortunately, attractive or not, the requisite pheromones never quite floated my way; I was head-over-heels, helplessly un-smitten.

"I've got some sketches of the east wall tile layout in my car," I said.

"Maybe later, okay?"

I talked about the design process; she talked about my blue eyes. I asked what kinds of indoor plants she liked while she emptied her first glass and asked about my failed marriage.

"We'll want to look at some lighting fixtures soon," I said, realizing the room we were in was illuminated with candles.

"I'm terrible at lighting fixtures. You pick them," she said, cranking up the stereo. "I'd rather dance."

In fact, I was taking tango lessons at the time. If the rest of the milonga had been in the room, I would have danced with Sara, tried to teach her about ochos, but this was different. "Bad knee," I said, wincing for effect.

Sara turned down the music. "You're kidding."

"Mountain biking accident," I said, omitting that the accident had happened two years before, and I was completely recovered.

"Tell me about it." She picked up my glass and refilled it.

"Over the handle bars," I said. "We call it 'soil sampling.'"

"I've got a bike," she said. "Maybe we should ride sometime. I bet I could keep up with you."

"I'm sure you could."

Sara knelt down on the rug by the fire and patted the space beside her. "Sit."

Feeling a kinship with obedient dogs, I sat, propping my knees between us. In another place, with another woman, the candlelit evening could have been memorable. Instead, it was awkward and superficial. The conversation stumbled on for another half-hour, two voices with two agendas. I managed to leave with my Boy Scout code intact. From my point of view, there was no harm done, and I hoped she thought the same.

In the days that followed, Sara treated our awkward encounter as if it had never happened, which I gratefully assumed to mean she had correctly interpreted my behavior. As the project progressed, she was clearly overwhelmed by the particulars of the building process and increasingly surrendered decisions to me, her omniscient architect. To the extent that I did my job well, her dependency appeared to her justified, and grew even stronger. As if to fortify our alliance, she became inexplicably suspicious of the contractor, turning to me constantly to confirm even his most reasonable assertions. The man was unequivocally honest and competent, but nothing I said would convince her. She needed to bond with me against a common enemy, and he was it. I had become the inadvertent white knight protecting a self-styled damsel-in-distress who needed no protection at all.

At about the time the roof was completed, my beloved Aunt Shirley died after a long and zesty life as an art gallery owner, dealer, and collector. She had arranged for me to inherit some of her outdoor sculpture, foremost of which were two magnificent, cast stone replicas of a pair of Francesco Boromini's lions — evocative of the lions in front of the New York Public Library, but considerably smaller. Since the funeral services were at her home in Illinois, I decided to fly out one-way, pay my respects, rent a truck, and bring the beasts home with me to New Hampshire. I explained the circumstances to Sara at our next meeting, and assured her that I would stay in touch with her and the builder by phone during the week I was away.

Sara seemed intrigued by the lions. "How tall are they?"

"Five or six feet, as I remember."

"And heavy?"

"Five to six hundred pounds each," I guessed.

"And you're going to tame them? Teach them some tricks?"

"Just the basics. Roll over, play dead ..."

"Lion tamer," she teased.

"I'll be lucky to get them home in one piece."

She picked at my sleeve. "Think you could tame me?"

I usually think of a snappy comeback line about three weeks after it's due. For some reason, the muse was on my shoulder that day, and I hardly knew what I'd said until after I'd said it. "Taming you would be a crime against nature."

I left for Chicago that night.

The absorbing sadness of the funeral was mixed with the paradoxical pleasure of remembering Aunt Shirley's colorful life. Cowgirl, aesthete, collector, world traveler, homebody — smoker, boozer, life of the party — she left so many friends with such good memories that the aftermath of her passing was mixed up with the feelings of loss and joy.

When the last of the family and friends finally departed, I had a forklift load the lions into the rental truck, said some sad goodbyes to her loyal neighbors, and drove home across the eastern flank of the continent.

I soon discovered that my over-loaded U-Haul was the tortoise of the Interstate. On the flats and downhills, I occasionally grazed the speed limit with the help of a stiff tail wind; the slightest uphill grades reduced me to a crawl. The only vehicles I passed were off the shoulder, broken down or abandoned. It wasn't until after midnight of the second day that I pulled up to my empty house, road weary and hungry.

Fumbling with the door key in the dark, I bumped into something unexpected. When the door was opened and the porch light turned on, I discovered three unmarked boxes stacked against the wall.

Was I expecting something?

I wasn't, and opened a pen knife. The first box contained a lightweight stool, four-legged with a round wooden top. I couldn't remember ordering such a thing, and there was no note, no mailing label or evidence of its origins. Curious, I opened the second box. Folded inside was a red, double-breasted jacket, forties' style, with wide, black satin lapels — a parody of a cheesy tuxedo jacket — and obviously brand-new. Again, no note, no sales slip, nothing. I wondered if one of my sisters was playing a joke — an expensive one at that — but where was the punch line? The third box contained a silk top hat. I impulsively tried it on and looked in the mirror. It fit. I looked ridiculous — but what was this all about? I made a sandwich, fell into bed, and slept like a — stone lion?

The next morning I found something I had missed the night before. A sturdy cardboard mailing tube, three inches in diameter and over six feet long, was propped up against the corner of the porch. A mailing label identified the source as an equestrian supply shop in Pittsburgh, Pennsylvania. Inside was a long-handled, braided whip — the kind used by trotting horse drivers.

Or lion tamers.

It suddenly all fit together: The stool, the ringmaster's jacket and hat — the whip. I'd been cast in a fantasy I hadn't signed up for. These gifts, and all they implied, were bizarre, but when I thought back on the arc of my relationship with Sara, they were not entirely surprising. I was the architect with all the answers. She counted on me to make her dream pool come true, as if only I knew the way. She saw me as saving her from an unscrupulous contractor, honest as he was. She called me for advice when her stereo wouldn't turn on, and again when her VCR broke. What I know about fixing stereos and VCRs could fit on the head of a six-penny nail, but she took my meager suggestions as if they'd been sent down from Circuit City Heaven. Yes, I showed up like clockwork for meetings, and she could have confused my obsessive Teutonic nature with an eagerness to see her, but I was just being myself. When she said sit, I sat. Yes, I patted her friendly old dogs and called them by name, Mutt and Chops, but I like dogs. I was literate, not entirely bald or obese, and brushed all my teeth twice a day. But I was not interested, and had tried to establish clear boundaries.

Or had I?

If my presence in her life was destined to be misinterpreted, there were plenty of opportunities for misunderstandings. Maybe I had contributed to this mix-up by being too personal, laughing at her suggestive jokes, but hadn't I made myself clear? Apologizing for something I hadn't done would have been humiliating for us both. I somehow felt guilty without knowing exactly why.

Considering what she'd left on my doorstep, I knew an acknowledgement of some kind would be required at our next meeting. How could I make myself abundantly clear, and simultaneously not hurt her feelings? I talked it over with Geoff, who felt sorry for Sara and urged me to be as delicate as possible.

Two days later, I willed myself to our weekly conference with dread. I arrived twenty minutes late, and went straight to the job site to review the progress made in my absence. During the meeting that followed, I kept the contractor with Sara and me as long as possible. We poured over the sub-contractors' schedules, deliveries, shop-drawings and invoices; all the pieces were timely and in perfect order. Finally, when every conceivable detail had been covered, and the contractor went back to his work, I was left alone with my tigress.

"How did your trip go?" she asked, curling up in her chair.

Looking more at my shoes than at her, I briefly recited the highs and lows.

"And the lions are home, safe and sound?"

"Guarding my house as we speak." A stillness followed, during which I resolved to remain silent until she spoke next.

"Did you get the stuff I left for you?"

"I found it when I got home." I said. "It was one a.m., something like that." I was seeking a perfect balance between polite acknowledgement and respectful indifference. "Long drive in a slow truck."

"And ...?" She pulled a pillow to her chest and wrapped her arms around it protectively.

"Well, I guess ..." A favorite family story suddenly came to the rescue: When my sisters were teenagers, my oldest sister brought home a new boyfriend. After he left, she asked my middle sister what she thought of him. My middle sister was unimpressed, but didn't want to say so. Her answer went something like, "He's so ... he's so ... he's so ... tall."

I tried a variation on the theme. "Well, I guess I was really ... surprised."

Sara tipped the pillow onto her knee and let it tumble to the floor. "Right," she said, standing up slowly and turning away. "I guess you were."

When I arrived for our next weekly conference, I noticed a beige, four-door Buick with Florida plates parked in the driveway. A neat bumper sticker posed the compelling question, "The Postal Mess — Who's To Blame?" Sara's dogs, who usually greeted me with goofy enthusiasm, were nowhere to be seen. I went over to the job site and found the contractor in a foul mood. He trudged back to the house with me, grumbling about nitpicky engineers. "You're not going to believe this bullshit," he said, nodding to the Buick.

As we entered the living room, Sara introduced me to Warren, an old friend of her father. Warren was in his late 60s, tall and thin with close-cropped hair and razor-sharp creases in his trousers. His breast pocket protector held no less than ten pens and pencils. He wore bifocals with flip-up sun glasses attached — flipped up — which gave him a startled look.

"Warren is an engineer," Sara said. "He'll be helping us out with the project."

"A few hours a week," he explained, "No big deal."

"He used to work for NASA, didn't you Uncle Warren?"

"Correct. Thirty-three years. Took full retirement in January."

The contractor and I exchanged furtive glances. Exactly where would uncle Warren fit into the chain of command here? This project wasn't a rocket bound for Mars. Did he know anything about light frame construction? Was he as uptight as he looked?

The meeting had none of the informality I was used to. Sara sat up straight in a straight-backed chair instead of curled into her customary upholstered wingback. It was the first time I'd seen her smoking a cigarette. Warren sat where I usually sat. The usual tray of juice and cookies were missing, but at least Mutt and Chops still lay at my feet. Sara rarely looked at me, but when she did, I saw taut lines around the corners of her mouth I'd never noticed before.

We made small talk with Warren about how well the pool was progressing, about how the mechanical system was designed to operate and about the schedule. What little he revealed of himself left me thinking he might be harmless — an asset, even. The timing of his appearance was ominous, however, and I couldn't discuss the dynamics leading up to the coincidence with the contractor.

Sara followed Warren's lead on the few changes he suggested, and directed no questions to me. She deliberately looked out the window the few times I spoke.

"So," I asked Warren, "Do you do structural, mechanical, or ... ?"

Sara answered for him. "It never hurts to have another pair of eyes."

"A little bit of everything," Warren said. "My specialty was aerospace aerodynamics."

"Glad to have you on the project," I lied.

"Me, too," the contractor mumbled.

In the three months that remained until the project was completed, Sara spent most of her time traveling, with brief stays at home every two or three weeks. Except for a few awkward conversations in the pool house, we had no interaction. I received no phone calls from her and never set foot in her house again. Warren made it clear that he would field all communications between us, and if I didn't mind — would I put mine in writing?

Warren visited the jobsite every few days with a tape measure and a note pad. We had no idea what he wrote on his pad, or in most cases, what he was measuring. He would say things like, "This wall is exactly eight feet, nine inches tall." And he would be correct. In the real world of architecture, some dimensions matter much more than others, but in Warren's tidy mind, they were all of equal importance.

More substantively, he'd say something like, "Sara wants you to make this door wheelchair accessible."

And I would say something like, "It is. The door schedule is on drawing #8, bottom left hand corner."

And he would say, "Of course. You bet. Just wanted to be sure."

And I would say, "Thanks for checking, Warren."

Warren was the kind of engineer I'd like to have working on a nuclear power plant if it was being built next door to my house. He was a belt-and-suspenders kind of thinker: If one little conduit was adequate, two big conduits were better. If twelve inches of insulation would keep the building toasty — why not twenty? If an idea could be quantified, Warren was the man to double it.

I will always wonder if Sara hired Uncle Warren to find fault with the project, or just to drive us crazy. As it turns out, he was an expert at both. Within the first week, the contractor began complaining about Warren's lurking around with his glasses down on the tip of nose, "Sniffing for trouble like a goddamned bloodhound."

One day I found Warren lying on the slab next to the pool with a six-foot level, scratching numbers into his note pad.

"Floor's out of level," he gasped, as he rose to his feet. "Sorry."

"Really?"

"A sixteenth in six feet." Warren tapped at his notes and swept his arm around the twenty-five-meter pool. "Three places."

I did a quick calculation: A sixteenth in six feet meant that the same pitch, extended ninety-six feet, would result in a rise of ... one inch. Oh boy. "Anything else?"

"A thirty-second over there," he added, "But I guess that's okay."

I wondered if Warren was married, if he kept a record of how many paper towels his wife used. "One thirty-second of an inch?"

He glanced at his notes. "A little less, actually."

"You're sure?"

He smiled apologetically. "Just keeping track."

Near the end of the job, Uncle Warren finally earned his keep. (I assumed Sara was paying him.) The dimension string on the foundation drawings showed the length of the building at ninety-six feet. As Warren inevitably discovered, the built structure measured ninety-five feet, eleven and three-eighths inches along one side, and ninety-six feet even along the opposite side.

"This end wall isn't square with the building," he said at a meeting with the contractor and me. "It ought to be corrected."

The contractor turned and spit a big, brown wad of Skoal into a trashcan.

I felt my face heating up. "But it's irrelevant, isn't it? Less than an inch in ninety-six feet?" It had no bearing on the building's soundness or aesthetics, especially given the violin curves.

Warren flipped down his sunglasses and stuck out his chest. "I've told Sara about it," he said, looking at me as if I were an errant schoolboy, "And she's very disappointed in you."

I understood well enough. She was disappointed in me in ways that her father's friend Warren could never begin to imagine.

The last chapter of the saga began with Warren's veiled threats of a lawsuit. "I hate to say it, but something will have to be done ..." Then came the withholding of a significant sum from the contractor's next bill. "The Sum" is familiar in contractors' circles: It approximates whatever a contractor would have to pay in legal fees to recover what he's owed. Most contractors write off the loss and move on, as this one did, and with good reason. I wrote several letters to Warren and Sara defending him — and myself — and got no reply. The contractor ultimately offered to fix the problem — reconfigure the offset and move the end wall at his expense — but Sara wasn't interested, and insisted on additional compensation.

The contractor continued to work until the job was finished, as did I. He was never paid the last ten percent he was owed, nor were my last two invoices paid. A lawyer advised me that although I was likely to win a lawsuit, the legal fees and the year or two of depositions and legal wrangling would approximate "The Sum," and not be worth the aggravation. I took his advice and went for an enjoyable bike ride.

Lamar was curious about the project as it progressed, and I kept him informed about the building, which turned out to be a gem despite Uncle Warren. When I showed him photos, he said: "I had no idea this sort of thing could be built in the wilderness. Who did you say the architect was?"

I underplayed the difficulties with his old girlfriend Sara. The worst thing I said was that she was "complicated."

"She put the moves on you, didn't she?"

"My lips are sealed."

"I knew she would."

"Is that why you recommended me — to test my integrity?"

"All the more reason I won't work for private clients," he said. "I have no integrity."

"You're so spoiled," I said.

"Of course, I might have been more diplomatic than you," he said

"You have no idea what diplomacy can lead to," I said, "Until you've declined to tame a lion."

"Which proves my contention that residential architecture is a circus."

"And the architects are the clowns?"

"You're finally catching on," he said.

As for the lion tamer's outfit and whip, they remained forgotten in the back of a closet for several years. I occasionally worried about what would happen if I were to suddenly die and they were discovered. The problem was solved with a visit by my New York theater friends Raoul and Eddie: The jacket fit Eddy perfectly, and he adored the top hat on Raoul. Neither admitted to taking the whip.

Telling Stories

In the winter of 1992, I taught a seminar titled "Architecture Meets Fiction" at the Cooper Union school of architecture in New York City. As an architect and author of two novels, it was clear to me that designing buildings and telling stories had much in common. Many of my houses, and both novels, were located in the Connecticut River border towns of New Hampshire and Vermont along the "Upper Valley," a region whose native population and hill-farm landscapes made me feel at home the moment I arrived in the late 1960s. I began writing fiction twenty years after I began making architecture, and I soon found that the creative decision-making for both the houses and the writing were informed by the same seasons, landscapes, personalities, and cultural environment. For me, recognition of place was essential to every decision. I figured that if my students of architecture could analyze how and why certain choices were made writing fiction, they could extrapolate what they learned and apply it to their work on the drafting board.

We began with a look at archetypical story-types. Admittedly simplistic, one accepted theory reduces them to: 1.) A stranger (relative, lover, fisherman, monk) comes into a town (house, workplace, kitchen, ship) and everything (something worth reading about) changes. Or, 2.) The same stranger, etc, leaves town, etc. and everything changes, as in, My wife ran away with my best friend Jim — and I miss him ...

Buildings fall into similarly basic archetypical forms: the tower, the cave, ziggurat, colonnade, box, and arena. But how are they similar to stories?

Access to a novel begins with an opening gambit by which the author leads the reader into a specific set of circumstances. The author's choices of locale, characters, details, and tone signal an intention of what's to come. If the time, place, dialogue and behavior of the characters ring true, the story seems "real." Add a hint of intrigue, and we are pulled into the tale.

Access to a building is similarly designed around the same necessities of orientation and intrigue. Choices of form and space (character), details, materials, and light give the building its first voice and tone. Bricks and mortar compose the "realness" of architecture, but it is the arrangement of these materials that begins to narrate the building's story. When the door is opened, the architect offers clues as to what will happen inside, and if the clues are evocative, we will be eager to explore the building.

On one of my rare visits to see Lamar in New York, we ducked into a prominent diamond merchant's showroom to get a sense of how architecture told the story of selling diamonds. It took a split second to realize I wasn't in Kansas anymore. The sales staff was dressed so impeccably that I felt like a vagrant. Lamar had purchased Simone's ring from them some years before, and they still remembered him, a repeat customer, no doubt. I found myself checking for mud on my shoes and wished I'd worn an ironed shirt. Even if I could have afforded the least expensive trinket on sale, I was certainly one of the most unlikely customers to have ever entered such a pantheon of preciousness.

The showroom's opening gambit was formulated around a simple theme — the refraction of light — a phenomenon at which flawless, multi-faceted diamonds are without peer. High ceilings, gorgeous woodwork, and brilliant halogen lighting spoke fluently of exclusivity. The hushed acoustics, Persian carpets and sparkling baubles without price tags suggested a story line between the eternal purity of diamonds, financial triumph, and chic ostentation. Okay, I got it — and wanted nothing more than to hurry over to Central Park and jog around the reservoir.

Instead, Lamar took me into a lobby of an office tower he'd helped design at SOM. The story I saw unfolding was one of immense corporate confidence and competence. The articulate vernacular of polished black granite, tinted glass, rubbed bronze, and dark mahogany said it all. I was sold at a glance: The narrative behind this sleek, modern design was meant to convince me that the occupants of this building were dedicated to doing serious, profitable business — and convinced I was.

Imagine another story, 1,500 miles away from the island of Manhattan. The rack of moose antlers hung above a hunting lodge door in Michigan's Upper Peninsula suggests a narrative occasion that leads inevitably to the primeval drama of predator and prey, life and death. The opening gambit includes a cold, early darkness, mouse-eaten mattresses, wood smoke, and hoar frost encrusted on cracked window panes at dawn. The particulars of place put the inexorable story line in motion: A hunter walks into the woods with a rifle, and everything changes ...

When I imagine the story suggested by the antique stone farmhouse in which I was raised, I see it framed within the architectural language of sturdiness, simplicity, and function. Its prior tenants, six generations of Pennsylvania Dutch farmers, had little use for grandiosity, ornament or idleness. Their huge, stone-ended barn attested to their agrarian ambitions and dedication to hard work. I like to think that the basic narrative provided by that sturdy stone house and barn was a reflection of their character, and helped form the better parts of mine.

The entry halls in nineteenth-century farmhouses like ours were used for formal occasions only — Sunday afternoon socials, weddings, and funerals. All other traffic came in through the back door where fragrant barn boots and soggy overcoats were left to dry outside the kitchen. When my parents remodeled the front hall to become the principal entrance, they shrank the floor space by adding closets and lost the formality it held for our predecessors. Ironically, they changed the opening gambit from formal to informal despite our family's access to culture and privilege. They brought the story level down a tone, and then scrambled to compensate with better furniture and art.

Mom was a romantic aesthete who made an effort to refine her life and her environment wherever she could. Her children were sent to artsy schools, given piano lessons, and encouraged to marvel at sunsets. Walking into her "simple" house, one couldn't miss the iconic antique Bristol clock on a wall bracket opposite the nouveau closet, the Chippendale foot stool, and the Audubon prints on the walls. This was not just a farmhouse story.

The old rooms had low ceilings (easier for a farmer to heat), eighteen-inch-thick outer walls (inexpensive materials — stone and mortar — plastered inside and out), and tulip-poplar floor boards (straight-grained, durable, local lumber). Against this undemanding, naturalistic narrative, my mother juxtaposed Persian carpets, furnishings, and art derived from a diverse storyline. Her capacity to embrace and encourage contrasting levels of simplicity and sophistication sanctioned the brand of agreeable cultural schizophrenia that would come to define my life.

My businessman father was a gifted athlete, genially supportive of his four children's interests, indisposed to serious literature, blind to art — and tone deaf. I'd come into the living room at night and find him reading a Mickey Spillane detective novel and humming a tune which bore no resemblance to what was playing on the hi-fi across the room. He liked Scotch on the rocks, fast horses, and poking fun at religious pomposities. For him, the greatest mystery in life was art. His definition of sculpture was something you bumped into when you backed away from one of those goddamned abstract paintings, whose only practical purpose was to hide a crack in the wall. But he taught me to work hard, play hard, shoot guns, drive fast, and fix the tractor. From him I learned to tend the garden, box and wrestle, appreciate good jokes, and see the good in people. The idea of our house representing a story would have perplexed him. He died too young, twenty years before my mother, but not before he got to see his four children succeed in the baffling fields of interior design, art, and architecture.

In her eighty-fifth year, Mom died at home, surrounded by the people and things she loved most. Her passing was difficult but dignified, expected yet shocking in its irrevocability. My sisters and I felt fortunate to have spent much of her last six months at her side. It was a long November goodbye, and little between us was left undone. The momentum of her life and love continues to pulse through our lives.

In the middle of the night after she passed, I lay awake in my old bedroom in the attic. The farmhouse was too warm and too quiet. My sisters were asleep in their childhood rooms, or perhaps they were awake like me. The furnace occasionally rumbled in the basement below, faithfully echoing a sound I've never forgotten. And although I couldn't see it, I knew the painting on the wall at the foot of my bed was alive with Apaches on galloping horses.

My mother furnished my childhood room differently from those of her daughters. Theirs were done in pastels — yellows, pinks and palest blue — with floral bedspreads and white lace curtains. Mine was decorated in 1950s, John Wayne desert-movie tones: rawhide, rock and sand — subtle manhood hints from blind-to-art Dad, no doubt, for a boy perhaps a bit too invested in drawing pictures and reading books in his Private-Do-Not-Enter tree houses.

As I fought with the bedclothes and ruminated on theories of nature vs. nuture, I mentally searched the house for clues to our family story, to our connectedness. Did our culturally schizoid, stone farmhouse and culturally nourishing mother lead us to the careers we chose, or was our passion for design biologically pre-ordained? From room to room I imagined the contents that might have fueled our enthusiasm. I pictured the Chinese screen in front of the living room fireplace, guardian of the embers, doorway to our childhood imaginations, and remembered us kids sitting by the hearth in our Mickey Mouse pajamas as the flames wove mesmerizing patterns through the decorative mesh. What was it we were thinking back then, these designers-to-be?

In the upstairs hall I pictured a painted wedding chest with the names of a Swedish couple scrolled across the top, dated 1829. When I was small, I hid in the chest during a game of hide-and-go-seek, and fell asleep. My sisters decided I had abandoned them and went off to pursue other things. I slept well until I heard my name called for supper.

Most of Mom's paintings came from her art-dealer sister, my aunt Shirley-of-the-stone-lions. Some of the paintings were abstract, some representational, and a few had become valuable over time. I admired Mom's range of taste and interpreted it as an absence of aesthetic dogma; she liked what she liked. As correlatives to her life, her modest accumulation of art and furniture was consistent with her sensibilities. In fact, they told her story better than the house she had chosen to live in; its stolid, Pennsylvania-Dutch practicality never managed to dampen her higher aspirations.

When the prospect of peaceful sleep seemed doomed, I began to count the houses I'd owned and lived in as an adult — five so far — two renovated, three built entirely new to my specifications. Perhaps there was a way to hold on to something of my mother by linking her to those houses, too. Maybe they and I were more connected to her than I knew.

The old New Hampshire farmhouse I renovated (when I should have been earning my salary in Cambridge) was the first. At the time, following the prescriptive modernist truths learned in school seemed easy, even when applied to an 1850s farmhouse. What masqueraded as truth, of course, was ideological and inappropriate, but I charged ahead, stripped away "outdated" antique features and put the project on a diet of "clean, spare" design. In the guest bedroom, for instance, I patched the plaster and painted the walls and ceiling stark white, refinished the wide pine floors, and installed three pieces of furniture: a bed, a chair, and a dresser — second-hand Danish modern. For baseboards, door and window casings, I used square-stock 1 x 4s. The tale I'd concocted was a thin account of modernist minimalism: It offered the reader little, risked nothing, and taught me even less. When my parents first came to visit, Mom thought the room was, "A bit bare." End of story. Good for her.

The second house was the one I built from scratch with the help of Peter Anderson. Enthusiastic as I was naïve, I fully emerged myself in design and construction techniques about which I knew next to nothing. Architecture school was four years behind, and the modernist idiom was still seductive. My first opportunity to tell a story using vivid language was not to be wasted. I tossed about cantilevers, sloped ceilings, towers, arches, curves, lofts, and balconies in every direction — at least one of each. There was no chapter on fine carpentry. When my parents toured the finished product, Mom was volubly silent about the melodramatic mix of form and space. The vivid spectrum of

oranges and purples I'd used for accent colors was fatally pro-
nounced "Interesting." I had failed Mom's aesthetic SATs; modernism and I had failed each other, and Dad wanted to know if
we'd ever be able to sell the house.

During the OPEC crisis of the '70s, I sold the unsellable
house, took a year off from design work, and hand-built an
earth-sheltered house. If one of the legitimate purposes of architecture was to conserve energy, I was officially legitimate: My
fuel oil company almost crossed me off its delivery schedule.
Beyond its efficiency, the house design was driven by a system of
curves, which I saw as adaptations of earth forms intended to
express undergrounded-ness. The structural system articulated a
simple dialect of lintel and arch, bearing walls, and beams. The
floors were finished with swirling waves of radiant-heated tile.
Ceilings were framed with massive timbers. The interior was
quiet and cozy with the warm tones of wood and tile. A twenty
mile view down the Connecticut River valley never failed to draw
my eye. Although the idea of growing grass on the roof exasper-
ated her, Mom thought the house was the first I'd done for
myself which was "at peace with itself." She was sorry when I sold
it to finance the fourth experiment.

My father died before he saw the River Road house. I was in
my late 40s and gaining insights about what architecture meant
to me, about how its success is based upon a mutually respectful
conversation between architect and client rather than upon an
architect's preconceived notion of style, the same, solipsistic
story re-told with minor variations. The new house was distinctly more conservative than my three previous efforts, and I think
Dad would have liked the absence of gratuitous architectural
"statements" built into my earlier work. Instead, the rooms
flowed graciously from one to another, the roof pitches made
sense, and the traditional detailing demanded, and showed, seri-

ous craftsmanship. Mom called it my first grownup house. It was sold after ten years to finance the postmodern farmhouse I live in today.

Has it been difficult to disconnect from these places that always seemed, at the outset, perfect? Like a snake shedding its skin, moving on to the next house has felt more like natural selection than an unnatural whim. The creative process is all about asking the question, "What happens if ...?" and we can't know the answer unless we risk the possibility of failure. Stories, buildings, and lives are all prone to design faults. They can break apart and fail, or knit together and transcend. What happens if they fail? We stay tuned and keep asking questions, keep looking for the true story line, the best solution. As the story of my life proceeds, I trust my ideas about life and architecture will continue to evolve. I can't accurately define what chapter I'm in until it's over, but today's perfect relationship, perfect story, perfect house is flowing through a continuing narrative.

In fact, what's been most difficult about moving every ten years or so is abandoning the plantings I've cared for. I cherish the buildings and the sometimes complicated memories they hold, but the gardens and trees I planted around them have always given me unconditional, uncomplicated pleasure. With or without me, they continue, dormant, storm-stunted, or blooming. Peonies planted thirty years ago are still outrageously spectacular in June. I've been granted visitation rights to prune apple trees on properties I sold long ago. Some of the new owners must think I'm crazy, but I've watched their flowers and trees grow up and mature; they're like family to me. Some have been cut down, some I never get to see, some are aging not so well. But every spring, those that survive will re-commence. Forget perfection. I feel much more blessed to be included within a circle of less-than-perfect gardens, trees, and family, and to know that they are more important to me than the promise of an abstracted, perfect architecture will ever be.

When my sisters and I divided up our mother's things in the weeks after her funeral, I was surprised by my sudden fondness for the painted, Swedish wedding chest. My middle sister, Judy, wanted it, too, but she wanted even more an antique writing desk and a set of china I could only pretend to admire. Gwyn coveted the Queen Anne, drop-leaf table that sat against the wall in the living room. She also inherited an old, carved, wooden mantle piece admired by Mom in a junk shop, brought home on a roof rack, but never installed in the farmhouse. (Gwyn eventually converted it into a bed's headboard.) Sue favored Mom's silverware, paintings, and sculpture. My sisters' happiness with their choices left me feeling less guilty about wanting the 1830s Bristol clock, and the faded, moss green, velvet foot stool with the Chippendale legs that once stood sentry in our front hall. But above all, I was happiest to have inherited the Chinese fireplace screen.

It's made of a tightly woven black steel mesh overlaid with delicate metal branches and leaves that suggest a forest of eucalyptus and bamboo. Hidden among the lower branches are a little pagoda at the edge of a lake, a fisherman in a sampan, and a three-arched bridge. We were told our grandparents bought the screen — we never knew where — in the 1920s. As a child, I imagined the forged iron landscape alive, and concocted a variety of stories, all of which had to include the fisherman in the sampan, the pagoda and the bridge. With a fire burning bright behind it, I could persuade the fisherman to move, unscathed, between the flames. Backlit with embers, I'd watch him sail his sampan into a fiery sunset until I fell asleep on the living room rug. The fisherman was habitually looking for something, and he was always me; his journeys were limited only by the limits of my inquiry.

Today, the screen covers the big stone fireplace in my New Hampshire living room. It links me to my parents and our home in Pennsylvania, and continues to be part of our unending story. I know that I will never see again what I saw through it in the innocence of youth, but I continue to think of the screen as a gateway to creativity. As I see it now, the forged iron forest has become a symbolic sanctuary, as so many real forests have been for me throughout my life. The pagoda stands for the challenge of designing a story — in prose or stone — in which the narrative links the artifact to the people, place and culture it serves. In the bridge, I see the means of freely crossing borders, connecting ideas to ideas, bricks and mortar to verbs and nouns. The fisherman's sampan, with me aboard, sails our imaginations into whatever waters we need to cross; the bait we use is: "What happens if ...?"

Epilogue

Tom's oldest son, Spencer — also an architect— married the distinctly lovely artist Briah Uhl on Saturday afternoon, September 17th, 2005. A hundred or so guests sat in folding chairs under the shade of a huge old tree while Ettie played a Scottish love song on her cello, *Come Give me Your Hand*. The justice of the peace, a tiny, grandmotherly woman whose stern, no-nonsense voice did little to conceal her sweetness, united the beaming bride and groom with Super-Glue authority. The air tingled with a collective sigh of approval when they kissed.

I usually cry at weddings, and credit my snifflings to empathic happiness for the bride and groom. My performance at Spencer and Briah's nuptials was no different, but something else — as awful as their union was wonderful—made the tears burn. At 5 a.m. on the day before the wedding, Tom got out of bed and went into his bathroom — the bathroom with the sash-less window looking out into the two-story room built into the granite cliff — and fell through the opening, head-first to the floor below.

Ettie was awakened by the crash, ran downstairs, and found him bleeding badly from a gash on the back of his neck. (He landed on a large piece of pottery.) He was barely conscious, in serious trauma, unable to move. Strapped to the gurney in the wailing ambulance, Tom realized he had no feeling below his shoulders. "Now I'm just a head," he said aloud. "This is going to be so interesting."

Spencer called early the next morning — his wedding day — to report that Tom was in critical condition in the ICU at Yale New Haven Hospital. It would take a few days, a week or two, to know the full extent of the damage. Tom's fourth vertebrae, C-4, was fractured, the nerves severely bruised — that was all anyone knew at the time. Tom was alert enough to insist that the ceremony proceed without him. Spencer was conflicted, but Tom was adamant: It would be crazy to call off the party!

I drove down I-91 in a daze, unable to accept the unacceptable, as if my mind were too small to let in such an unsolicited enormity. Tom was as robust and energetic as anyone half his age. He rowed every day. He swam. He had built ingenious climbing structures in children's museums all over the continent — and now this?

Tom taught me to live below the water line during my divorce. He cured every adversity with humor, taught me about having fun for fun's sake, about questioning everything, about how you never get to really know people until you've stayed up very late with them sharing large quantities of lethal beverages. By his example, Tom taught me to love without hedging, to see my children as perfect gifts, to find the good in everyone, no matter how difficult they might be. He had helped me and so many others so much, and now we were helpless to help him. I bargained with God: In exchange for a miracle, I would become a true believer.

At the hospital, a cluster of Tom's closest friends and family were waiting in the Hall outside the ICU. We hugged one another hard with the knowledge of what might be coming. What was there to say? There were no updates on Tom's condition, no star to wish upon. Time hung about us heavily, a surreal dimension. Long, awkward silences were suddenly interrupted with innocuous chit-chat. "How was your drive from ____?" Even among my old friends gathered there, I felt desperate. Lamar was on a three-year assignment in Hong Kong and had yet to be notified, a task I hoped would fall to someone else. We had lost touch over the past few years, so much so that I felt entirely disconnected. Just ten minutes face-to-face would presumably bring us back into focus, but those ten minutes never seemed to materialize.

When it was my turn to see Tom, I followed a nurse down a bright corridor to Tom's room. His battered head was propped up on pillows, disheveled, tubes inserted everywhere; he looked awful. Ettie stood protectively beside him, gaunt with worry. As I approached, she whispered my name. With huge effort, Tom turned his head, half-a-degree in my direction. I had to remind myself to breathe as I bent down to kiss his damp forehead. Tom made a sound in response, a sign of recognition, but indecipherable. I wanted so badly to say something useful, to offer some comfort, but the phrases frozen to my lips were Hallmark Card-ridiculous: I'm so sorry. How are you feeling?

I heard myself croaking, "I love you." If the situation had been reversed, Tom would have told me I looked beautiful — and meant it — and he would have looked around the hospital room and commented on how amazing it all was, the technology, the cleanliness, the kind nurses — and then he would have told me he loved me, and that this was the beginning of an exciting chapter of my life.

I was neither so eloquent nor wise. The best I could do was press my thighs hard against his bed frame and will into him a transfusion of strength and endurance. Take all I've got — please — take it all. The nurse looked at her watch. It was time to make way for the next loved one. Tom was barely conscious, but before I left, his eyes sparked at mine for an instant, and I knew what he was thinking: "It may look like I'm fucked, but don't worry; I'm not."

I worried anyway, as did everyone else. Days passed, and the news was never as good as we wished for. Tom moved a finger. Could he do it again? Sometimes yes, mostly no. His doctors and nurses were peerless, but they had no magic cure. The two-week benchmark passed and there were none of the signs we needed. If someone asked about his prognosis, I found myself explaining that, statistically, things looked bad, but Tom had never thought much of statistics, and that if anyone were to turn the numbers around, his name would be Tom Luckey.

A tracheotomy made it impossible for Tom to speak louder than a silent whisper. For a month, he was held captive not only by his body, but to silence as well. His family learned to interpret the whispers, but even they were often mystified by what he was trying to say. My hour-long, bedside conversations with him were comedic exercises in intuition. He'd mouth a paragraph's worth of words, and I would repeat what I thought he'd said. When I got it right, he'd grin and nod his head. When I got it wrong, he'd just grin.

With his trache-tube removed, Tom talked non-stop about plans to continue his latest project in a partnership with Spencer. In the next few months, as his stamina improved, they began to work together. Spencer would tape drawings to the wall in front of Tom's bed, and the discussion would begin. It wasn't all easy. The classic father-son dynamic inspired some zesty exchanges over issues of aesthetics, scheduling, costs, and, most painfully — authority — but they completed the Boston Children's Museum climbing structure in March of 2007, eighteen months after Tom's accident — and they are still best of friends. While they were working, Laura Longsworth, a gifted documentary film-maker (and, incidentally, my daughter-in-law), filmed a made-for-TV documentary of their collaboration; we expect to it see aired in 2008.

As I write this, Tom is beginning to move a few fingers and toes at will. Medically speaking, he's not supposed to be able to do this, but he has always excelled at doing the impossible. He's already joking about being "More than just a head."

The Children's Museum is planning a gala reception for the Fall of 2007; they will open their newly remodeled areas to the public and introduce Tom's work. He'll be there in his electric-powered wheelchair, resplendent in his most outrageous party shirt. I can hear him insisting, "Isn't this," — and by "this" he means everyone present, the weather, the food, the speeches, the museum, and everything in it — "Isn't this just fabulous?"

Acknowledgements

I wrote this book slowly, which I ordinarily blame on my primitive typing skills, uncomfortable sitting position and the inscrutable treacheries of my computer, but I was also writing at a desk in my architecture office surrounded by uncompleted drawings, phones, faxes, and e-mails. As I reflect on how this multi-tasked arrangement worked, I'm tempted to believe it helped further inform the contrast between a romanticized version of pristine architecture and the boisterous reality of clients' and contractors' demands.

As for the many who helped nourish this book to fruition, I'll start by thanking Phil Pochoda, who began pestering me ten years before I yielded to his flattery and began to scribble. I owe a huge debt of gratitude to a quartet of loyal writer-group friends — William Craig, Matson Sewell, John Griesemer and Allan Stam — each of whom helped immensely with the shape and texture of the evolving chapters, and could always be counted upon to rescue me from disaster when I was tempted to jump the shark. My appreciation for their skills extends as well to several indispensable readers of the first completed draft, including the inimitable W.D. Wetherell, my dear and dauntless pals Sydney Lea, Neil and Margot Goodwin, Utah's undisputed Queen of the Desert, Laurie Hutchinson, and the ever-perceptive Cynthia Huntington and Nicola Newton. To Robert King, I owe a Rocky Mountain high five for judicious counsel. Among family members with many helpful hints are my astute son and daughter, Luke and Oona, and my tough-as-nails, sharp-as-tacks, take-no-prisoners sisters Susan,

Judy and Gwyn. Merci beaucoup as well to my cupid-playing, cello-making, crème-brûlée-baking, immigration-law-breaking sister-in-law, Michele Ashley.

For keeping my tormented, chair-bound vertebrae adjusted, I thank the world's best chiropractor, Todd Mosenthal and his wily henchmen Scott and Jeff. Harvey "Not-a-geek" Brotman, computer genius extraordinaire, rescued me more than once from the evil machinations of my degenerate Dell. My agent, Colleen Mohyde deserves a halo and a Rolls Royce for her invaluable help. Jim Gold and Penny McConnell put me together with Ib Bellew and Carole Kitchel Bellew at Bunker Hill Publishing — many thanks. And through it all, my wife Melinda read every word, gave solid, sound advice and the kind of support and wisdom that only comes from someone as smart and steady and loving as she has always been to me.